Selected Poems of Bernard Barton, the 'Quaker Poet'

Selected Poems of Bernard Barton, the 'Quaker Poet'

Edited by
Christopher Stokes

ANTHEM PRESS

Anthem Press
An imprint of Wimbledon Publishing Company
www.anthempress.com

This edition first published in UK and USA 2025
by ANTHEM PRESS
75–76 Blackfriars Road, London SE1 8HA, UK
or PO Box 9779, London SW19 7ZG, UK
and
244 Madison Ave #116, New York, NY 10016, USA

First published in the UK and USA by Anthem Press in 2020

© 2025 Christopher Stokes editorial matter and selection

The moral right of the authors has been asserted.

All rights reserved. Without limiting the rights under copyright reserved above,
no part of this publication may be reproduced, stored or introduced into
a retrieval system, or transmitted, in any form or by any means
(electronic, mechanical, photocopying, recording or otherwise),
without the prior written permission of both the copyright
owner and the above publisher of this book.

British Library Cataloguing-in-Publication Data
A catalogue record for this book is available from the British Library.

Library of Congress Control Number: 2024946861

ISBN-13: 978-1-83999-418-0 (Pbk)
ISBN-10: 1-83999-418-5 (Pbk)

This title is also available as an e-book.

CONTENTS

List of Figures	ix
Acknowledgements	xi
List of Abbreviations	xiii
Introduction	1
A Note on Quakerism	13
1812–19: Anonymous Beginnings	**17**
My Lucy	19
Stanzas on the Anniversary of the Abolition of the Slave Trade	21
Ode to an Æolian Harp	24
A Guess at the Contents of Lalla Rookh	26
Stanzas ("The Heaven was Cloudless")	27
The Convict's Appeal [Stanzas 1–15]	29
On Silent Worship	32
Playford. A Descriptive Fragment.—1817	34
Written in a Lady's Album	37
Stanzas, Addressed to Some Friends Going to the Sea-Side	38
Sonnet to the Deben ['Thou hast thrown aside thy summer loveliness']	40
Stanzas, to Helen M— M—	41
Haunts of Childhood	43
Sonnets to Charlotte M— [1818 and 1828]	46
Drab Bonnets	48

1820–25: Emergence of the 'Quaker Poet' — 51

The Ivy, Addressed to a Young Friend	53
The Valley of Fern	55
Verses, Supposed to be Written in a Burial-Ground Belonging to the Society of Friends	60
Leiston Abbey	65
Stanzas, Addressed to Percy Bysshe Shelley	71
To Lydia	73
Winter	74
A Dream	75
A Day in Autumn [Invocation]	78
A Day in Autumn [The River Orwell]	80
The Quaker Poet. Verses on Seeing Myself So Designated	84
To L.E.L.	87
Napoleon [Stanzas 28–90]	88
The Contrast	106
To a Robin	110
Verses on the Death of Bloomfield, the Suffolk Poet	114
Bishop Hubert	118
Pity for Poor Little Sweeps	121
A Memorial of John Woolman; a Minister of the Gospel, Among the Quakers	124
A Memorial of James Nayler, the Reproach and Glory of Quakerism	127
A Memorial of Mary Dyer, One of the Early Worthies and Martyrs in the Society of Quakers	131
Verses on the Approach of Spring, Addressed to my Little Play-Fellow	132
Bealings House	134
To a Butterfly. Translated from the French	135
On a Portrait of Beatrice Cenci	137
On the Death of Samuel Alexander, of Needham-Market	139
Bow Hill	142

CONTENTS

1826–29: Literary Fame — 145

A Grandsire's Tale — 147

Stanzas, Composed During a Tempest — 151

A Prophet's Old Age — 152

Ruth's Love — 154

The Vanity of Human Knowledge — 156

A Soliloquy — 157

A Reflection — 159

Tears — 161

Walking in the Light — 163

Which Things Are a Shadow — 164

Prefatory Sonnet [to *A Widow's Tale, and Other Poems*] — 165

Caractacus — 166

Sonnet; to a Grandmother — 169

Stanzas, Written for a Blank Leaf in Sewell's History of the Quakers — 170

The Vale of Tears — 173

Concluding Verses, to a Child Seven Years Old — 175

Sonnet to William and Mary Howitt — 178

Sonnet to the Same — 179

The Daughter of Herodias — 180

Godiva — 182

On a Portrait by Spagnoletto — 184

Fireside Quatrains, to Charles Lamb — 187

England's Oak — 189

Summer Musings — 192

Epistle to the Editor of Friendship's Offering — 194

1830–49: Late Barton — 197

The Coronation of Ines de Castro — 199

To the White Jasmine — 201

To Wm. Kirby, Rector of Barham, Suffolk	202
The Sea-Shell	204
A Negro Mother's Cradle-Song	205
The Bible ['Lamp of our feet!']	206
A Clerico-Politico Portrait	208
First Scripture Lessons	211
On a Drawing of the Cottage at Aldborough, Where Crabbe Lived in Boyhood	214
An Epistle to a Phonographic Friend; Or a Few Words on Phonography	217
To the B.B Schooner, on Seeing Her Sail Down the Deben for Liverpool	219
Sonnet, to a Friend Never Yet Seen, But Corresponded with for Above Twenty Years	220
A Postscript to 'To the Dead in Christ'	221
The Yellow-Hammer; A Song, by a Suffolk Villager	222
To E.F. [Elizabeth Fry], On Her Reappearance Among Her Friends at the Yearly Meeting, 1845	224
Sonnet, to Job's Three Friends	225
Sonnets, Written at Burstal	226
Poetical Illustrations from *Natural History of the Holy Land*	230
A Prefatory Appeal for Poetry and Poets	237
Contextual Material	243
Notes	261
Bibliography	327
Index of Titles and First Lines	329

FIGURES

1. Jusepe de Ribera [Lo Spagnoletto], *Man, Wine Bottle and Tambourine* (1631). Oil on canvas. Gösta Serlachius Fine Arts Foundation, Mänttä, Finland. Photographer: Yehia Eweis. Reproduced with the kind permission of the Gösta Serlachius Fine Arts Foundation — 183
2. *Philip Doddridge as a child being taught the Old and New Testaments by his mother using ceramic tiles around the fireplace.* Engraving by G. Presbury after J. Franklin. Wellcome Collection. Reproduced under the terms and conditions of the Creative Commons Attribution licence (CC BY 4.0). https://wellcomecollection.org/works/a62hdt7g. This image was used as the accompanying illustration to 'First Scripture Lessons' in *Fisher's Juvenile Scrap-Book* (1839) — 210
3. *The Elk*, engraved by T.[homas?] Dixon. Plate from Lucy Barton, *Natural History of the Holy Land* (1856). Reproduced from editor's own copy, with the kind assistance of the University of Exeter's Digital Humanities Lab. Photographer: Emma Sherriff — 232
4. *The Heron*, engraved by T.[homas?] Dixon. Plate from Lucy Barton, *Natural History of the Holy Land* (1856). Reproduced from editor's own copy, with the kind assistance of the University of Exeter's Digital Humanities Lab. Photographer: Emma Sherriff — 233
5. *Butterflies*. Plate from Lucy Barton, *Natural History of the Holy Land* (1856). Reproduced from editor's own copy, with the kind assistance of the University of Exeter's Digital Humanities Lab. Photographer: Emma Sherriff — 234
6. *The Serpent of the Isle of Celebes*, engraved by T.[homas?] Dixon. Plate from Lucy Barton, *Natural History of the Holy Land* (1856). Reproduced from editor's own copy, with the kind assistance of the University of Exeter's Digital Humanities Lab. Photographer: Emma Sherriff — 235

7. *Barbary Ape & Ouran Outang*, engraved by T.[homas?] Dixon. Plate from Lucy Barton, *Natural History of the Holy Land* (1856). Reproduced from editor's own copy, with the kind assistance of the University of Exeter's Digital Humanities Lab. Photographer: Emma Sherriff   236

ACKNOWLEDGEMENTS

Since first reading Charles Lamb's account of silent prayer in 'Imperfect Sympathies' and finding my curiosity so piqued as to go in search of Quaker poets of the Romantic era, this project has grown to absorb considerable amounts of (mostly pleasurable!) time and attention. There are inevitably many acknowledgements.

As it has developed, I have always appreciated the support and ideas of my immediate colleagues at both campuses of the University of Exeter: I owe a general debt to the Penryn Humanities department, but would offer particular thanks (in no particular order) to Jim Kelly, Tim Cooper, Jason Hall, Kate Hext, John Plunkett, Andrew Rudd and Joseph Crawford. For invaluable aid in the archival process, I'd like to thank Elly Babbedge; for research support, Annie Sheen; and for broader help with the project, Ivy Wrogg. Jeremy Greenwood and Melanie Bill both aided a research visit to Woodbridge during which I got to walk in Barton's footsteps and visit many places mentioned in these poems. My anonymous reviewers, across two stages of manuscript preparation, gave helpful and incisive feedback, and of course I am also grateful to all at Anthem Press.

Preparing this volume has involved the help of many archives and institutions, and I'd like to thank the staff at the Cadbury Research Library at the University of Birmingham; the British Library; Special Collections at the University of Delaware; the Devon and Exeter Institution, the libraries and Digital Humanities Lab of the University of Exeter; the Gainsborough's House Museum; Special Collections at the University of Leeds; Senate House Library at the University of London; the John Rylands Library at the University of Manchester; the Gösta Serlachius Fine Arts Foundation in Mänttä, Finland; the New York Public Library and the curators of the Carl H. Pforzheimer Collection of Shelley and his Circle; the Library of the Society of Friends in London; and the Friends Historical Library at Swarthmore College.

All substantial reproduction of text within this volume is of previously published material where the relevant term of copyright has expired. All archival material has been cited with the permission of the holding archive.

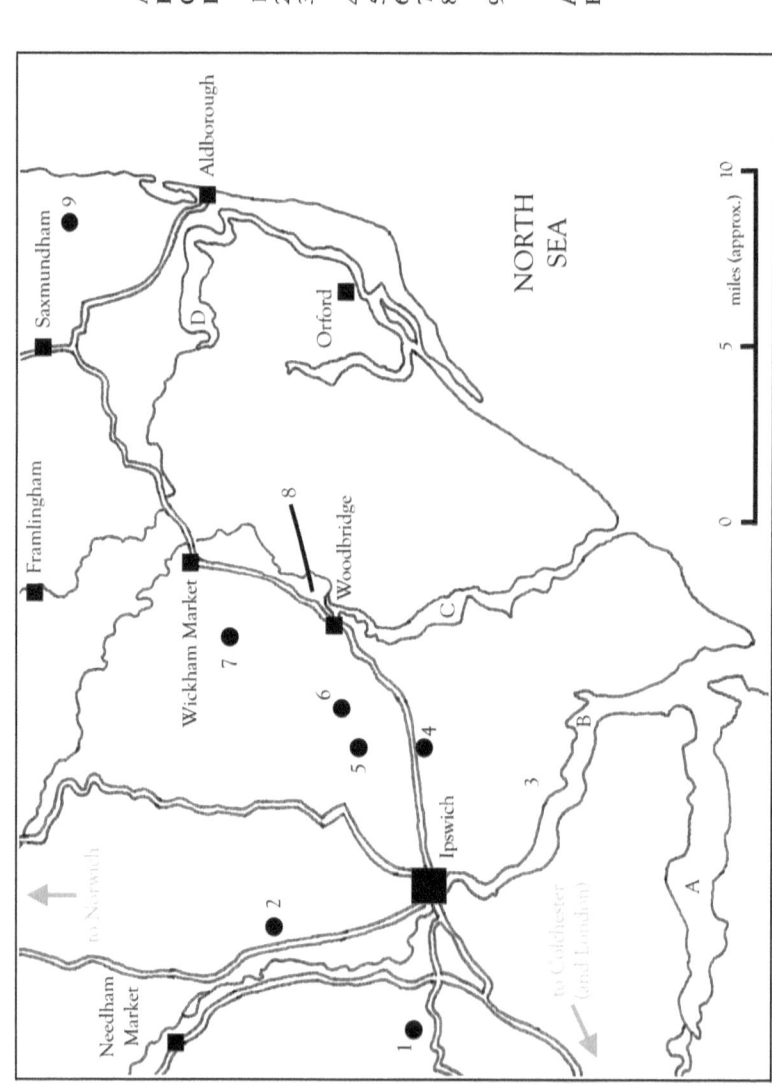

Map 1. Map of Barton's Suffolk.

A   River Stour
B   River Orwell
C   River Deben
D   River Alde/River Ore

1   Burstal
2   Barham
3   Downham Reach ['A Day in Autumn']
4   Kesgrave
5   Playford
6   Great Bealings
7   Bredfield
8   Leeks Hill ['The Valley of Fern']
9   Leiston Abbey

Aldborough = Aldeburgh
Burstal = Burstall

ABBREVIATIONS

Lamb *The Letters of Charles and Mary Lamb 1821–42*, ed. E.V. Lucas (London: Methuen, 1912)
LCBB *The Literary Correspondence of Bernard Barton*, ed. James E. Barcus (Philadelphia: University of Pennsylvania Press, 1966)
SPL *Selections from the Poems and Letters of Bernard Barton*, ed. Lucy Barton (London: Hall, Virtue, 1849)

INTRODUCTION

In 1831 the poet laureate Robert Southey wrote simply 'who has not heard of Bernard Barton?'[1] It is an ironic question for the modern reader – or even the modern scholar – for whom his poetry has passed into almost total obscurity. Yet certainly for the reader of the 1820s and 1830s, he would have been immediately familiar as the author of several volumes of verse, a key devotional poet, and a prolific contributor to periodicals and literary annuals. Reputedly, an English actor called Barton was announced in a Paris theatre in 1822 and 'the audience called out to inquire if it was the Quaker poet'.[2] Indeed, one could argue that Barton did not even need to be named: a reference to 'the Quaker Poet' or 'broad brims' in the pages of a journal was enough to elicit instant recognition. Friendships and correspondence with the Romantic essayist Charles Lamb and Edward FitzGerald (translator of *The Rubáiyát of Omar Khayyám*) ensured his work remained culturally visible after his death in 1849, but by the time of E. V. Lucas's biography in 1893, his star was waning – before being eclipsed entirely. This occlusion is a shame. His is a unique nineteenth-century poetic voice: one of sun-dappled Suffolk woodland and heath; gentle reflections on history, time and loss; and affectionately painted domestic scenes. It is influenced by Wordsworth, Cowper and Pope; the sentimental conventions of late Romantic writing; and fellow county poets such as George Crabbe and Robert Bloomfield. Nor is he limited to one strain: across his work one finds devotional verse, political writing, *ekphrasis* and even zesty satire.

One special and distinctive element that shapes this poetic voice is Quakerism. Southey's rhetorical question was asked in the context of a remarkable emergence: in 1815, William Hazlitt had concluded that 'a Quaker poet would be a literary phenomenon' and almost a contradiction in terms.[3] The Society

---

[1] 'Art III. – *Essays on the Principles of Morality, and on the Private and Political Rights and Obligations of Mankind*. By Jonathan Dymond', *Quarterly Review* 44 (January 1831), p. 83.
[2] *SPL*, p. xv.
[3] 'The Round Table. No. 19', *Examiner* 402 (10 September 1815), p. 587. See 'The Friends: Letter to the Editor of the Examiner' in the contextual material for a response likely penned by Barton.

of Friends, a once revolutionary seventeenth-century sect that had retreated into quietism in the eighteenth century, appeared quintessentially unpoetic. They eschewed fashion and decoration, never attended concerts or dances, proscribed novels and tightly controlled practices of reading among members. They were plain, pious and, on their own account, 'peculiar'. Although it is not true to say there were no Quaker poets whatsoever – Thomas Ellwood, John Scott of Amwell and the Lake District writer Thomas Wilkinson are three examples – the not entirely invalid perception was that Quakers had no poetic tradition of which to speak.[4] Barton was therefore a trailblazer and helped lay the ground for a striking proliferation of Quaker poetry in the nineteenth century, such as that of William, Mary and Richard Howitt; Hannah Mary Rathbone; Jeremiah Wiffen; Sarah Hoare; Amelia Opie and others (including John Greenleaf Whittier in America). This volume aims to understand and present Barton as both a serious Romantic writer and a seminal Quaker poet – and indeed a Quaker Romantic – by collecting a modern selection of his verse for the first time.

'A Maker of Literary Luxuries': Barton's Life

Barton was born on 31 January 1784 in Carlisle. He knew little of his parents, John and Mary (*née* Done) Barton. Mary died days after giving birth, and indeed Barton only learnt at school that his father's second wife, Elizabeth Horne (1760–1833), was not his biological mother, although this appears to have had no traumatic effect whatsoever. His father – a manufacturer who had married into the Friends, and one of nine Quakers among those who founded the Society for Effecting the Abolition of the Slave Trade – died in 1789. Elizabeth moved to be close to her parents in Tottenham, and the young Barton hence spent his days between London and a short-lived but well-respected Quaker boarding school in Ipswich.[5] At 14, he was apprenticed to an Essex shopkeeper, Samuel Jesup, and in 1807 married his master's niece, Lucy Jesup (1781–1808). By this time, he had moved to Woodbridge in Suffolk, the small town that would effectively define his life: most of his poems refer no further than a 15-mile radius around it. However, tragedy struck and history repeated itself when his wife died giving birth to their daughter, also named Lucy. Grief-stricken, he dissolved his commercial interests (a corn and

---

[4] Barton himself wrote in 1820 that his *Poems* were 'an *experiment* how far a QUAKER POET might hope to win attention'. See William Jerdan, *The Autobiography*, 4 vols (London: Arthur Hall, 1853), III, p. 116.

[5] See C. Brightwen Rowntree, 'Friends' Schools at Ipswich (1790–1800) and Colchester (1817–1917)', *Journal of the FHS* 35 (1938), pp. 50–64.

INTRODUCTION

coal business with his brother-in-law Benjamin Jesup) and left to become a private tutor in Liverpool. When he returned, a year later, he became a clerk in a bank run by the Quaker Alexander family, a position he would hold until his death 40 years later.

It is about this time that Barton began to write. Initially, this appears to have been in the provincial press under the curious pen name 'Marcus': the earliest poem I have identified is 'To Walter Scott, Esq., On Perusing His Lady of the Lake', in the *Suffolk Chronicle* of 9 June 1810. By 1812 he had enough verses to compile his first volume *Metrical Effusions*; this was followed in 1818 by *Poems, by an Amateur*, printed for the author by subscription. Both these volumes were anonymous, as was all his work of this decade (or under the initials B.B.). The 1818 list of subscribers is a good indication of the poet's social networks and the type of friendships he cultivated throughout his career, as well as his life in the 1810s specifically – the latter a period for which evidence like letters is scant. They include extended family, Quaker connections near and far, clergymen from Suffolk villages, individuals from Woodbridge and Ipswich (some of whom are also the subjects of poems in the volume), and influential gentry and other county worthies. Poets William Wordsworth, Thomas Moore and Robert Southey are also included. Yet the print run of *Poems, by an Amateur* was extremely limited at around 150 copies. It was only in the following decade that his poetic career truly prospered and he was catapulted into prominence, spurred by the first volume under his own name – *Poems* (1820), which gathered much of his best earlier verse with new material, and eventually ran to four editions with revisions and additions.

It was the beginning of a prolonged and prolific phase in his literary life. Across the 1820s, he published no fewer than six major volumes. He became a frequent contributor to the newly relaunched *London Magazine*, which printed Thomas de Quincey's *Confessions of an English Opium-Eater* and many other major figures. Not only did his contributions to the *London* raise his literary profile, but some accounts also suggest that he met one of his closest correspondents, Charles Lamb, at one of its dinners. The decade also saw the first of the literary annuals, Frederic Shoberl's *Forget-Me-Not*, quickly followed by a slew of imitators. These were popular commercial offerings, released for Christmas and New Year, dominated by sentimental poetry and interspersed with engravings. Barton would go on to publish much of his poetry in such gift books. He was reviewed well, reprinted regularly and even received a generous annuity to support his work organised by sympathetic Quakers led by Joseph John Gurney. Although he followed some famous advice from Charles Lamb not to abandon his clerkship at the bank, his poetic labour was intensive: letters from the time are abuzz with concern about reviews and royalties, and Robert

Southey even counsels him to avoid the fate of Henry Kirke White, the consumptive, proto-Keatsian genius supposedly destroyed by overwork.

His pace slackened in the 1830s. Although he never ceased to write, his late phase includes only two major volumes: *The Reliquary* (1836), jointly authored with his daughter, and 1845's *Household Verses*. He continued living in Woodbridge, now in more spacious accommodation (his first cottage, which still stands, is a conspicuously narrow timber-framed house). He deepened old social connections and formed new ones, one of the most important being with Edward FitzGerald, who would go on to enter into an entirely unsuitable and short-lived marriage with Barton's daughter Lucy after the Quaker poet's death. Barton had been a keen walker, but was increasingly sedentary, grumbling half-comically about exercise – although he never lost his love for the local landscape and seascape. He rarely left Woodbridge and was an amiable fixture in town life. An 1855 article recalls his kind and cheerful demeanour on making a local visit, describing a deceptively young-looking man on whose knee the house's cat, Stalker, was enthusiastically purring.[6] We have a richer picture of his life and opinions at this time, due to the survival of far more letters now scattered across various archives. In 1849, after a few months of worsening health, he rang the bell from his room having gone to bed with a candle: a friend and his daughter ran upstairs to find him having a heart spasm, and he was laid to rest in the same Woodbridge burial ground where Lucy Jesup had been buried some four decades earlier. He was 65.

'Light winds sweeping o'er a late-reap'd field': Barton's Style

The judgements of Romantic-era contemporaries on Barton's style are relatively consistent. He writes many different kinds of poems, and is surprisingly experimental in his variety of forms: rolling anapaestic rhythms broadly based on three syllable units (e.g. 'On its **sides** no proud **for**ests, their **fo**liage **wav**ing'), polysyllabic or 'feminine' rhymes, and considerable variety in sonnet structure are just three stylistic traits he favours repeatedly. Despite this, the perception of Barton overall is clear. He does not aspire towards the force or ambition characteristic of 'Romantic genius', and there is a tendency to thematic repetition in his work. Lamb teasingly asks, 'do children die so often, and so good in your parts?'[7] Yet he is seen as sincere, lucid and tender. As critics understood it, his was the poetry of the affections rather than the passions,

---

[6] 'Reminiscences of Bernard Barton', *The Leisure Hour: A Family Journal of Instruction and Recreation* 159 (11 January 1859), pp. 27–30.
[7] Letter of 2 July 1825, *Lamb*, p. 736.

INTRODUCTION

and he is marked as particularly successful in the pathetic and descriptive strains – indeed, we can detect a slight feminisation in his cultural reception. Above all, in an era which revalued simplicity – in peasant poets like John Clare and Suffolk-born Robert Bloomfield, and in Wordsworth's aesthetic of common speech – his own simplicity found a ready resonance. Like William Cowper and Samuel Taylor Coleridge, Barton's diction and flow often veer towards the conversational, and his figuration is rarely excessive: things tend to bear straightforward allegorical morals while the verse's texture is, with some interesting exceptions, not sensuous or visionary but delicate and reflective. Perhaps his favourite form is the nine-line Spenserian stanza, utilised in the Romantic period not so much for its past tendencies towards bejewelled richness, but for open and flexible simplicity.[8]

This unaffected aesthetic is one of the main ways in which readers began to negotiate the 'phenomenon' or paradox of a Quaker poet. The Society of Friends was known for several things in the period, ranging from their role in anti-slavery campaigning to a strong commercial reputation which would eventually underwrite well-known firms including Clarks, Cadbury and Barclays. However, the most conspicuous thing in everyday encounters would have been plain dress; this meant drab colours, simple and functional fabrics, no decorative embroidery or tailoring (e.g. frills, flounces, lace) and, famously, broad-brimmed hats for men and bonnets for the women. Nearly all of Barton's initial reviews evoke the analogy of Quaker fashion, and, as the *British Review* commented in 1822, there is a sense that the quiet and reserved simplicity of his verse 'is in some degree a new department, and it offers itself to the genius of this amiable Quaker as his own by right of occupancy and natural claim'.[9] Other reviews talked about the Quaker muse or Quaker beauties. There is plenty of evidence that Barton himself also saw these affinities. For instance, in 'The Quaker Poet, Verses on Seeing Myself So Designated' (1821), he justifies Quaker poetry by arguing that quietly expressed feeling is more authentic than intense emotion superficially enfolded with 'gayer robes'. In a characteristic analogy, the shaded stream is deeper and more beautiful than the sparkling brook open to the sunlight.

This latter comparison is also marked by Barton's exemplary stylistic gesture, one which the reader will find articulated again and again: a version of

---

[8] The Spenserian stanza (ABABBCBCC, with a lengthened final line) originated with Edmund Spenser (1552–1599) but enjoyed a Romantic-era revival, especially among the second generation poets. See my own 'Poetics at the Religious Margin: Bernard Barton and Quaker Romanticism', *Review of English Studies* 70, no. 295 (2019), pp. 509–26, which includes a discussion of Barton's use of the stanza.
[9] 'Art. XVIII. Poems by Bernard Barton', *British Review* 20 (December 1822), p. 408.

litotes, understood in its classical sense of simplicity, understatement and strategic negation. Across his oeuvre, something lesser is privileged over something superficially more arresting, in the form that 'X is not Y, but nevertheless…' Thus, winter beauties can outmatch spring and summer, the Valley of Fern is more affecting than Romantic mountain scenery, Quaker bonnets delight over fashionable head-dresses, the modest ivy is chosen instead of spring-time birches, and the rustic pastoral of Crabbe and Bloomfield makes its own claim over classical traditions. Explicit or implicit *litotes* determines Barton almost completely as a Romantic-era nature poet. As E. V. Lucas argues, 'Had [he] been painter instead of poet he would have given us landscapes in the style of Gainsborough.'[10] His verse is shaped by the gentle topography of Suffolk, of its villages, fields, woodlands, meadows, heaths, winding rivers and North Sea beaches. This is not Snowdon or even the Lakes, but was never meant to be. Like Gainsborough's early paintings of the same environs, Barton is heavily influenced by the notion of the picturesque: varied and irregular, often rustic, less perfect than beauty but less spectacular than the sublime. Such was a natural mode for him.

The other analogy Lucas offers with the visual arts – not inappropriately, since Barton loved pictures – was the painter George Morland, famed for his warm scenes of rural life, influenced by Dutch and Flemish styles. This speaks to another unpretentious side of Barton's poetic output: his tendency to the domestic, and a modest sentimentality which made him a natural fit for the popular periodicals and annuals. Occasionally, this is expressed in narrative verse or pastoral registers – for example 'The Yellow-Hammer', framed as a Suffolk villager's song, or the Wordsworthian 'A Grandsire's Tale' – but more commonly it appears drawn from life. In particular, both his extensive correspondence and the already cited local networks generated many informal poems of friendship and sociability. Like many Romantics, he repeatedly idealises children and childhood, and as touchstones of pure feeling they are frequent addressees and subjects. These gentle affections predominate almost entirely over stronger passions. When all these strands of humble sensibility are combined with moral and pious sentiments, as they generally are in Barton's work, we can see yet another set of poetic decisions that contribute to an overall aesthetic of simplicity. As the aforementioned poem 'The Quaker Poet' reminds us in one of its central images, the nightingale is a songbird 'of sober plume' who sings, even while the peacock slumbers.

---

[10] E. V. Lucas, *Bernard Barton and his Friends: A Record of Quiet Lives* (London: Edward Hicks, 1893), p. 181.

INTRODUCTION

'I must e'en be a Quaker still': Barton and Religion

If readers found it hard to disentangle Barton's style from his Quakerism, there were also plenty of poems that took openly Quaker subjects and presented this world poetically to nineteenth-century audiences for arguably the first time. *Poetic Vigils* (1824) includes a triptych of memorials to Quaker martyrs, and the earlier 'Verses, Supposed to be Written in a Burial-Ground Belonging to the Society of Friends' is an explicitly Quaker re-writing of Gray's famous 'Elegy Written in a Country Churchyard'. There are also more indirect motifs. In particular, vocabularies of light and silence, although hardly absent from other Romantic-era writing, have evocative resonance in the Quaker context. The former implicates one of its most important doctrines, the 'inward Light', or the presence of God within the individual which enacts a potentially prophetic discerning of spiritual truths. The latter cannot help but evoke the values of a Quaker spirituality based on silence: without form or liturgy, Friends' meetings would often pass with no speech whatsoever, as a practice of prayerful waiting. It is hence notable that light and silence are frequently deployed in moments of sacramental feeling or expression within Barton's verse.

Such theologies of light and silence had their origins in the seventeenth century, and it is worth underlining that Barton's Quakerism generally adhered to the denomination's most traditional forms, as can be seen in his letters to Quaker correspondent Mary Sutton. This is important because the nineteenth century was a period of fundamental transformation for the Friends: Evangelical Christianity was vibrant and expansive, and quietistic Quaker orthodoxy was being displaced due to its influence (see the 'Note on Quakerism' for further detail). Barton, however, held fast to the faith in which he had been brought up, even though many around him were leaving the Society of Friends or adopting Evangelical practices. To Sutton, he averred that 'a sprinkling, or water sprinkled, sacrament-taking Quaker is a sort of incongruous medley I can neither classify nor understand.'[11] However, his traditionalist positions were not held in hostility or with any desire to enter conflict with others. He disliked polemic, division and vain dispute, and his one solely religious volume of poetry, the important *Devotional Verses* (1826), shows how he could smoothly transcend potentially fraught issues. The place of scripture was an inner fault-line for the Society of Friends, and lay behind the most significant schism of nineteenth-century British Quakerism, the Beaconite Controversy of the 1830s. Yet *Devotional Verses* is almost entirely structured around Biblical verses: Barton simply saw no incompatibility worth

---

[11] *SPL*, p. 49.

contending over between scripture and the Light, either in Quaker tradition, or in his present moment.

Devotional Verses also speaks to Barton's wider religious reach. As the *Athenaeum* noted in an 1827 review of *A Widow's Tale*, extracted in this volume, there was an irony in the fact that despite coming from a small and distinctive sect Barton was one of the leading religious poets of the day. Although Barton's Quakerism is orthodox, his religious sensibility was broad, sensitive and Biblically literate. At a time when the amorality and infidelity of literature (most obviously in the pervasive shadow cast by Byronism) was an anxiety for many readers, Barton's religious verse and the more or less oblique religiosity of much of his other poetry appeared pure and even pleasingly chaste. It probably helped that Barton – an ironically tolerant member of a denomination already known for its toleration – conceived faith in open and generous terms. He had keen friendships with many Anglican clergy, and his poetry could be sympathetic to Roman Catholics, Methodists and others. The long poem 'Leiston Abbey', set amongst a Suffolk ruin and written in 1819, is an excellent example of his reflections on religious identity, shared Christianity and the violent upheavals and persecutions of sectarian history.

A final aspect of Barton's religion with a clear effect on his poetry is Quakerism's forceful commitment to social causes of the period. Barton's politics in the conventional sense were predictable and unassuming: he was a Whig, like most Dissenters, and had close connections with the liberal MP for East Suffolk, Robert Newton Shawe, and his family. He could write direct and even stinging political poetry (e.g. 'A Clerico-Politico Portrait'). Yet more important and certainly more overt was the larger Quaker humanitarian impulse which shaped poems from 1812's 'Stanzas on the Anniversary of the Abolition of the Slave Trade' onward. The Society of Friends had been at the centre of eighteenth-century opposition to the slave trade and continued to address a range of political and social issues, including the continuation of slavery in the British Empire and elsewhere, the working condition of chimney sweeps, and prison reform. In 1796 they founded the first modern asylum for the mentally ill, the York Retreat, based on William Tuke's 'moral treatment'. And the Quakers had maintained the tenet of radical pacifism in their opposition to the long, gruelling Napoleonic Wars. Barton supported many of these causes, and poems involving one or the other of them appear across his many volumes. It is a reminder that quietism in the spiritual sense need not mean retreat from the world in an ethical sense: although no-one would position Barton as a radical, in the sense John Thelwall or Percy Bysshe Shelley were radicals, his instincts were fundamentally humane.

INTRODUCTION

An Edition of Bernard Barton

Almost immediately after Barton's death, Lucy Barton and Edward FitzGerald collaborated on a volume entitled *Selections from the Poems and Letters of Bernard Barton*, published by Hall, Virtue & Co. While 1818's *Poems, by an Amateur* by the virtually unknown Barton had possessed a short list of subscribers, the list in 1849 goes on for 24 pages and includes Queen Victoria and 10 copies for Sir Robert Peel, the former Prime Minister who had gifted Barton a £100 pension in 1846. It is a fascinating text, containing a useful memoir penned by FitzGerald and many interesting footnotes. As a collection of poetry, however, it is very limited even taking into account its Victorian provenance. Its selection is biased towards the work of the 1840s and one senses poems about local acquaintances and friends have been privileged. Moreover, while its editors have a conscious and perceptive sense of Barton's aesthetic weaknesses – notably dragging out fine descriptive verses with a somewhat trite moral – they act on this by radically altering and shortening many of the texts included.

This edition attempts instead to give a selection of Barton's work underpinned by modern scholarship and a retrospective critical standpoint. Out of over seven hundred poems from his major volumes alone, I have picked out around 80. In making the selection several principles have guided me. Firstly, I have drawn from all periods of his career (albeit with an inevitable concentration on the 1820s) and striven to represent a full range of tonal and thematic variety. This means giving roughly equal weight to his three major modes: nature poetry, religious verse (both specifically Quaker and more generally devotional), and texts of friendship, domesticity and feeling. In addition, I have sought to represent his historical and political engagement (not least via a very substantial extract from his longest work 'Napoleon'), as well as including several pieces that engage the arts, such as poems on paintings and verses addressed to other writers. Secondly, I have attempted to mirror both nineteenth-century and contemporary interests. On one hand, if a poem appeared especially striking to Barton's contemporaries or was repeatedly noted by reviewers (e.g. 'The Ivy' or 'A Dream'), I have usually included it. On the other hand, I have also tried to select pieces that will most engage a modern readership and reflect up-to-date scholarly concerns: hence, for example, I give considerable attention to his anti-slavery poetry, and include a generous illustrated selection from the posthumous *Natural History of the Holy Land*. Last but not least, I have opted for poems that seem aesthetically striking and which I personally enjoy. Barton was not a poet of the first rank, as his contemporaries would put it, but he is a fascinating writer capable of delicately arresting beauty.

In textual terms, Barton does not present an editor with a vast array of variation. Even at the compositional stage, he preferred the immediacy of the initial expression. As he states apologetically in his preface to *Napoleon, and Other Poems* (1822):

> It has not been from indolence that the author has not bestowed more elaborate revision on his compositions; nor is it with any affected contempt of refined taste, or in wilful disrespect of critical opinion [...] in his judgement, his poetry is not of a description which long and laborious revision would essentially improve (p. xiv).

It is clear that much the same judgement applied later on in the literary process too. There are inevitably slight changes in wording when multiple versions exist, and the Advertisement to the fourth edition of *Poems* notes that his publisher had refined its typographical appearance. Nevertheless, it is a relatively simple editorial decision to consistently base reading texts on *the first printed appearance of the poem* – or at least the first appearance my research has been able to uncover. Not only does this locate the reading text close to each poem's origin, it better evidences the diverse range of print contexts – literary annuals, periodicals, anthologies, provincial newspapers – in which his work was met and oeuvre evolved. In a few cases, I have departed from this practice and used a later base text, giving further explanation in the head-note. There is a limited set of Barton manuscript poems in archives: I have consulted these wherever possible. My notes indicate any significant variations between versions of a poem: very minor verbal variants and differences in typography and punctuation have not been recorded. Due to the posthumous nature of the 1849 *Selections from the Poems and Letters*, and the editorial interventions of Lucy Barton and Edward FitzGerald in the preparation of that text, those variants are not noted.

The date of first printed publication also determines the chronological arrangement of the poems, not least because the evidence for when Barton wrote a given piece is usually non-existent. While this does create a few minor anomalies when a date of composition is known – particularly notable where Barton himself has provided one at the foot of the poem, which is reproduced – it is a more consistent approach than trying to combine clashing chronologies. I have attempted to reflect these other dates to some extent when sequencing poems from the same source; in most other cases I simply follow the volume's own original ordering. The reader is advised to consult the notes if interested in the precise detail of what is known about textual and publication histories. In any case, this volume accurately charts Barton's unfolding career and can be used to trace what phases do exist in his work. The table

INTRODUCTION

of contents has been structured to suggest one fourfold division: the early anonymously published work of the 1810s; the period of emergence between 1820 and 1825 which begins with his contributions to the *London Magazine* and concludes with the final revised edition of *Poems*; the intensely productive phase in the late 1820s that encompasses three major volumes and much of his literary annual verse; and finally the less prolific output of the 1830s and 1840s crowned by *Household Verses*. While it is true that his aesthetic does not develop as radically as some poets, one can detect subtle thematic and stylistic changes: the slow fading of initially raw grief for his wife Lucy, greater imaginative ambition and stylistic range in volumes of the late 1820s, or the emergence of increasingly condensed and allegorical nature poetry, to name but three. Whilst E. V. Lucas, aiming to characterise Barton as an artist out of the flow of time, claimed that his literary identity was utterly static – 'from the death of his wife in 1808, until his own death in 1849, he lived through one long, level day' – it is hoped that this selected poems will illustrate a poet whose undoubted continuities do nonetheless contain multitudes.[12]

---

[12] Lucas, p. 12.

A NOTE ON QUAKERISM

Although I have drawn attention in the notes to specific Quaker contexts where they are relevant, the following brief note offers a simplified overview of Quakerism which the reader may find helpful. The 'further reading' section of the bibliography includes several works offering full and scholarly accounts of Quaker history, culture and thought.

The Society of Friends – or Quakers – are a religious group that emerged in the religious and social tumult of the English Civil War era, led by George Fox (1624–1691). Like many radical Protestant sects in the seventeenth century, they rapidly became a persecuted minority, although as time went on their charismatic and disruptive beginnings (most infamously going naked as a sign) gave way to greater degrees of organisation. Theologically, the same period saw the evolution of a quietist spirituality based on simplicity, unique forms of worship and detachment from society. This was codified in Robert Barclay's *Apology for True Christian Divinity* (1676) and became the dominant (if not only) current of Quakerism across the eighteenth century.

The basic unit of Quakerism is the Meeting. Although there are ministers and elders, there is no formal hierarchy: any member may speak if they feel a spiritual prompting and Quakerism permitted female preaching from early in its history. Barton belonged to the Woodbridge Meeting, the old Meeting House of which still stands and beside which the poet is buried. Meeting Houses were grouped into Monthly and then Quarterly Meetings which oversaw matters of organisation and spiritual discipline among members at district and regional levels: this discipline was especially crucial to the eighteenth-century identity of Quakerism, as inherited by Barton. Yearly Meetings stand at the apex of this pyramid, and the London Yearly Meeting formalised doctrine for Friends in Britain through the issue of epistles. These were collated into what was known as the *Book of Discipline* or *Extracts from the Minutes and Advices of the Yearly Meeting* (its descendent is now entitled *Quaker Faith and Practice*). As at all levels, decision making at the Yearly Meeting was carried out not via a formal process but through intuiting the 'sense of the meeting' as it developed among all members.

Quakerism in Barton's time had developed a series of practices that seemed remarkable to outsiders. These included idiosyncratic speech-ways (e.g. using 'thou' instead of 'you' on the basis of radical equality, or refusing oaths because all speech should be truthful); rejecting fashion, ornament and luxury in favour of plainness; and filling their burial grounds with unmarked graves. The aforementioned system of discipline, overseen by elders and the Meetings, created a distinctive partition from mainstream society: Quakers could not attend theatres, balls or concerts, and the Society was rigorous in their attitude towards debtors (indeed, the latter was one of the most common reasons for which members were 'disowned'). They prayed largely in silence, their Meeting Houses were unadorned, and Quaker spirituality had its own unique vocabulary: 'discerning' for the uncovering of truth, or 'convincement' for conversion, for instance. While the Quaker stance on slavery eventually aligned with a mounting social consensus in favour of abolition, their radical pacifism and opposition to all violence and trade in arms remained (and remains) unusual.

Yet – as Barton's friend Thomas Clarkson explored in his sympathetic three volume *Portraiture of Quakerism* (1806) – these apparently strange aspects of identity coherently expressed a deeply held theology. One element of this is simply a radical Christianity: a commitment to truthfulness, benevolence and a desire to stand against the world in the name of simplicity. This impulse goes back to the earliest days of Fox. Another derives from perhaps Quakerism's most distinctive theological concept: the inward Light. Each believer has an inward guide and spiritual sense which means religion is levelled among equal individuals. Quaker Meetings are silent, non-hierarchical and anti-ceremonial because they are acts of jointly waiting and listening for the prompts of the inward Light, rather than the performance of set external forms under the auspices of a priestly figure. Due to this privileging of individual inwardness, the theology of the Society of Friends has sometimes shifted the authority of Scripture to a subsidiary place.

As already noted in the introduction, this potential tension between the Bible and the Light became one key conflict between established Quaker orthodoxy and the rising tide of Evangelical Christianity in the nineteenth century. Others included the importance of sacraments (especially baptism) to the new style of faith, and the Evangelical emphasis on conversion and growth versus Quakerism's cultural introversion and birthright membership. Schisms were triggered within the Society of Friends on both sides of the Atlantic in the face of Evangelical influence, and many left the Quakers – these included all of Barton's closest relatives. Quakerism would thus be reshaped and altered in Barton's lifetime, especially from the 1830s onwards when British Friends split sharply over the so-called Beaconite Controversy. However, despite its

A NOTE ON QUAKERISM

strong scriptural sense, Barton's poetry is best seen as an expression of the more classical tenets of the denomination, and the poet's own opinions (see the contextual material) are relatively clear in adhering to the faith of his 'father's house'.

Note on dates: in some places within the text, the reader will find Barton's own rendering of dates in Quaker form. Due to the pagan origins of the names of the month, Quaker practice was to refer to months by number (e.g. 1st Mo. = January).

1812–19: ANONYMOUS BEGINNINGS

MY LUCY

"No idly-feign'd poetic pains
    My sad love-lorn lamentings claim;
No shepherd's pipe, Arcadian strains;
    No fabled tortures, quaint and tame:
The plighted faith; the mutual flame;
    The oft attested pow'rs above:
The promis'd father's tender name:
    These were the pledges of my love!"
BURNS.

Oh, Thou! from earth for ever fled!
Whose reliques lie among the dead
With daisied verdure overspread,
                  My Lucy!

For many a weary month gone by,   5
How many a solitary sigh
I've heav'd for thee, no longer nigh,
                  My Lucy!

And if to grieve I cease awhile,
I look for that enchanting smile   10
Which all my cares could once beguile,
                  My Lucy!

But ah! in vain. The blameless art,
Which sooth'd to peace my troubled heart,
Is lost with thee, my better part!   15
                  My Lucy!

Thy converse innocently free,
That bade the fiends of fancy flee—
'Tis there I find the want of thee,
          My Lucy! 20

Nor is it for myself alone,
That I thy early death bemoan:
Our infant now is *all my own*,
          My Lucy!

Couldst thou a guardian angel prove 25
To the dear offspring of our love,
Until it reach the realms above,
          My Lucy!

Could thy angelic spirit stray,
Unseen companion of my way, 30
As onward drags the weary day,
          My Lucy!

And, when the midnight hour shall close
My eyes in short unsound repose,
Couldst thou but whisper off my woes, 35
          My Lucy!

Then, though thy loss I must deplore
Till next we meet to part no more,
I'd wait the grasp that from me tore
          My Lucy! 40

For, be my life but spent like thine,
With joy shall I that life resign,
And fly to thee, for ever mine,
          My Lucy!

STANZAS ON THE ANNIVERSARY OF THE ABOLITION OF THE SLAVE TRADE

Respectfully Inscrib'd to the Members of the African Institution

 Again the rapid flight of time brings round
   The sacred hour to virtue justly dear:
 My muse! commemorate, with joyful sound,
   An hour which unborn ages shall revere.
 E'en that glad hour which wip'd the bitter tear   5
   From Afric's cheek, and cast her chains away:
 Freedom, humanity, and justice, hear!
   To you I dedicate this votive lay,
And consecrate to you this ever glorious day.

 All hail, ye heavenly band! your holy fire   10
   Inflam'd with virtuous ardour CLARKSON's breast;
 Awoke that zeal which labour ne'er could tire,
   Danger affright, nor av'rice lull to rest.
 He saw poor Afric's sable sons opprest;
   Saw them, transported from their native shore,   15
 Meet stern-eyed death in all his horrors drest,
   Or life more horrible than death deplore.
Such were the scenes he saw—scenes we behold no more.

 CLARKSON! and WILBERFORCE! thrice honour'd names!
   Ye shine conspicuous 'mid that chosen band,   20
 Whose steady zeal a nation's reverence claims,
   Whose generous labours have redeem'd the land.
 And could a humble poet's trembling hand
   Present to merit half the tribute due,

Thy name, illustrious G<small>LOSTER</small>! forth should stand 25
    Amid the bold disinterested few,
Who prejudice defied, and spurn'd her venal crew.

Among the hosts who hail with just applause
    This joyful hour, my partial eyes survey
A sect, whose ardent zeal in virtue's cause, 30
    Prompts me the tribute of respect to pay.
Ye F<small>RIENDS</small> OF P<small>EACE</small>! to you this glorious day
    Is doubly sanctified, is doubly dear;
On Afric's shores no more shall martial fray
    Infringe that sacred law your souls revere; 35
But strife and war shall cease, and happier days appear.

On Guinea's coast, where once the shriek of wo
    Proclaim'd the reign of anguish and despair;
Where avarice sunk the man the brute below,
    And christian monsters mock'd the captive's prayer; 40
A different aspect shall that region wear:
    There scenes of bliss shall once more greet the eye;
The festive song the evening gale shall bear
    In broken accents to the distant sky—
Blest sounds of peaceful mirth, and village revelry. 45

O Thou! whose sceptre sways this earthly ball,
    This trivial atom in creation's round;
"Who seest with equal eye as God of all,"
    A Negro fetter'd, or a Monarch crown'd:
O Thou! whose power and goodness none can bound, 50
    Heal Afric's wrongs, and pardon Europe's crime;
Proclaim through torrid wastes that joyful sound,
    Which Jordan's vallies heard in earlier time:
Salvation's gladdening voice, and Gospel truths sublime!

E'en while I sing, behold! a beam of light 55
    Shines tremulously o'er my raptur'd mind,
Foreboding that the soul's protracted night
    Shall, like the body's patient sufferings, find
An end at last; for charity, more kind
    Than proud munificence could ever boast, 60
To leave no entrance for regret behind,

    Hath rais'd of pious ranks a countless host,
Who rear her standard high, and shout from coast to coast.

    The B<small>IBLE</small>! sacred pledge of love divine,
        The christian's treasure, now the heathen's prize,   65
    Shall soon complete redemption's grand design,
        And bring salvation home to Afric's eyes.
    Soon shall the sun of righteousness arise,
        And shine o'er every zone from pole to pole:
    Then, O my Country! ever just as wise,   70
        'Till planets in their orbits cease to roll,
Shalt thou remain enshrin'd in every grateful soul.

ODE TO AN ÆOLIAN HARP

Sweet instrument! whose tones beguile the ear
    With mingled strains of sadness and delight,
Recal the scenes to melancholy dear,
    Or to the bowers of former bliss invite;
The sweet aerial sylph, or seraph bright,   5
    That sweeps thy strings with more than mortal skill,
Although of frame too subtle for the sight,
    May well a bard's imagination fill.

Hark! what a heavenly strain was there!
    A dirge for some departed soul   10
Angels have taken to their care,
    With kindred spirits to enrol.
Such were the sounds that softly stole
    Erewhile on Cowper's faltering sense,
As onward he survey'd the goal   15
    That hasten'd his departure hence.

A bolder and a bolder note
    To gladness now directs my mind,
Like distant bells whose changes float
    Across the water on the wind;   20
To hail some married pair, design'd
    For mutual love, or mutual strife;
By habit or by will inclin'd
    To strange vicissitudes of life.

And while the rapid chariot rolls,   25
    In noisy pride, the streets along;
Attracts the gaze of vulgar souls,
    And mocks and interrupts my song;

ODE TO AN ÆOLIAN HARP

How I despise the restless throng,
    Who scorn the meed of sober thought; 30
Whose pulses beat with rapture strong,
    Whose transient bliss is dearly bought!

That dying fall, which now succeeds
    The uproar that subdued thy sound,
Tells me of many a heart that bleeds 35
    With guilt in fashion's giddy round;
Who never since their childhood found
    A day, an hour of cheap repose,
But vainly thought their wishes crown'd.
    When riot with the morning rose. 40

The lofty song, the sprightly dance,
    To them was life, to them was all.
The studied sigh, the wanton glance,
    And all the arts that grace the ball,
My unapproving heart appal; 45
    But while I listen to thy strains,
I fit my mind for duty's call,
    And bless the lot that pride disdains.

The trumpet tells of streaming blood,
    Of valour's feats, of victory's prize, 50
Of broken hearts, and many a flood
    Of tears that gush from widows' eyes.
But thy celestial breath supplies
    With thoughts of peace and joy my mind;
It lifts my soul above the skies 55
    To transports for the just design'd.

And when, arising on the final day,
    Mortals shall hear the first immortal sound;
When millions shall reluctantly obey
    The call, and look in mute amazement round; 60
Sensations purer still than e'er I found
    From the light breeze, as over thee it blew,
Shall realize the fancied spell that bound
    My grosser sense, and prove the pleasure true.

A GUESS AT THE CONTENTS OF LALLA ROOKH

Sunshine and Moonshine by hook or by crook;
With Bowers, and Flowers, and many a Brook;
Fairy regions which never were dreamt of by Cook;
Rosy lips, rosy cheeks too, and tresses, which, shook
By the amorous breezes, inchantingly look;   5
With bright eyes which glance into every nook,
Speaking language which might even puzzle Horne Tooke,
If Purley his spirit from Pluto could hook;—
In short, you can't guess what you'll find in the Book
Which Tom Moore has written, and call'd Lalla Rookh!   10

STANZAS ("THE HEAVEN WAS CLOUDLESS")

The Heaven was cloudless—the Ocean was calm,
    For the breeze which blew o'er it scarce ruffl'd its breast;—
Not a sight, not a sound, that might waken alarm,
    Could the eye, or the ear, of the wanderer molest.

As I roam'd on the beach, to my memory rose,   5
    The bliss I had tasted in moments gone by;
When my soul could rejoice in a scene of repose,
    And my spirit exult in an unclouded sky.

I thought of the *past*—and, while thinking, THY NAME
    Came uncall'd to my lips:—but no language it found: 10
Yet my heart felt how dear, and how hallow'd its claim;
    I *could* think, though my tongue dared not utter a sound.

I did not forget how with THEE I had paced
    On the shore I now trod—and how pleasant it seem'd;
How my eye then sought thine, and how gladly it traced   15
    Every glance of affection which mildly it beam'd.

The *beginning* and *end* of our loves were before me;—
    And both touch'd a chord of the tenderest tone;
For thy SPIRIT, then near, shed its influence o'er me,
    And told me that still THOU wast truly my own.   20

Yet—I thought at the moment—how dear was the thought!
    That there still was a union, which death could not break;
And if with some sorrow the feeling was fraught,
    Yet even that sorrow was sweet for *thy* sake.

Thus musing on THEE, every object around 25
    Seem'd to borrow thy sweetness to make itself dear;
Each murmuring wave reach'd the shore with a sound
    As soft as the tone of *thy* voice to my ear.

The lights and the shades on the surface of ocean
    Seem'd to give back the glimpses of feeling and grace, 30
Which once so expressively told each emotion
    Of thy innocent heart, as I gaz'd on thy face.

And when I look'd up to the beautiful sky,
    So cloudless and calm—O! it harmoniz'd well
With the gentle expression which spoke in *thy* eye, 35
    Ere the curtain of death on its loveliness fell!

How proud is the prize which thy virtues have won,
    When their *memory* alone is so precious to me,
That this world cannot give what my soul would not shun,
    If it tore from my breast the remembrance of THEE! 40

THE CONVICT'S APPEAL
[STANZAS 1–15]

The hours fly fast, and soon the beam
    Of life's last day must break;
And soon must be fulfill'd the dream,
    From which 'twas joy to wake.

I dreamt just now, when feverish sleep   5
    My heavy eye-lids seal'd,
I could not sigh, I could not weep,
    My heart was sear'd and steel'd.

I stood, methought, in mute despair,
    Upon the scaffold's height,   10
And mark'd the thousands gather'd there,
    To gaze upon the sight.

O pardon, Heav'n! the impious thought,
    For impious it must be,
Which in that dreadful hour was brought,   15
    Unconsciously to me.

Forgive me, if I wildly pray'd,
    The yawning earth might ope,
And swallow those who thus survey'd,
    A being 'reft of hope.   20

'Twas frenzied anguish brought that prayer,
    To slumbering misery;
Yet sure 'twas cruel to come there,
    My wretched death to see.

For there were *Fathers*, *Husbands* too,   25
    Who wives and daughters had;
And even *Mothers* came to view,
    While mine!—it made me mad!

A suffocating thirst, a swell,
    Which seem'd my breath to choak,   30
Came over me:—it broke the spell
    Of sleep, and I awoke.

Though momentary the relief,
    It seem'd a respite given;
A something to give vent to grief,   35
    To weep, and kneel to Heaven.

Now, thanks to God's most gracious name,
    That frenzied hour is past;
Yet still o'erwhelm'd with grief and shame,
    I can but dread the last.   40

Must I then meet my death so soon?
    Can they who power possess,
To grant of life the glorious boon,
    Be deaf to my distress?

From Virtue's paths though I have swerv'd,   45
    And injur'd man, can I,
For bloodless crimes, have e'er deserv'd
    That dreadful doom—TO DIE?

Such is, it seems, the *Law's* decree,
    No mercy can be shown;   50
My life the sacrifice must be,
    Though ill it can atone.

To Thee, O God! who, through thy Son,
    Hast proffer'd life to all,
Who feel themselves by sin undone,   55
    I turn,—before Thee fall;—

And supplicate with streaming eyes,
   And heart with anguish rife,
From Thee, that mercy man denies,
   From Thee, eternal life.   60

ON SILENT WORSHIP

"Thou worshipp'st at the temple's inner shrine,
God being with thee when we know it not."
WORDSWORTH.

Though glorious, O GOD! must thy temple have been
    On the day of its first dedication,
When the Cherubim's wings widely waving were seen
    On high, o'er the ark's holy station;—

When even the chosen of Levi, though skill'd   5
    To minister, standing before Thee,
Retir'd from the cloud which the temple then fill'd;—
    And Thy Glory made Israel adore Thee:—

Though awfully grand was thy majesty then;—
    Yet the worship thy Gospel discloses,   10
Less splendid in pomp to the vision of Men,
    Far surpasses the ritual of Moses.

And by whom was that ritual for ever repeal'd?
    But by HIM, unto whom it was given
To enter that *Oracle*, where is reveal'd   15
    Not the Cloud,—but the brightness of Heaven!

Who, having once enter'd, hath shown us the way,
    O GOD! how to worship before Thee;
Not with shadowy forms of that earlier day,
    But *in Spirit* and *Truth* to adore Thee!   20

This, this is the worship the Saviour made known
    When She of Samaria found Him

ON SILENT WORSHIP

By the Patriarch's well, sitting weary, alone,
    With the stillness of evening around Him.

How sublime, yet how simple the worship he taught   25
    To her, who enquir'd by that fountain,
If J<small>EHOVAH</small> at Solyma's Shrine would be sought?—
    Or ador'd on Samaria's mountain?—

Woman!—believe me, the hour is near,
    When H<small>E</small>, if ye rightly would hail Him,   30
Will neither be worshipp'd *exclusively* here,
    Nor yet at the altar of Salem.

For GOD is a Spirit!—and they who aright
    Would perform the pure worship he loveth,
In the heart's holy temple will seek with delight   35
    That Spirit the Father approveth.

And many that Prophecy's truth can declare,
    Whose bosoms have livingly known it;
Whom GOD hath instructed to worship him there,
    And convinc'd that his mercy will own it.   40

The Temple which Solomon built to his Name
    Now lives but in History's story;
Extinguish'd long since is its altar's bright flame,
    And vanish'd each glimpse of its glory:—

But the Christian—made wise by a wisdom divine,   45
    Though all human fabrics may falter,
Still finds in his heart a far holier shrine
    Where the fire burns unquench'd on the Altar!

PLAYFORD. A DESCRIPTIVE FRAGMENT.—1817

Hast thou a heart to prove the power
   Of a landscape lovely, soft, and serene?
Go—when its fragrance hath left the flower,
   When the leaf is no longer glossy and green;
When the clouds are careering across the sky,   5
And the rising winds tell the tempest nigh,
Though the slanting sunbeams are lingering still,
On the tower's grey top, and the side of the hill;—
   Then go to the village of Playford, and see
     If it be not a lovely spot;   10
   And, if Nature can boast of charms for thee,
     Thou wilt love it, and leave it not,
Till the shower shall warn thee no longer to roam,
And then thou wilt carry its picture home;
To feed thy fancy when far away,   15
A source of delight for a future day.
Its sloping green is verdant and fair,
   And between its tufts of trees
Are white cottages, peeping here and there,
   The pilgrim's eye to please:—   20
A white farm-house may be seen on its brow,
And its grey old hall in the valley below,
   By a moat encircled round;
And from the left verge of its hill you may hear,
If you chance on a Sabbath to wander near   25
   A sabbath-breathing sound:
'Tis the sound of the bell which is slowly ringing
   In that tower, which lifts its turrets above
The wood-fring'd bank, where birds are singing,
And from spray to spray are fearlessly springing,   30

PLAYFORD. A DESCRIPTIVE FRAGMENT.—1817

    As if in a lonely and untrodden grove;
For the grey church-tower is far over head;
    And so deep is the winding lane below,
They hear not the sound of the traveller's tread,
    If a traveller there should chance to go:—   35
But few pass there, for most who come
At the bell's loud summons have left their home,
    That bell which is tolling so slow.
And grassy and green may the path be seen
        To the village-church that leads;   40
For its glossy hue is as verdant to view
        As you see it in lowly meads.
And he who the ascending pathway scales,
By the gate above, and the mossy pales,
    Will find the trunk of a leafless tree,   45
        All bleak, and barren, and bare;—
    Yet it keeps its station, and seems to be
        Like a silent monitor there:—
    Though wasted and worn, it smiles in the ray
    Of the bright warm sun, on a sunny day;   50
        And more than once I have seen
    The moonbeams sleep on its barkless trunk,
    As calmly and softly as ever they sunk
        On its leaves, when its leaves were green;
And it seem'd to rejoice in their light the while,   55
Reminding my heart of the patient smile
Resignation can wear in the hour of grief,
When it finds in Religion a source of relief,
And stript of delights which earth had given,
Still shines in the beauty it borrows from heaven!   60
    But the bell hath ceas'd to ring;—
    And the birds no longer sing;—
And the grasshopper's carol is heard no more;—
    Yet sounds of praise and prayer
    The wandering breezes bear,   65
Like the murmur of waves on the ocean shore.
All else is still!—but silence can be
    More eloquent far than speech;
And the valley below, and that tower and tree,
    Through the eye to the heart can reach.   70
Could the sage's creed, the historian's tale,

Utter language like that of yon silent vale?
As it basks in the beams of the sabbath-day,
And rejoices in Nature's reviving ray;
While its outstretch'd meadows, and autumn-ting'd trees   75
Seem enjoying the sun, and inhaling the breeze.
And hath not that church a lovely look
In the page of this landscape's open book?
Like a capital letter, which catches the eye
Of the reader, and says a new chapter is nigh;   80
So its tower, by which the horizon is broken,
Of prayer, and of praise, a beautiful token,
Lifts up its head, and silently tells
Of a world hereafter, where happiness dwells.
While that scathed tree seems a link between   85
   The dead and the living!—'Tis barren and bare,
But the grass below it is fresh and green,
   Though its roots can find no moisture there:—
Yet still on its birth-place it loves to linger,
And evermore points with its silent finger   90
   To the clouds, and the sun, and the sky so fair!
   * * * * * * *

WRITTEN IN A LADY'S ALBUM

Like one who, fruitlessly perchance,
   Engraves his name upon a tree,
In hopes to win a casual glance,
   And woo remembrance still, when he
A distant wanderer may be:—   5
   Thus have I claim'd a page of thine;
Be it but reckon'd worthy thee,
   And I shall proudly own it mine.

Jan. 5, 1818.

STANZAS, ADDRESSED TO SOME FRIENDS GOING TO THE SEA-SIDE

Since Summer invites you to visit once more
The haunts she most loves on the ocean's cool shore,
Where billows are foaming, and breezes are free,
Accept at our parting one farewell from me.

I can easily picture the pleasures in view,   5
Because before now I have shar'd them with you;
But unable this season to taste them again,
I must feast on such pleasures as flow from my pen.

Let fancy then give me what fate has denied,
And grant me at seasons to roam by your side;   10
Nor will I repine while remembrance can be
Still blest with the moments I've spent by the sea.

The ramble at morning, when morning first wakes,
And the sun through the haze like a beacon-fire breaks;
Illuming to sea-ward the billows' white foam,   15
And tempting the loiterer ere breakfast to roam;—

The stroll after breakfast, when all are got out;
The saunter, the lounge, and the looking about;
The search after shells, and the eye glancing bright,
If cornelian, or amber, should come in its sight:—   20

Nor must I forget the last ramble at eve,
When the splendors of day-light are taking their leave;
When the sun's setting beams with a tremulous motion
Are reflected far off on the bosom of ocean.

STANZAS, ADDRESSED TO SOME FRIENDS

This, this is the time, when I think I have found　　25
The deepest delight from the scenery round:
There's a freshness in morning's enjoyments, but this
Brings with it a feeling of tenderer bliss.

I remember an evening, though years are gone by,
Since that evening was spent;—to my heart and my eye　　30
It is present by memory's magical power,
And reflects back its light on this far distant hour.

'Twas an evening the loveliest that Summer had seen,
The sky was unclouded, the ocean serene;
The sun's setting beams so resplendently bright,　　35
On the billows were dancing like streamers of light.

So soothing the sounds were which faintly I heard,
They were sweeter than notes of the night-loving bird;
And so peaceful the prospect before me, it seemed
Like a scene of delight of which fancy had dreamed.　　40

There's a pensive enjoyment the pen cannot paint;
There are feelings which own that all language is faint;
And such on that eve to my heart were made known,
As I mus'd by the murmuring billows alone.

But enough—may your sea-side excursion fulfil　　45
Every hope you have formed, be those hopes what they will;
And may I, although absent, in fancy create
Those joys which on you in reality wait.

SONNET TO THE DEBEN ['THOU HAST THROWN ASIDE THY SUMMER LOVELINESS']

Thou hast thrown aside thy summer loveliness:—
   And those who sought thy banks are well content
   To spend at home in social merriment
Their wintry day; no loitering footsteps press
Thy cheerless border; yet I must confess 5
   I love thee still; and think an hour well spent
In walking by thee; for thy winter dress
   To many a lonely hour a charm hath lent.—
Instead of summer's sun; and rippling tide,
   Flowing so softly that it seem'd to creep 10
In silence to thy banks; are now descried
   Dark gathering clouds; and o'er thy bosom sweep
The wintry winds, until thou seemst to be
To fancy's eye some little inland sea.

STANZAS, TO HELEN M— M—

"O! mayst thou ever be, what now thou art,
Nor unbeseem the promise of thy spring;
As fair in form, as warm, yet pure in heart."
BYRON.

Believe not that absence can banish
    The memory of moments gone by;
Could I deem they so lightly would vanish
    I should think on the past with a sigh.
But thy image was never intended   5
    The source of one sorrow to be;
For pleasure and hope are both blended
    In each thought which arises of thee.

'Tis not love—as that passion is painted,
    Its revival I never shall prove;   10
For, long ere we two were acquainted,
    I had ceas'd e'en to think about love.
The attachment I feel is another,
    'Tis passion from penitence free;
And had I to choose as a Brother,   15
    I would look for a Sister in thee.

Thou need'st not, dear Helen, to doubt me,
    When I fondly and frankly confess,
That thought in this bosom about thee
    Is busier than words can express.   20
And when such ideas are springing,
    They touch such a tone and a key;
If my hand on my harp I am flinging,
    Its strings must be vocal to thee.

When the sun, in his rising from ocean, 25
    Foretels a bright day by his dawn;
With eager and joyful emotion
    We exult in the beauties of morn.
Such thine—be thy noontide the same too,
    And may age, from infirmity free, 30
Calm, peaceful, as earth can lay claim to,
    In life's close, be still lovely in thee.

O grant that the picture thus painted,
    The world may not wantonly mar!
Keep thy soul in its whiteness untainted, 35
    And may innocence still be its star.
Then whatever the station assign'd thee,
    Though distant that station may be;
The remembrance of friends left behind thee
    Shall dwell with delight upon thee. 40

For affection bids distance defiance,
    Its ardour no absence can change;
And the links of its holy alliance
    Can reach through creation's vast range.
Those links have so lovingly bound us, 45
    That, when thou art far over sea,
Thy image shall hover around us,
    And tenderly whisper of thee.

HAUNTS OF CHILDHOOD

"O long be my heart with such memories fill'd!
Like the vase in which roses have once been distill'd;
You may break, you may ruin the vase if you will,
But the scent of the roses will hang round it still."
MOORE.

Who has not known and felt the soothing charm
Of looking back to hours, so clear and calm,
They seem as if they scarce were spent on earth,
But ow'd to mere imagination birth?
He most enjoys them, who in childhood slighted   5
Their present bliss;—whose eager eye delighted
The shadowy joys of future years to scan,
And sigh'd, most foolishly, to be a man!
  * * * * * * *
We need not sleep to dream.—I was not sleeping;
But busy memory was her vigils keeping;   10
And on my mind past images were thronging,
Bringing those feelings to the past belonging;
They came so thick about me, that at last,
I fairly lost the present in the past;
And, for a time, a happy boy again,   15
I lost in memory's pleasure, manhood's pain.
I stroll'd along a winding lane: a stream
Flow'd on one side of it; the sun's bright beam
Was here and there reflected, gaily glancing,
As o'er its pebbly bed that brook was dancing: 20
Sometimes, so narrow were its banks, the eye
Could scarcely trace it in its revelry;
Half hid by stunted bushes, on it flow'd;
Now still, now murmuring sweetly on its road:—

A wooden bridge then cross'd it, and I stood 25
Awhile upon that bridge in pensive mood,
To look around me.

        Straight before me rose
A house, where all was hush'd in calm repose;
For 'twas a summer morning, bright and fair,
And none of human kind were near me there: 30
Before the house there were some lofty trees,
Whose topmost branches felt the morning breeze,
And glisten'd in the sunbeams; these among
Were numerous rooks, attending on their young,
Whose clamorous cawings, as they hover'd round, 35
Seem'd to my ear like Music's sweetest sound.
Below, before the house, there was a space,
Where in two rows were set, with bloomy grace,
Orange and lemon trees; which to the sun
Open'd their fragrant blossoms every one; 40
And round them bees all busily were humming,
Cheerily to their morning labours coming:—
And in the centre of each space beside,
An aloe spread its prickly leaves with pride.
    *   *   *   *   *   *   *
Now in the garden of that house I stray'd, 45
Its flowers, its mossy turf, its walks survey'd;
Explor'd each nook, and roam'd through each recess,
With pleasure, and light-hearted carelessness:
Nor was it long before I found a walk
Where I could think, or to myself could talk;— 50
A grassy walk, with lime trees on one side,
Bordering a pond which yet they did not hide;
For here and there upon its rippling bosom
The water lily op'd her dewy blossom;
And at the end of this sweet walk I found 55
A grotto, where I listen'd to the sound
Of turtle-doves, which in a room above,
Were tremulously telling tales of love.
    *   *   *   *   *   *   *
But wherefore dwell upon these recollections,
These hallow'd haunts of childhood's warm affections? 60
Why? but because they rise with wings of healing,

HAUNTS OF CHILDHOOD

And hover round me; softly, sweetly stealing
Its bitterest pang from pain, its sting from sorrow,
And from past blessedness fresh blessings borrow.
O! ere such dreams as these for ever leave me,   65
Or manhood of such blameless bliss bereave me;
Memory, and life itself, must both be past,
For while I live, at times, must their remembrance last.

SONNETS TO CHARLOTTE M—[1818 AND 1828]

Thou art but in life's morning, and as yet
   The world looks witchingly: its fruits and flowers
   Are fair and fragrant, and its beauteous bowers
Seem haunts of happiness, before thee set,
All lovely as a landscape freshly wet 5
   With dew, or bright with sunshine after showers;
   Where pleasure dwells, and Flora's magic powers
Woo thee to pluck joy's peerless coronet.
   Thus be it ever:—wouldst thou have it so,
Preserve thy present openness of heart;— 10
Cherish those generous feelings which now start
   At base dissimulation, and that glow
Of native love for ties which home endears;
And thou wilt find the world no vale of tears.

[1818]

"Thou art but in life's morning!"—Years have sped
   Their silent flight since thus my idle rhyme
   Addressed thee in thy being's opening prime;
If since that hour some clouds at times have spread
Their shadow o'er thy path, these have not shed 5
   On thee their anger; but, from time to time,
   Have led thy thoughts tow'rd sunnier heights to climb;
Communing with the loved, lamented dead!
And still thou art but in the glowing morn
   Of thy existence: hearts of finest mould, 10
   And warm affections claim their right to hold

SONNETS TO CHARLOTTE M—[1818 AND 1828]

Those purer, nobler feelings with them born,
Which will not let them droop, of hope forlorn,
   Nor in a few brief years be changed and cold.

[1828]

DRAB BONNETS

Verses occasioned by reading in a Morning Paper, that at a Meeting convened in London, for some charitable purpose, "among other Ladies we observed a considerable number, whose Drab Bonnets bespoke them Members of the Society of Friends."

They may cant of costumes, and of brilliant head-dresses,
    A la Grecque—a la Françoise—or what else they will;
They may talk of tiaras, that glitter on tresses
    Enwreath'd by the Graces, and braided with skill:
Yet to my partial glance, I confess the drab bonnet   5
    Is the loveliest of any,—and most when it bears
Not only the bright gloss of neatness upon it—
    But, beneath,—the expression Benevolence wears!
Then let Fashion exult in her vapid vagaries,
    From her fascinations my favourite is free: 10
Be Folly's the head-gear that momently varies,
    But a Bonnet of drab is the sweetest to me.

Though stately the ostrich-plume, gracefully throwing
    Its feathery flashes of light on the eye;
Though tasty and trim the straw-bonnet, when glowing   15
    With its ribbons so glossy of various dye:—
Yet still I must own, although none may seem duller
    Than a simple drab Bonnet to many a gaze—
It is, and it will be, the favourite colour,
    Around which my fancy delightedly plays:—   20
And it well suits my muse with a garland to wreathe it,
    And echo its praises with gratefullest glee,—
For, knowing the goodness that oft lurks beneath it,
    The Bonnet of drab beats a turban with me.

DRAB BONNETS

Full many a rare gem,—the poet has chaunted,— 25
    In the depths of the ocean flings round it its sheen;—
And many a floweret, its beauties unvaunted,
    Springs to life, sheds its perfume, and withers unseen:
And well do I know that our sisterhood numbers,
    Array'd in the liv'ry that coxcombs reprove,— 30
Forms as fair as e'er rose on a poet's sweet slumbers,
    And faces as lovely as ever taught love.
This I know, and have felt;—and, thus knowing and feeling,
    A recreant minstrel I surely should be,
If, my heart-felt attachment ignobly concealing, 35
    The Bonnet of drab past unhonour'd by me!

I have bask'd in the blaze of both beauty and fashion,—
    Have seen these united with gifts rich and rare,
And crown'd with a heart that could cherish compassion,—
    And by sympathy soften what sorrow must bear. 40
Yet acknowledging this,—which I can do sincerely,—
    Far the highest enjoyment this bosom e'er knew,
The glance which it treasures most fondly, most dearly,
    Beam'd from under a Bonnet of drab-colour'd hue.
'Twas my pleasure,—my pride!—it is past, and has perish'd, 45
    Like the track of a ship o'er the dark-heaving sea;
But its loveliness lives, its remembrance is cherish'd,
    And the Bonnet of drab is still beauteous to me!

1820–25: EMERGENCE OF THE 'QUAKER POET'

THE IVY, ADDRESSED TO A YOUNG FRIEND

Dost thou not love, in the season of spring,
    To twine thee a flowery wreath,
And to see the beautiful birch-tree fling
    Its shade on the grass beneath?
Its glossy leaf, and its silvery stem,   5
O! dost thou not love to look on them?

And dost thou not love, when leaves are greenest,
    And summer has just begun,
When in the silence of moonlight thou leanest,
    Where glist'ning waters run,—   10
To see, by that gentle and peaceful beam,
The willow bend down to the sparkling stream?

And O! in a lovely autumnal day,
    When leaves are changing before thee,
Do not nature's charms, as they slowly decay,   15
    Shed their own mild influence o'er thee?
And hast thou not felt, as thou stood'st to gaze,
The touching lesson such scene displays?

It should be thus at an age like thine;
    And it has been thus with me;   20
When the freshness of feeling and heart were mine,
    As they never more can be,—
Yet think not I ask thee to pity my lot,
Perhaps I see beauty where thou dost not.

Hast thou seen, in winter's stormiest day,   25
    The trunk of a blighted oak,

Not dead, but sinking in slow decay
    Beneath time's resistless stroke,—
Round which a luxuriant ivy had grown,
And wreath'd it with verdure no longer its own?   30

Perchance thou hast seen this sight, and then,
    As I, at thy years might do,
Pass'd carelessly by, nor turned again
    That scathed wreck to view.
But now I can draw, from that mould'ring tree,   35
Thoughts which are soothing and dear to me.

O smile not! nor think it a worthless thing,
    If it be with instruction fraught;
That which will closest and longest cling
    Is alone worth a serious thought!   40
Should aught be unlovely which thus can shed
Grace on the dying, and leaves not the dead?

Now in thy youth beseech of HIM
    Who giveth, upbraiding not,
That his light in thy heart become not dim,   45
    And his love be unforgot;—
And thy God, in the darkest of days, will be,
Greenness, and beauty, and strength to thee!

THE VALLEY OF FERN

Part I.

    There is a lone valley, few charms can it number,
        Compar'd with the lovely glens north of the Tweed;
    No mountains enclose it where morning mists slumber,
        And it never has echoed the shepherd's soft reed.
    No streamlet of crystal, its rocky banks laving,   5
        Flows through it, delighting the ear and the eye;
    On its sides no proud forests, their foliage waving,
        Meet the gales of the Autumn or Summer wind's sigh;
    Yet by me it is priz'd, and full dearly I love it,
        And oft my steps thither I pensively turn;   10
    It has silence within, Heaven's proud arch above it,
        And my fancy has nam'd it the Valley of Fern.

    O deep the repose which its calm recess giveth!
        And no music can equal its silence to me;
    When broken, 'tis only to prove something liveth,   15
        By the note of the sky-lark, or hum of the bee.
    On its sides the green fern to the breeze gently bending,
        With a few stunted trees, meet the wandering eye;
    Or the furze and the broom their bright blossoms extending,
        With the braken's soft verdure delightfully vie;—   20
    These are all it can boast; yet, when Fancy is dreaming,
        Her visions, which Poets can only discern,
    Come crowding around, in unearthly light beaming,
        And invest with bright beauty the Valley of Fern.

    Sweet Valley! in seasons of grief and dejection,   25
        I have sought in thy bosom a shelter from care;
    And have found in my musings a bond of connexion
        With thy landscape so peaceful, and all that was there:

In the verdure that sooth'd, in the flowers that brighten'd,
   In the blackbird's soft note, in the hum of the bee,   30
I found something that lull'd, and insensibly lighten'd,
   And felt grateful and tranquil while gazing on thee.
Yes! moments there are, when mute nature is willing
   To teach, would proud man but be humble and learn;
When her sights and her sounds on the heart-strings are thrilling;   35
   And this I have felt in the Valley of Fern.

For the bright chain of being, though widely extended,
   Unites all its parts in one beautiful whole;
In which Grandeur and Grace are enchantingly blended,
   Of which GOD is the Centre, the Light, and the Soul!   40
And holy the hope is, and sweet the sensation,
   Which this feeling of union in solitude brings;
It gives silence a voice—and to calm contemplation,
   Unseals the pure fountain whence happiness springs.
Then Nature, most lov'd in her loneliest recesses,   45
   Unveils her fair features, and softens her stern;
And spreads, like that Being who bounteously blesses,
   For her votary a feast in the Valley of Fern.

And at times in its confines companionless straying,
   Pure thoughts born in stillness have pass'd through my mind;   50
And the spirit within, their blest impulse obeying,
   Has soar'd from this world on the wings of the wind:—
The pure sky above, and the still scene around me,
   To the eye which survey'd them, no clear image brought;
But my soul seem'd entranced in the vision which bound me,   55
   As by magical spell, to the beings of thought!
And to HIM, their dread Author! the Fountain of Feeling!
   I have bow'd, while my heart seem'd within me to burn;
And my spirit contrited, for mercy appealing,
   Has call'd on his name in the Valley of Fern.   60

Farewell, lovely Valley!—when Earth's silent bosom
   Shall hold him who loves thee, thy beauties may live;—
And thy turf's em'rald tint, and thy broom's yellow blossom,
   Unto loiterers like him soothing pleasure may give.
As brightly may morning, thy graces investing   65
   With light, and with life, wake thy inmates from sleep;

And as softly the moon, in still loveliness resting,
    To gaze on its charms, thy lone landscape may steep.
Then, should friend of the bard, who hath paid with his praises
    The pleasure thou'st yielded, e'er seek thy sojourn,   70
Should one tear for his sake fill the eye while it gazes,
    It may fall unreprov'd, in the Valley of Fern.

1817.

Part II.

Thou art chang'd, lovely spot! and no more thou displayest
    To the eye of thy votary, that negligent grace,
Which, in moments the saddest, the tenderest, the gayest,   75
    Allur'd him so oft thy recesses to trace.
The hand of the spoiler has fallen upon thee,
    And marr'd the wild beauties that deck'd thee before;
And the charms, which a poet's warm praises had won thee,
    Exist but in memory, and bless thee no more.   80
Thy green, palmy fern, which the softest and mildest
    Of Summer's light breezes could ruffle,—is fled;
And the bright-blossom'd ling, which spread o'er thee her wildest
    And wantonest hues,—is uprooted and dead.

Yet now, even now, that thou neither belongest,   85
    Or seem'st to belong, unto Nature or Art;
The love I still bear thee is deepest and strongest,
    And thy fate but endears thee the more to my heart.
Thou art passing away, like some beautiful vision,
    From things which now *are*, unto those that *have been!*   90
And wilt rise to my sight, like a landscape elysian,
    With thy blossoms more bright, and thy verdure more green.
Thou wilt dwell in remembrance, among those recesses
    Which fancy still haunts; though they *were*, and *are not*;
Whose loveliness lives, and whose beauty still blesses,   95
    Which, though ceasing to be, can be never forgot.

We know all we see in this beauteous creation,
    However enchanting its beauty may seem,
Is doom'd to dissolve, like some bright exhalation,
    That dazzles, and fades in the morning's first beam.   100

The gloom of dark forests, the grandeur of mountains,
    The verdure of meads, and the beauty of flowers;
The seclusion of valleys, the freshness of fountains,
    The sequester'd delights of the loveliest bowers:
Nay, more than all these, that the might of old ocean,   105
    Which seems as it was on the day of its birth,
Must meet the last hour of convulsive commotion,
    Which, sooner or later, will uncreate earth.

Yet, acknowledging this, it may be that the feelings
    Which these have awaken'd, the glimpses they've given,   110
Combin'd with those inward and holy revealings
    That illumine the soul with the brightness of heaven,
May still be immortal, and destin'd to lead us,
    Hereafter, to that which shall not pass away;
To the loftier destiny God hath decreed us,   115
    The glorious dawn of an unending day.
And thus, like the steps of the ladder ascended
    By angels, (beheld with the patriarch's eye,)
With the perishing beauties of earth may be blended
    Sensations too pure, and too holy to die.   120

Nor would Infinite Wisdom have plann'd and perfected,
    With such grandeur and majesty, beauty and grace,
The world we inhabit, and thus have connected
    The heart's better feelings with nature's fair face,
If the touching emotions, thus deeply excited,   125
    Towards Him who made all things, left nothing behind,
Which, enduring beyond all that sense has delighted,
    Becomes intellectual, immortal, as mind!
But they do; and the heart that most fondly has cherish'd
    Such feelings, nor suffer'd their ardour to chill,   130
Will find, when the forms which inspir'd them have perish'd,
    Their spirit and essence remain with it still.

Thus thinking, I would not recall the brief measure
    Of praise, lovely valley! devoted to thee;
Well has it been won by the moments of pleasure   135
    Afforded to some, justly valued by me.
May their thoughts and mine, often silently ponder
    Over every lov'd spot that our feet may have trod;

And teach us, while through nature's beauties we wander,
    All space is itself but the temple of God!   140
That so, when our spirits shall pass through the portal
    Of Death, we may find, in a state more sublime,
Immortality owns what could never be mortal!
    And Eternity hallows some visions of Time!

1819.

VERSES, SUPPOSED TO BE WRITTEN IN A BURIAL-GROUND BELONGING TO THE SOCIETY OF FRIENDS

What though no sculptur'd monuments around,
    With epitaphs engraven, meet me here,
Yet conscious feeling owns, with awe profound,
    The habitation of the dead is near:
With reverend feeling, not with childish fear,   5
    I tread the ground which they, when living, trod,
Pondering this truth, to Christians justly dear,
    Whose influence lends an interest to the sod
That covers their remains:—The dead still live to God!

Is it not written in the hallow'd page   10
    Of Revelation, God remains to be
The Lord of all, in every clime and age,
    Who fear'd and serv'd him living? Did not He,
Who for our sins expir'd upon the tree,
    Style him of Abram, Isaac, Jacob,—Lord!   15
Because they liv'd to Him? Then why should we,
    (As if we could no fitter meed afford,)
Raise them memorials *here?*—Their dust shall be restor'd.

Could we conceive Death was indeed the close
    Of our existence, Nature might demand   20
That, where the reliques of our friends repose,
    Some record to their memory should stand,
To keep them unforgotten in the land:—
    Then, then indeed, urn, tomb, or marble bust,
By sculptor's art elaborately plann'd,   25
    Would seem a debt due to their mouldering dust,
Though time would soon efface the perishable trust.

But, hoping, and believing; yea, through Faith,
    Knowing, because H<small>IS</small> word has told us so,
That Christ, our Captain, triumph'd over Death,   30
    And is the first fruits of the dead below;—
That he has trod for man this path of woe,
    Dying—to rise again!—we would not grace
Death's transitory spell with trophied show;
    As if that "shadowy vale," supplied no trace   35
To prove the grave is not our final dwelling-place.

The poet's page, indeed, would fain supply
    A specious reason for the sculptor's art;
Telling of *"holy texts that teach to die:"*
    But much I doubt they seldom reach the heart   40
Of church-yard rovers. How should truths impart
    Instruction, when engraven upon stone,
If unconfess'd before? The Christian's chart
    Records the answer unto Di-ves known,
Who, for his brethren's sake, pleaded in suppliant tone.   45

"If Moses and the Prophets speak unheard,
    Neither would they believe if spoke the dead."
Then how should those, by whom unmov'd the word
    Of greater far than such, has oft' been read,
By random texts, thus "strewn around," be led   50
    Aright to live, or die? And how much less
Can false and foolish tributes, idly spread,
    In mockery of truth and tenderness,
Awaken solemn thoughts, or holy themes impress?

And, therefore, would I never wish to see   55
    Tombstone, or epitaph obtruded here.
All has been done, requir'd by decency,
    When the unprison'd spirit sought its sphere:
The lifeless body, stretch'd upon the bier
    With due solemnity, was laid in earth;   60
And Friendship's parting sigh, Affection's tear,
    Claim'd by pure love, and deeply cherish'd worth,
Might rise or fall uncheck'd, as sorrow gave them birth.

There wanted not the pall, or nodding plume,
    The white-rob'd priest, the stated form of prayer;   65

There needed not the livery'd garb of gloom,
    That grief, or carelessness alike might wear;
'Twas felt that such things "had no business there."
    Instead of these, a silent pause, to tell
What language could not; or, unconn'd by care   70
    Of rhetoric's rules, from faltering lips there fell
Some truths to mourners dear, in memory long to dwell.

Then came the painful close—delay'd as long
    As well might be for silent sorrow's sake;
Hallow'd by love, which never seems so strong,   75
    As when its dearest ties are doom'd to break.
One farewell glance there yet remain'd to take:
    Scarce could the tearful eye fulfil its trust,
When, leaning o'er the grave, with thoughts awake
    To joys departed, the heart felt it must   80
Assent unto the truth which tells us—we are dust!

The scene is past!—and what of added good
    The dead to honour, or to soothe the living,
Could then have mingled with the spirit's mood,
    From all the empty show of man's contriving?   85
What worthier of memory's cherish'd hiving
    With miser care? In hours of *such* distress
Deep, deep into itself the heart is diving;
    Aye! into depths, which reason must confess,
At least mine owns them so, awful and fathomless!   90

Oh! 'tis not in the bitterness of grief
    Bereavement brings with it, the anguish'd mind
Can find in funeral mummeries relief.
    What matters, to the mourner left behind,
The outward "pomp of circumstance," assign'd   95
    To such a sacrifice? What monument
Is wanted, where affection has enshrin'd
    The memory of the dead? Grief must have spent
Itself, before one thought to such poor themes is lent.

And, when it hath so spent itself, does it   100
    Need other pile than what itself can build?
O no!—it has an epitaph unwrit,

WRITTEN IN A BURIAL-GROUND BELONGING TO THE FRIENDS

  Yet graven deeper far than the most skill'd
Of artists' tool can reach:—the full heart thrill'd,
  While that inscription was recording there;   105
And, till his earthly course shall be fulfill'd,
  That tablet, indestructible, must bear
The mourner's woe, in lines Death can alone outwear.

Then, be our burial-grounds, as should become
  A simple, but a not unfeeling race: 110
Let them appear, to outward semblance, dumb,
  As best befits the quiet dwelling-place
Appointed for the prisoners of Grace,
  Who wait the promise by the Gospel given,—
When the last trump shall sound,—the trembling base   115
  Of tombs, of temples, pyramids be riven,
And all the dead arise before the hosts of Heaven!

Oh! in that awful hour, of what avail
  Unto the "spiritual body," will be found
The costliest canopy, or proudest tale   120
  Recorded on it?—what avail the bound
Of holy, or unconsecrated ground?
  As freely will the unencumber'd sod
Be cleft asunder at that trumpet's sound,
  As Royalty's magnificent abode: 125
As pure its inmate rise, and stand before his GOD.

Then THOU, lamented and beloved Friend!
  Not friend alone, but more than such to me;
Whose blameless life, and peaceful, hopeful end,
  Endear, alike, thy cherish'd memory;   130
Thine will a joyful resurrection be!
  Thy works, before-hand, unto judgment gone,
The second death shall have no power o'er thee:
  On thee, redeem'd by his beloved Son,
Thy FATHER then shall smile, and greet thee with, "WELL DONE!"   135

  Could I but hope a lot so blest as thine
   Awaited me, no happier would I crave:
  That hope should then forbid me to repine
   That Heaven so soon resum'd the gift it gave;

That hope should teach me every ill to brave;— 140
   Should whisper, 'mid the tempest's loudest tone,
Thy spirit walk'd with me life's stormiest wave;
   And lead me, when Time's fleeting span was flown,
Calmly to share thy couch, which needs no graven stone.

9th Mo. 14th, 1819

LEISTON ABBEY

Beautiful fabric! even in decay
    And desolation, beauty still is thine:
As the rich sunset of an autumn day,
    When gorgeous clouds in glorious hues combine
To render homage to its slow decline,   5
    Is more majestic in its parting hour;
Even so thy mouldering, venerable shrine
    Possesses now a more subduing power,
Than in thine earlier sway with pomp and pride thy dower.

To voice of praise or prayer, or solemn sound   10
    Of sacred music, once familiar here,
Thy walls are echoless; within their bound,
    Once holy deem'd, and to religion dear,
No sound salutes the most attentive ear
    That tells thy former destiny; unless   15
It be when fitful breezes wandering near
    Wake such faint sighs, as feebly might express
Some unseen spirit's woe for thy lost loveliness.

Or when on stormy nights the winds are high,
    And through thy roofless walls and arches sweep,   20
In tones more full of thrilling harmony
    Than art could reach; while from the neighbouring deep
The roar of bursting billows seems to keep
    Accordant measure with the tempest's chime;
Oh, then! at times have I, arous'd from sleep,   25
    Fancied that thou, even in thy proudest prime,
Couldst never have given birth to music more sublime.

But to the *eye*, revolving years still add
    Fresh charms, which make thee lovelier to the view;

For nature has luxuriantly clad
   Thy ruins; as if wishing to renew
Their claim to homage from those hearts that woo
   Her gentle influence: with indulgent hand
She has aton'd for all that time could do,
   Though she might not his ravages withstand;
And now thou art her own: her skill thy beauties plann'd.

The mantling ivy's ever-verdant wreath
   She gave thee as her livery to wear;
Thy wall-flowers, waving at the gentlest breath,
   And scattering perfume on the summer air,
Wooing the bee to come and labour there;
   The clinging moss, whose hue of sober grey
Makes beautiful what else were bleak and bare;
   These she has given thee as a fit array
For thy declining pomp, and her delightful sway.

Yet is it not her power, or these alone
   That make thee interesting as thou art;
The merely beautiful, however prone
   We are to prize it, could not touch the heart.
Mere form and colour would not thus impart,
   Unto the pensive, contemplating mind,
Thoughts which might almost cause a tear to start
   In eyes not given to weep: there is assign'd
To thee a stronger power in deeper feeling shrin'd.

It is a consciousness of what thou wert,
   Compar'd with what thou art; a feeling sense
Which even steals upon the most inert,
   Who have the least conception how, or whence
Such mixt sensations should arise from thence;
   But so it is, that few there are can gaze
Upon the wrecks of old magnificence,
   Nor own the moral that their fate conveys,
How all that man can build his own brief power betrays.

And most of all this truth arrests the heart,
   When edifices that were meant to be,
Not mere mementos of the builder's art,

LEISTON ABBEY

    That future ages should with wonder see;
But monuments of wealth and piety,
    To the Most High for ever consecrate;
When *these*, too, share the fate now fallen on thee,   70
    Who can with stoic coldness contemplate
Their splendour thus defac'd, their pomp thus desolate.

    No Catholic am I, in whom the sight
        Of glories tarnish'd, altars overthrown,
    Aught of revengeful feeling could excite: 75
        Pope, Cardinal, and Abbot, I disown
    Alike, as empty titles; seldom shown
        More insignificant and profitless,
Than where they once assum'd their haughtiest tone;
    Yet do I feel what words cannot express,   80
Viewing the faded pride of fancied holiness.

    Of *fancied* holiness! O say not so,
        Nor judge unkindly of another's creed;
    The intent and motive God alone can know,
        And these condemn, or sanctify the deed.   85
    Ave-maria, crucifix, and bead
        Are nothing in themselves; but if they were
    Imagin'd helpful in the votary's need,
        Although a faith more spiritual may spare
Such outward aids to seek, from blame it may forbear.   90

    And thus this gorgeous edifice, if rear'd
        By piety, which sought with honest aim
    The glory of The Lord, should be rever'd,
        Even for that cause, by those who seek the same.
    Perchance the builders err'd; but who shall blame   95
        Error, nor feel that they partake it too?
    Then judge with charity, whate'er thy name,
        Be thou a Pagan, Protestant, or Jew;
Nor with a scornful glance these papal reliques view.

    I grant that Popery's was a galling yoke,   100
        Its ritual, one that reason must disdain;
    And much I venerate their names who broke
        The fetters, and releas'd us from the chain.

Dreadful indeed is superstition's reign,
    And priestcraft has pollution in its touch;   105
Yet, as extremes beget extremes again,
    There is a danger, or there may be such,
That we in turn may *doubt*, as they *believ'd*, too much.

To give implicit credence to each tale
    Of monkish legends; reliques to adore;   110
To think GOD honour'd by the cowl or veil,
    Reckless or who, or what, the emblem wore;
Indeed is mockery, mummery, nothing more:
    But if cold scepticism usurp the place
That superstition held in days of yore,   115
    We may not be in much more hopeful case
Than if we still implor'd the Virgin Mary's grace.

There is a medium, could we find it out,
    (And all may find it if they seek aright,)
Between extreme credulity and doubt;   120
    A safe and middle path, not gain'd by might
Or wisdom of our own; a path, whose light
    "Shines more and more unto the perfect day;"
Not overcast by bigotry's dark night,
    Nor faintly lit by reason's twilight ray;   125
But cloudless, straight, and plain; a high and holy way.

And those who walk therein, with humble trust
    In Him who cast it up, and led them there,
Remembering this, that they are form'd of dust,
    The gifts they have receiv'd with meekness bear: 130
Reason and faith are such; a peerless pair,
    Would man but *use* them both with holy awe,
And of the *abuse* of each, in turn, beware,
    They would instruct him what to love—to abhor,
And how to live in peace, and keep GOD's righteous law.   135

But I have wander'd widely from my theme,
    And some perhaps may think have wander'd long;
Yet others more indulgently may deem,
    Nor chide the minstrel for his sober song:
It could not well be gay, thus fram'd among   140

LEISTON ABBEY

The desolate ruins of departed days
And years gone by, whose presence wakes a throng
  Of pensive thoughts, compelling me to raise,
In contemplative mood, chasten'd and solemn lays—

Congenial to the scene; and, as is fit, 145
  Imprest with somewhat of its temper'd hues;
One, if no more, I trust will cherish it,
  When she, the past retracing, shall peruse
This frail memorial of an humble muse:
  For she will then remember how, erewhile, 150
Far from her home upon the banks of Ouse,
  She wander'd with me through this ruin'd pile,
When autumn's setting sun shed round his softest smile.

Yes, thou, my young friend, will not soon forget,
  Nor shouldst thou, visiting this lovely scene; 155
Because upon thy brow thou bear'st as yet
  Youth's joyous chaplet of unblighted green,
Surpassing far the poet's bay, I ween;
  For the fresh dews which unto thine dispense
Its living loveliness—its charm serene, 160
  Rise from the fount of early innocence,
That makes in happy hearts its hidden residence.

Thou art exactly at the age, when all
  Within, each outward beauty can enhance;
When bliss has too much novelty to pall, 165
  As it does afterwards in life's advance,
Even reality may seem romance;
  It often does, while yet delight is new;
And time, and place, and trivial circumstance,
  That feed the eager fancy, charm the view, 170
At such an age as thine, may last existence through.

Therefore do I believe, that in thy heart
  These ruins will their own remembrance keep;
And, sketch'd with them on memory's faithful chart,
  Will be, the wild walk to the mighty deep, 175
The lone and shady spot for washing sheep,
  Where the tall, trembling aspens ceaseless play,

And we stood still to hear the light winds sweep
    Their rustling leaves, while, in the unseen bay,
We heard the billows' dash: these shall not pass away!   180

Nor will the scene that hail'd us at the close
    Of our wild ramble, less survive to each;
When we exchang'd the stillness and repose
    Of the lone common, for the open beach;
And saw before us, far as eye could reach,   185
    The bursting breakers fling their foam on high,
And felt how poor was all the power of speech
    To paint the grandeur and rude melody
That spoke, in nature's tone, to heart, and ear, and eye.

Farewell! I may not lengthen out a strain   190
    Already too protracted; then, farewell!
Nor shall I think that I have writ in vain,
    If they, who love such scenes, whose bosoms swell
With those pure feelings that delight to dwell
    In yet untroubled hearts; if such shall own   195
That I have spoken what their tongues would tell,
    Returning from such haunts: that praise alone
Shall recompence me well, and for the task atone.

9th Mo. 20th, 1819.

STANZAS, ADDRESSED TO PERCY BYSSHE SHELLEY

Forests, and lakes, the majesty of mountains,
    The dazzling glaciers, and the musical sound
Of waves and winds, or softer gush of fountains:
    In sights and sounds like these thy soul has found
Sublime delight; but can the visible bound   5
    Of this small globe be the sole nurse and mother
Of knowledge and of feeling? Look around!
    Mark how one being differs from another;
Yet the world's book is spread before each human brother.

Was this world, then, the parent and the nurse   10
    Of him whose mental eye outliv'd the sight
Of all its beauties?—Him who sang the curse
    Of that forbidden fruit, which did invite
Our first progenitors, whom that foul sprite,
    In serpent-form, seduc'd from innocence,   15
By specious promises, that wrong and right,
    Evil and good, when they had gather'd thence,
Should be distinctly seen, as by diviner sense?

They pluck'd, and paid the awful penalty
    Of disobedience: yet man will not learn   20
To be content with knowledge that is free
    To all. There are, whose soaring spirits spurn
At humble lore, and, still insatiate, turn
    From living fountains to forbidden springs;
Whence having proudly quaff'd, their bosoms burn   25
    With visions of unutterable things,
Which restless fancy's spell in shadowy glory brings.

Delicious the delirious bliss, while new;
    Unreal phantoms of wise, good, and fair,
Hover around, in every vivid hue   30
    Of glowing beauty; these dissolve in air,
And leave the barren spirit bleak and bare
    As alpine summits: it remains to try
The hopeless task (of which themselves despair)
    Of bringing back those feelings, now gone by,   35
By making their own dreams the code of all society.

"All fear, none aid them, and few comprehend;"
    And then comes disappointment, and the blight
Of hopes, that might have bless'd mankind, but end
    In stoic apathy, or starless night: 40
And thus hath many a spirit, pure and bright,
    Lost that effulgent and ethereal ray,
Which, had religion nourish'd it, still might
    Have shone on, peerless, to that perfect day,
When death's veil shall be rent, and darkness dash'd away.   45

Ere it shall prove too late, thy steps retrace:
    The heights thy muse has scal'd, can never be
Her loveliest, or her safest dwelling-place.
    In the deep valley of humility,
The river of immortal life flows free   50
    For thee—for all. Oh! taste its limpid wave,
As it rolls murmuring by, and thou shalt see
    Nothing in death the Christian dares not brave,
Whom faith in GOD has given a world beyond the grave!

TO LYDIA

Midnight has stol'n upon me! sound is none,
Save when light, tinkling cinders, one by one,
Fall from my fire; or its low, fluttering blaze,
A faint and fitful noise at times betrays;
Or distant baying of the watch-dog, caught   5
At intervals. It is the hour of thought!
Canst thou then marvel, now that thought is free,
Memory should wake, and Fancy fly to thee?—
That she should paint thee, wrapp'd in peaceful sleep?
While round thy happy pillow spirits keep   10
Their post unseen: those watchers of the night,
Who, o'er the innocent, with fond delight
Stand centinels, and, by their guardian power,
Preserve from evil, Virtue's slumbering hour.
Calm, healthful, and refreshing be thy rest!   15
And be thy dreams as blissful, as e'er blest,
In Fancy's sweetest, purest, loveliest mood,
The hours of stillness and of solitude!

WINTER

Thou hast thy beauties: sterner ones, I own,
    Than those of thy precursors; yet to thee
    Belong the charms of solemn majesty
And naked grandeur. Awful is the tone
Of thy tempestuous nights, when clouds are blown   5
    By hurrying winds across the troubled sky;
    Pensive, when softer breezes faintly sigh
Through leafless boughs, with ivy overgrown.
    Thou hast thy decorations too; although
        Thou art austere: thy studded mantle, gay   10
    With icy brilliants, which as proudly glow
        As erst Golconda's; and thy pure array
Of regal ermine, when the drifted snow
    Envelopes nature; till her features seem
        Like pale, but lovely ones, seen when we dream.   15

A DREAM

Thou art not one of the living now;
    And yet a form appears
At times before me, such as thou
    In days of former years:
It rises, to my spirit's sight,   5
In thoughts by day, in dreams by night.

Nor can I choose, but fondly bless
    A shade, if shade it be,
Which, with such soft expressiveness,
    Recalls one thought of thee: 10
I own it, in itself, ideal;
Its influence o'er my heart is real.

I grant that dreams are idle things,
    Yet have I known a few,
To which my faithful memory clings;   15
    They seem'd so sweet and true,
That, let who will the fault condemn,
It was a grief to wake from them.

One such came lately in the hours
    To nightly slumber due;   20
It pictur'd forth no fairy bowers
    To fancy's raptur'd view;
It had not much of marvels strange,
Nor aught of wild and frequent change:—

But all seem'd real.—Aye! as much,   25
    As now the page I trace
Is palpable to sight and touch:

Then how could doubt have place?
Yet was I not from doubt exempt,
But ask'd myself if still I dreamt. 30

I felt I did; but, spite of this,
   Even thus *in dreams* to meet,
Had much, too much of dearest bliss,
   Though not enough to cheat:
I knew the vision might not stay, 35
And yet I bless'd its transient sway.

But oh, *thy* look!—It was not one
   That earthly features wear;
Nor was it aught to fear or shun,
   As fancied spectres are: 40
'Twas gentle, pure, and passionless,
Yet full of heavenly tenderness.

One thing was strange.—It seem'd to me
   We were not long alone;
But many more were circling thee, 45
   Whom thou on earth hadst known:
Who seem'd as greeting thy return
From some unknown, remote sojourn.

To them thou wast, as others be
   Whom on this earth we love; 50
I marvell'd much they could not see
   Thou camest from above:
And often to myself I said,
"How can they thus approach the dead?"

But though all these, with fondness warm, 55
   Said, "Welcome!" o'er and o'er,
Still that expressive shade, or form,
   Was silent, as before!
And yet its stillness never brought
To *them* one hesitating thought. 60

I only knew thee as thou *wert*;
   A being not of earth!

A DREAM

Yet had I not the power to exert
    My voice to check their mirth;
For blameless mirth was theirs, to see 65
Once more, a friend belov'd as thee.

And so apart from all I stood,
    'Till tears, though not of grief,
Afforded, to that speechless mood,
    A soothing, calm relief: 70
And, happier than if speech were free,
I stood, and watch'd thee silently!

I watch'd thee silently, and while
    I mus'd on days gone by,
Thou gav'st me one celestial smile— 75
    One look that cannot die.
It was a moment worthy years!
I woke, and found myself in tears.

In tears; but not such tears as fall
    From sorrow's waking eye; 80
Nor such as flow at feeling's call
    From woman's.—Mine are dry;
Save when they melt with soft'ning bliss,
And love, in some such dream as this!

A DAY IN AUTUMN [INVOCATION]

"It was a day that sent into the heart
    A summer feeling!"—and may Memory, now,
Its own inspiring influence so impart
    Unto my fancy, as to teach me how
To give it fitting utterance. Aid me, thou   5
    Most lovely season of the circling year!
Before my leaf of life, upon its bough,
    In the chill blasts of age shall rustle sere,
To frame a votive song to hours so justly dear.

Autumn! soul-soothing season! thou who spreadest   10
    Thy lavish feast for every living thing;
Around whose leaf-strew'd path, as on thou treadest,
    The year its dying odours loves to fling,
Their last faint fragrance sweetly scattering;
    O! let thy influence, meek, majestic, holy,   15
So consciously around my spirit cling,
    That its delight may be remote from folly,
In sober thought combin'd with gentle melancholy.

If, in the morning of my life, to Spring
    I paid my homage with a heart elate;   20
And with each fluttering insect on the wing,
    Or small bird, singing to his happy mate,
And Flora's festival, then held in state;—
    If joyous sympathy with such was mine;—
O! still allow me now to dedicate   25
    To Thee a tenderer strain: that tone assign
Unto my murmuring lyre, which Nature gives to thine;—

A DAY IN AUTUMN [INVOCATION]

A tone of thrilling softness, now, as caught
    From light winds sweeping o'er a late-reap'd field;
And, now and then, be with those breezes brought   30
    A murmur musical, of winds conceal'd
In coy recesses, by escape reveal'd:
    And ever and anon, still deeper tone
Of winter's gathering dirge, at distance peal'd
    By harps and hands unseen, and only known   35
To some enthusiast's ear when worshipping alone.

A DAY IN AUTUMN
[THE RIVER ORWELL]

I must not linger, though well pleas'd I might,
   (And Memory would enjoy the dear delay)
Upon each hour that wing'd its noiseless flight
   Over my head on that delightful day.
Yet would I not, in this my faint essay   5
   To trace its tranquil pleasures, wrong it so,
As not endeavour briefly to portray
   Our morning's ride; though lacking power to show
Those lovely scenes attir'd in Autumn's richest glow.

For they indeed were beautiful! we drove   10
   Through bowering lanes; their lofty trees between,
Whose leaves were ting'd with colours far above
   Spring's gayest flowers, or turf of freshest green:
Their blending shades of every tint were seen;
   Pale amber, half transparent in the ray   15
Of the bright sun; while others, in his sheen
   Assum'd more gorgeous beauty; others, gray,
Wither'd, and lifeless now, bestrew'd our narrow way.

Nor was the distant scenery aught surpass'd
   By nearer objects: there, expanding wide,   20
And by unclouded sunshine brightly glass'd,
   Flow'd, ORWELL! thy serenely rippling tide,
Hemm'd in by hilly slopes on every side,
   Whose tufted woods upon its margin break,
It more resembled, as by us descried,   25
   Some quietly reposing inland lake,
Than ocean's briny branch, which ebb and flow o'er-take:

A DAY IN AUTUMN [THE RIVER ORWELL]

And on its bosom, mark'd by vivid gleam
    Of sunny glory, peacefully did sleep
A single vessel, whose white sail might seem   30
    The lonely monarch of its little deep:
And where its banks arose abruptly steep,
    Though cliffs it boasts not, lines of lengthen'd shade
Over its silvery breast appear'd to creep:
    Yet those soft shadowy lines but lovelier made   35
Its sparkling radiance seem, by contrast's height'ning aid.

Orwell! lov'd stream, at thought of thee I pause,
    To pay that tribute thou mayst justly claim,
Scene of my boyish pleasures! for that cause
    Worthy such song as Muse of mine can frame.   40
Not mine the power to bid thy cherish'd name
    To aught of classic dignity aspire;
Yet all I can bestow of fleeting fame
    Thy sweet recesses from my song require,
And well might these demand a worthier, louder lyre.   45

England may boast of streams more beautiful,
    More boldly grand, romantically wild;
From whose enchanting banks a bard might cull
    Rich flowers of fancy as he rov'd beguil'd,
With rocks on rocks around him rudely piled,   50
    Whose clustering pinnacles half hide the sky:—
But storm has seldom lower'd, or sunshine smil'd
    Upon a stream, whose features could supply
With harvests passing thine a poet's quiet eye.

The bolder forms of mountain scenery,   55
    When floating mist, or gleam of partial light,
With picturesque effect enchants the eye,
    Command that praise thy quiet charms *invite*:
But though the former fill the roving sight
    With mute astonishment, ere long it grows   60
Sated with wonder, and, bewilder'd quite,
    Longs for some scene on which it may *repose*;
Such scenes as thy sweet banks so lavishly disclose.

Thus in the deepest, strongest fascination
    Beauty can boast, in woman's lovely face,   65
Charms there may be that waken admiration,
    When *first* beheld, that have no dwelling-place
On Memory's tablet; while thereon we trace
    Features less perfect, and less mark'd at first,
But made indelible by softer grace;   70
    Too unobtrusive all at once to burst
Upon the gazer's soul:—once known, for ever nurs'd

With cherish'd fondness, for the much lov'd sake
    Of purest happiness, which these alone
Have had the power within our hearts to wake,   75
    By loveliness peculiarly their own.
Such faces live, e'en when that life is flown
    Which made their smiles so truly eloquent,
And gave such harmony to every tone
    And accent, that, united with them, lent   80
Unto their passing spell an influence permanent.

They rise upon us in our sweetest dreams
    By night; they break on sorrow's cloudiest day;
And on the soul far more than sunshine gleams
    From their blest smiles: it seems a heavenly ray   85
Vouchsaf'd to dash the darkness all away,
    And let in glorious light upon the soul.
Alas! too rare their visits, brief their stay;
    Such soothing visions own not our control;
They rise, they shine, they set—like orbs in heaven that roll.   90

Orwell, farewell! thy cherish'd image must
    Be with me as a thing that cannot die,
Until my memory shall resign its trust
    Of what life's brightest moments can supply—
Hopes, friendships, love, that charm'd me, and pass'd by: 95
    Though far apart, perchance, we may not sever;
And sometimes I may gaze, with pensive eye,
    Upon thy winding shores; yet never, never,
Canst thou recal again enjoyments fled for ever!

A DAY IN AUTUMN [THE RIVER ORWELL]

And now our morning's ride is ended; past 100
    Another social meal; and closing eve
Tells him who frames this legend, that at last
    Of the kind circle he must take his leave.
Nor would he foolishly repine, or grieve,
    Though some there be whom he may meet no more; 105
E'en should it prove so, why should this bereave
    His breast of some sweet thoughts unknown before,
Which friends till then unmet have added to its store?

THE QUAKER POET. VERSES ON SEEING MYSELF SO DESIGNATED

"The Quaker Poet!"—is such name
   A simple designation;—
Or one expressive of my shame,
   And thy vituperation?—

If but the former—I, for one,   5
   Have no objection to it;
A name, as such, can startle none
   Who rationally view it.

But if such title would convey
   Contempt, or reprobation,   10
Allow me, briefly as I may,
   To state my vindication.

It is not splendour of costume
   That prompts harmonious numbers;—
The nightingale, of sober plume,   15
   Sings, while the peacock slumbers.

The shallow brooks, in spring so gay,
   In summer soonest fail us;
Their sparkling pride has pass'd away,
   Their sounds no more regale us.   20

While the more deep, but quiet streams,
   By alders overshaded,
Flow on, in spite of scorching beams,
   Their beauties uninvaded.

And on their peaceful verge we see 25
    Green grass, fresh flowers, and round them
Hover the butterfly and bee,—
    Rejoicing to have found them.

Is it the gayest of the gay,
    The votaries of fashion, 30
Who feel most sensibly the sway
    Of pure and genuine passion?

No!—hearts there be, the world deems cold,
    As warm, as true, as tender
As those which gayer robes enfold, 35
    However proud their splendour.

Of mine I speak not:—He, alone,
    Who form'd, can truly know it;
Nor of my verse;—I frankly own
    Myself no lofty poet. 40

But I contend the Quaker creed,
    By fair interpretation,
Has nothing in it to impede
    Poetic aspiration:

All that fair nature's charms display 45
    Of grandeur, or of beauty;
All that the human heart can sway,
    Joy, grief, desire, or duty;—

All these are ours—The copious source
    Of true poetic feeling:— 50
And wouldst thou check their blameless course,
    Our lips in silence sealing?

Nature, to *all* her ample page
    Impartially unfolding,
Prohibits neither saint, nor sage, 55
    Its beauties from beholding.

And thus the muse her gifts bestows
    With no sectarian spirit,
Her laurel wreaths invest the brows
    Which such distinctions merit.   60

Through every age, in every clime,
    Her favour'd sons have flourish'd;
Have felt her energy sublime,
    Her pure delights have nourish'd.

From Lapland's snows, from Persia's bowers,   65
    Their songs are still ascending,
Then, Quaker Poets, try your powers!
    Why should you fear offending?

Still true to nature be your aim,
    Abhorring affectation;   70
You, with peculiar grace may claim
    Each simpler decoration.

And, with such, you may blend no less,
    Spite of imputed weakness,
The god-like strength of gentleness,   75
    The majesty of meekness!

The blameless pride of purity,
    Chast'ning each soft emotion;
And, from fanaticism free,
    The fervour of devotion!   80

Be such your powers;—and in the range
    Of themes which they assign you,
Win wreaths you need not wish to change
    For aught that fame could twine you.

For never can a poet's lays   85
    Obtain more genuine honor,
Than whilst his GIFT promotes the praise
    Of HIM, who is its Donor!

TO L.E.L.

On his or her Poetic Sketches in the Literary Gazette.

To me there's more of Minstrel stealth
   In thy brief overflowings
Of fancy,—more of Thought's best wealth,—
   And Feeling's sweetest glowings;—
Than I can find in many a tome,   5
O'er which, from page to page, I roam.

Such gentle music may pass by
   The cold, or careless hearer;—
To me, it's witching melody
   Is, from it's softness, dearer: 10
Its gushing forth, its dying fall,
Surpass the notes of Nourmahal.

I know not who, or what thou art;
   Nor do I seek to know thee,
While Thou, performing thus thy part,   15
   Such banquets canst bestow me.
Then be, as long as thou shalt list,
My viewless, nameless Melodist.

NAPOLEON [STANZAS 28–90]

XXVIII.

But is there then no medium? or, because
    Napoleon's name alternately has been
A theme for indiscriminate applause
    And fiercest censure, must we blindly lean
To either? Truth is, surely, found between.   5
    And he who has not mingled in debate
With those who loudest talk when least they mean,
    May, without erring widely, estimate
Napoleon's lasting claim to be consider'd GREAT.

XXIX.

True greatness is not won by POWER alone,   10
    Even if that power be nobly, fairly gain'd;
But as its influence unto GOOD is prone,
    The plaudits of the virtuous are obtain'd.
By this sure test alone may be explain'd
    All genuine greatness;—it has made mankind   15
Wiser, and happier; it has never stain'd
    Its fame by selfishness, but borne in mind,
That glory, to be true, must be with good combin'd.

XXX.

GOD is not *great* because *omnipotent*!
    But because power, in Him, is understood,   20
And felt, and prov'd, to be benevolent,
    And wise, and holy;—thus it ever should!
For what HE wills, we know, is pure and good,
    And has in view the happiness of ALL:

Hence love and adoration;—never could
    The contrite spirit at his footstool fall,
If Power, and Power *alone*, its feelings did appal!

XXXI.

If then divinest power be truly so,
    Because its end and object is to bless;
It follows, that all power which man can know,
    The highest even monarchs can possess,
Displays alone their "less than littleness,"
    Unless it seek the happiness of man,
And glory of the Highest;—nothing less
    Than such a *use* of power one moment can
Make its possessor great, on Wisdom's godlike plan.

XXXII.

Thus judg'd, Napoleon was not truly great;
    Because his *actions* to the world have shown,
In language which admits of no debate,
    Self-aggrandizement was his end alone.
He us'd his power, as conquerors are prone,
    And ever were, for selfish ends; and sought
To extend his sway, and fortify his throne;
    Not by those gentler arts, with blessings fraught,
But by War's ruthless spoil, with blood and rapine bought.

XXXIII.

I will not say that he had no excuse,
    With those who judge by worldly policy;
But this can never justify the abuse
    Of power, to Truth's discriminating eye:
All the apology it can supply
    Amounts to this, alas! and little more;
"He did but do, as some, in days gone by,
    Have done before him: it *was* thus of yore,
And *will be so*, howe'er the fact we may deplore."

XXXIV.

THIS brings me, then, unto the main intent,
    Which first inspir'd this unelaborate strain;
And, O! could I, by force of argument,

Or by appeal to sympathy, obtain
Even brief audience, surely not in vain
   Precepts, to which all Christians ought to bow,
Might be again declar'd: Messiah's reign
   Of peace once more announc'd! "Assist me, Thou
Who worest, for our sakes, around thy patient brow,

XXXV.

"The thorny diadem! may thy meek Spirit,
   Which all who bear thy name should, in degree,
By word and action, prove that they inherit,
   May this alone my inspiration be!
The glorious cause is Thine! for unto Thee
   Was given, before thy sway on earth began,
A holy kingdom from contention free;
   And angels thus announc'd its scope and plan,
Glory to God on high! peace and good will to man!

XXXVI.

"Since Thou art fitly styl'd the Prince of peace!
   And unto thee all power by love is given,
So shed abroad thy Spirit, so increase
   Its influence upon earth; that hearts, now riven
With angry feelings, which too long have striven
   To injure, may each harsher thought disown;
And thy pure law of love, revered in heaven,
   May be on earth in human actions shown,
Proving thy kingdom come, the heart of man thy throne.

XXXVII.

"And unto them whose hearts anticipate,
   With earnest prayers, thy pure and peaceful reign,
Give wisdom, meekness, zeal—to advocate
   The good they hope for; patience to sustain
Its slow fulfilment; power to '*turn again*
   The battle to the gate;' that these, made strong
By Thee alone, may steadfastly remain
   Oppos'd to every violence and wrong;
Seeking, by holy love, what Seers have promis'd long.

XXXVIII.

"And, on this feeble effort to extend
   Thy gentle government and quiet creed,
May that pure blessing through thy power descend,
   Which giveth good, and maketh wise indeed.
Suffer THY SPIRIT for itself to plead,   95
   With its own energetic eloquence,
That *some* who these unstudied lines shall read,
   May find them answer'd by that inward sense,
Which gives awaken'd thought sublime intelligence."

XXXIX.

His blessing crav'd, revert we to our theme,   100
   And let us humbly ask ourselves, what right
The Christian has, upon the Gospel scheme,
   To employ of force the all-unhallow'd might,
And wrong unmerited, by wrong requite?
   My kingdom is not of this world, if 'twere,   105
The Saviour said, then would my followers fight:
   And can we, who profess his name to bear,
In spite of his commands, for murderous strife prepare?

XL.

Put up thy sword! the cup my Father gives
   Shall I not drink? 'Twas thus our Master spake;   110
And he who in his Spirit breathes and lives,
   Like him will patiently injustice take,
And bear it meekly, for his Pattern's sake:
   Knowing who hath immutably decreed—
"Vengeance is MINE alone!" he dares not wake   115
   For apprehended wrongs, in word or deed,
Wrath's devastating woes, or to redress proceed.

XLI.

But not by insulated precepts, strown
   Throughout the Gospel, war is prov'd to be
Unlawful: that unlawfulness is shown   120
   By Christianity's whole tendency:
This should be happiness and harmony;

For *all* its doctrines uniformly prove
How genuine is its holy sympathy,
   With peace, and gentleness, and joy, and love 125
To all on earth below, and all in heaven above.

XLII.

The wrath of man works not, nor can it work,
   The righteousness of God; because in it
That latent evil cannot fail to lurk,
   Which proves it for such glorious task unfit: 130
In characters of blood its deeds are writ;
   Nor has it learnt that lesson, first and best,
Religion teaches, calmly to submit,
   And all its wishes, cares, and griefs to rest
On His disposing power, and bow to its behest. 135

XLIII.

These are hard sayings; who can such receive?
   Not they who, easily provok'd by ill,
Resent it promptly, and themselves believe
   Fit arbiters of retribution still;
Although their purpose is but to fulfil 140
   The puny wrath of disappointed pride;
Whose judgment is the dictate of the will,
   Uncurbed by reason, and unsanctified
By meek Religion's laws, which fitlier would decide.

XLIV.

Now, he who has been tutor'd in the school 145
   Of Christ, and by its precepts has been taught
To judge of all things by that nobler rule,
   Which revelation, by its light, has brought
To bear upon those secret springs of thought
   Whence actions flow—sees how unfit is man, 150
Viewing himself as truth proclaims he ought,
   His own imagin'd injuries to scan,
And chastisement inflict, ev'n where he safely can.

XLV.

They know but little of the human heart,
   Nor have they ever studied well their own, 155

Who have not learnt with what insidious art
   To what we *will* our sophistry is prone.
Our better reason will not speak alone;
   Passion will plead, and selfishness be heard;
And these, combin'd, will overpower the tone   160
   Of conscience, whose inspeaking heavenly word
Should be unquestion'd there, and unto all preferr'd.

XLVI.

But is there not a reason, yet unnam'd,
   That home to every human heart should come;
Which, if it were on glory's field proclaim'd,   165
   Ay! on the verge of conflict! when the drum,
The echoing trumpet, and the mingled hum
   Of hosts were heard—at once should break the spell?
Appal each Christian's heart, and render dumb
   The boldest voice?—oh! let us ponder well,   170
How different are the *hopes* on which IN PRAYER we dwell!

XLVII.

"Father! forgive our trespasses, AS *we*
   Others forgive, who trespass against us!!"
If, when we supplicate Heaven's majesty,
   Our words have ANY meaning, is it thus   175
We show forgiveness? praying now with HUSS,
   And then with ZISCA fighting! Oh! in vain
May sciolists minuter points discuss;
   This outward rite reject, and that retain;
We cannot, must not hide so palpable a stain.   180

XLVIII.

Is there a man,—I ask not of his creed
   On minor points of faith,—whose lips have been
Accustom'd thus to pray, that does not need
   Forgiveness from his God? with unblench'd mien
Is he prepar'd to dye the verdant green   185
   He stands on with a brother's blood? and then
Present himself with countenance serene,
   Before his Maker, with his fellow men,
And thus for mercy plead, by mercy shown again?

XLIX.

I write in charity, and freely make
    Ample allowance for unconscious crime;
I grant all any disputant could take
    For views and habits, which the poet's rhyme
Has cherish'd long, from bards of olden time
    To those of latter days: my heart can thrill,
I trust it can, with patriot hopes sublime:
    Yet, feeling thus, to me all war is still
Forbidden by the law which says, Thou shalt not kill.

L.

Tradition, custom, habit, cannot plead
    Excuse for what is evil: well I know
That many who have own'd the Christian creed,
    And have in part *adorn'd* it, o'er a foe
Have fought, and conquer'd; and, in doing so,
    Have render'd, as they thought, a patriot's due;
But, owning this, I cannot so forego
    My views of right and wrong, of false and true,
As think them right *in this*, and own the Gospel too.

LI.

Nay more, I have delightful converse held
    On themes of lofty thought, with some who wear
The livery of war; and, uncompell'd,
    Most grateful testimony I could bear,
Not to their moral worth alone, and care
    To walk uprightly in the sight of men,
But more than this; nor would my spirit dare
    To doubt for such divine acceptance, when
The final trump shall sound, the dead shall rise again.

LII.

But can e'en such examples, while I feel
    Renewedly their force still unforgot,
Th' express command of God himself repeal,
    Or from his book its brightest precept blot?
Christians may err, but surely Christ could not;
    And he declar'd the simple, touching sign
Of holiest fellowship with him was—what?

Wrathful contention? no! but love benign!
"By this shall all men know that ye are mine!" 225

LIII.
As for the common-place, heroic rant
    Of wreaths by fame twin'd round a warrior's head;
Such move me not, if gather'd from a plant
    Nurtur'd by tears and blood; of valiant dead,
Gloriously laid on honour's gory bed, 230
    From whence they look to Heav'n with noble pride
Of such things I have often heard and read,
    "In sorrow, not in anger;" misapplied
Indeed, are words like these to men who thus have died!

LIV.
"Die for thy country! thou romantic fool! 235
    Seize, seize one plank, thyself, and get to shore."
The bard upbraids not thus the hireling tool,
    Who fights for sordid pay, and asks no more;
Content to fall as thousands fell before,
    And millions will, when he is senseless clay: 240
But those of nobler natures would implore
    To pause, and seriously reflect, if they,
By dying for its sake, a patriot's debt can pay.

LV.
He pays it better, surely, who still lives,
    Blessing, and blest; who, in his humble sphere, 245
To aid the poor his scanty pittance gives,
    Befriends the orphan, dries the widow's tear;
Or if by poverty forbade to cheer,
    Even with trivial boons, the lot of woe,
By kindness, and by sympathy sincere, 250
    Gives more, perhaps, than affluence can bestow,
To mitigate those griefs the suff'rers only know.

LVI.
And oh! how much of these have war's wide pest,
    And those harsh feelings from whence wars arise,
Inflicted upon man! He who, at rest 255
    Under his vine or fig-tree, feasts his eyes

On scenes of peace alone, can sympathize
   Imperfectly with all those horrors which
Attend the foul, unnatural sacrifice,
   To Moloch offer'd, only to enrich   260
The blood-stain'd altar plac'd before an idol's niche.

LVII.

We read of battles won, and battles lost,
   "The Senate's thanks, the Gazette's pompous tale;"
Our streets are by triumphal arches cross'd,
   The rustic quaffs his mug of nut-brown ale;   265
Pride pours the wine-cup; music fills the gale;
   And all to celebrate a feat, which few,
Who thus rejoice, could see, and not turn pale
   Which many could not for a moment view,
Nor cry "Forgive them, God! they know not what they do."   270

LVIII.

Allow me, therefore, reader, not to paint
   The scene itself; I will not trust so far
My own imperfect powers of verse; too faint
   Even to sketch the actual strife of war,
Where dying groans on music's concord jar: 275
   I would but paint a quiet, peaceful scene,
Not meant, methinks, for man himself to mar;
   First, in its native loveliness serene;
Last, as it may be found when glory there has been.

LIX.

Come, take thy stand upon this gentle ridge,   280
   Which overlooks yon sweet secluded vale;
Before us is a rude and rustic bridge,
   A simple plank; and by its side a rail
On either hand, to guide the footsteps frail
   Of first or second childhood; while below   285
The murm'ring brooklet tells its babbling tale,
   Like a sweet under-song, which, in its flow,
It chanteth to the flowers that on its margin grow.

LX.

For many a flow'ret blossoms there to bless
    The gentle loveliness whose charms imbue   290
Its border;—strawberry of the wilderness;
    The star-like daisy; violet brightly blue;
Pale primrose, in whose cup the pearly dew
    Glistens till noon-tide's languid, listless hour;
And last of all, and sweetest to the view,   295
    The lily of the vale, whose virgin flower
Trembles at every breeze within its leafy bower.

LXI.

Now glance thine eye along the streamlet's banks
    Up through yon quiet valley; thou wilt trace
Above, the giant mountains in their ranks,   300
    Of bold and varied outline; little space
Below their summits, far above their base,
    Umbrageous woods; and, last of all, thine eye
Will rest on many an humble dwelling-place
    Of happy human beings; and descry   305
The lowly temple where they worship the Most High

LXII.

How quietly it stands within the bound
    Of its low wall of grey, and mossy stone!
And like a shepherd's peaceful flock around
    Its guardian gather'd,—graves, or tombstones strown,   310
Make *their* last narrow resting-places known,
    Who, living, lov'd it as a holy spot;
And, dying, made their deep attachment shown
    By wishing here to sleep when life was not,
That so their turf, or stone, might keep them unforgot!   315

LXIII.

It is a bright and balmy afternoon,
    Approaching unto even-tide; and all
Is still except that streamlet's placid tune,
    Or hum of bees, or lone wood-pigeon's call,
Buried amid embow'ring forest tall,   320

Which feathers, half way up, each hill's steep side:
Dost thou not feel such landscape's soothing thrall;
   And wish, if not within its bowers t'abide,
At least to explore its haunts, and know what joys they hide?

LXIV.
Nor need'st thou wish a truer luxury 325
   Than in its depths, delighted, thou might'st share;
I will not say that nought of agony,
   Blest as it is, at times may harbour there,
For man is born to suffer, and to bear:—
   But could I go with thee from cot to cot, 330
And show thee how this valley's inmates fare,
   Thou might'st confess, to live in such a spot,
And die there in old age, were no unlovely lot.

LXV.
But time suffices not to loiter so:
   Then let us take, as sample of the rest, 335
That lowly hut, where blooming wall-flowers grow
   Above the ivy time has made its vest,
Like glist'ning foam-wreaths on a green wave's crest:
   On one side of its porch, poor, old, and weak,
A patriarch sits, in homely raiment drest; 340
   A woman opposite, whose faded cheek,
Though younger far than his, some lines of sorrow streak.

LXVI.
Yet in her form, once beautiful, is seen
   Still fair proportion, natural elegance;
And though most matronly is now her mien, 345
   And meekly chasten'd is the downward glance
Of her dark eye, who looks on it, perchance
   May well conjecture, from its beauty, how,
Ere grief had dimm'd by painful circumstance
   Its lustre, from beneath its arching brow 350
It sparkled at love's tale, fill'd at affection's vow.

LXVII.
And though that cheek is not, as youth's may be,
   In blooming beauty drest, 'tis lovely yet;

And whoso looks upon it, soon may see
    That disappointed hope, and keen regret,   355
Have marr'd, but not effaced, the charms that met
    In softest union on those features mild:
Still may be traced the stamp which nature set
    Upon them, when sweet Agnes, then a child,
Here warbled, like a bird, her carols free and wild.   360

LXVIII.

She lov'd, and married one, who long had been
    First playmate, then companion;—only son,
And child, of that old man before her seen;
    And for a time existence smoothly run
In a calm current; children many a one   365
    Were theirs, and if not wealth, at least content;
Childless, and widow'd, is she now; for none
    Of those rich blessings bounteous Heaven had lent,
Are left to call her own,—one after one they went.

LXIX.

But though it cost poor Agnes many tears   370
    To see first one and then another die
Of those sweet children, loveliest of their peers,
    At least they seem'd so in a mother's eye;
And though it was still deeper agony
    When the pale messenger the last time came   375
To call her husband hence; no impious sigh
    Impeach'd Omnipotence: she felt His claim
"Who gives, and takes away; and bless'd his holy name!"

LXX.

The woes which God inflicts, he gives the power
    To bear; or would, did man but supplicate;   380
And this the sufferer found; yet many an hour,
    Or casual incident, would lay in wait,
As if to make her feel more desolate,
    In this her desolation, by the view
Of happy objects, which her stript estate   385
    Renewedly recals; but patience too
Is given to bear them all. This moment proves it true!

LXXI.

Behold, two lovely children now have stray'd
    From some near cottage to that bowery tree;
And Agnes sees them coming, half afraid390
    To trust herself a sight like this to see:
A girl, the eldest, who perhaps may be
    Ten summers old, assumes her sagest look,
Sits down, and opens wide upon her knee
    Her youngling brother's well-conn'd spelling-book,395
Who turns from thence his eye to yonder bubbling brook.

LXXII.

For sweetest flow'rets are up-springing there,
    Which he would rather pluck than learn to spell;
But when he hears his teacher's lips declare
    That he shall have those flowers he loves so well,400
As guerdon of his labour—to compel
    His fix'd attention, there requires no more;
The task is learnt, repeated; then pell-mell
    They scamper forth amid that shining store;
His pupilage is past, her gravity is o'er.405

LXXIII.

Among those flowers the happy playmates quaff
    Delight as innocent as flowers are fair;
And Agnes hears the frequent shout, the laugh,
    Break on the stillness of the balmy air.
But now a tenderer scene ensues;—look where410
    The sister quietly resumes her seat
Under that tree of blameless knowledge there,
    And hears him, kneeling by her side, repeat
His evening prayer to God, in lisping accents sweet!

LXXIV.

That done, his rosy cheek the guileless boy415
    Rests on her knee, upturns his eyes to hers,
And glances of affection, truest joy,
    Between their hearts are still interpreters.
The sun, meantime, behind those sable firs,
    Is softly sinking; but his lingering streak420
Is on those lovely children:—zephyr stirs

The glistening locks which hide *his* cherub cheek,
And many a kiss *she* prints, a sister's love to speak!

LXXV.

This is no sight for Agnes to behold
    Unmov'd;—nor can she, viewing it, forget 425
How her own darling us'd to be of old
    Just such, and so employ'd. But though regret
May thrill her heart, its better hopes are set
    Upon its inward comforter and stay;
She rises up, and going forth, has met 430
    Those young companions on their homeward way;
They know her kindness well, and childhood's greetings pay.

LXXVI.

She kisses each with tenderness, and smiles
    As meekness only can, when tears supprest
Are felt—though viewless:—they, with gentle wiles 435
    Of playful innocence, by her carest,
Whom next to their own parents they love best,
    Beguile her from herself;—till when they part
Even she is sooth'd, nor thinks her lot unblest,
    Since still she can, though tears at seasons start, 440
Partake in others' joys with no ungrateful heart!

LXXVII.

Why do I linger o'er this portraiture
    Of idle fancy?—wherefore—but to show
How much there is of beauty to allure
    In peaceful quietude; did man but know, 445
And knowing, seek, what is most truly so.
    O much there is to be most thankful for,
E'en in this world, despite of all its woe,
    Would we but love each other, and abhor
Each harsh and cruel thought that leads to strife and war. 450

LXXVIII.

But to that happy valley turn once more,
    When War's destroying angel there has been:—
Had Winter's devastations, or the roar
    Of elements, alone, deform'd the scene;

Still, in its ruins, it had worn the mien 455
   Such natural scourges mostly leave behind;
Some of its features yet had smil'd serene,
   Ev'n in the absence of all human-kind,
And with our darkest fears a hope might be combin'd.

LXXIX.

Now its once rustic bridge is lopp'd away 460
   By some rude pioneer's regardless stroke;
Each peaceful homestead, blest but yesterday,
   A shapeless mass of ruins, black with smoke:
The graceful birch, tall pine, and sturdy oak,
   Which bosom'd the sweet hamlet, too, are hewn; 465
And hideous, maim'd, half putrid corpses choke
   The murmuring brook, which on that afternoon,
Had music in its flow of most delightful tune.

LXXX.

Nor have they spared the solitary tree,
   Beneath whose boughs that child her brother taught;— 470
Agnes, the patient Agnes! where is she?
   And her old helpless father? He who caught,
From her meek smiles and accents, feelings fraught
   With more than joy. Those lovely children too,
Where are they all? We dare not trust our thought 475
   To tell their tale, nor follow fancy's clue;
Lest e'en the very worst should fearfully prove true.

LXXXI.

Perhaps—but why conjecture? can we guess
   Horrors more foul than War itself supplies?
The blood of age staining its silver tress; 480
   Childhood, or fright, or famine's sacrifice;
The ruin'd maiden's unavailing cries:—
   All these might be their lamentable lot,
Whose home was late so lovely in our eyes:
   We know but this—they were! and *here* are not! 485
And feel we stand indeed on an ACCURSED SPOT!

LXXXII.

O War! thou art indeed the deadliest curse
   Which Heaven can suffer, or the world endure;
However pride thy glories may rehearse,
   Or hopes of fame thy votaries may allure.   490
Volcano, earthquake, pestilence impure,
   Are evils; but they poison not the spring
Of thought and feeling: lenient time may cure
   Their devastations; but to thine there cling
Resentment, rooted hate, and each unholy thing.   495

LXXXIII.

"But what," perhaps some reader may exclaim,
   Weary at last of this digression long,
"Has War to do with him, who gives its name
   And title to thy Poem?"— Am I wrong?
Or are there not an almost countless throng   500
   Of thoughts, to which Napoleon's name gives rise,
Blended with war?—on which the poet's song,
   The historian's page, alike should moralize,
If either hope to please the virtuous or the wise?

LXXXIV.

What is Napoleon *now*—admitting all   505
   His former talents, enterprise, and power?
The time has been, nor distant, when the thrall
   Of his portentous name made monarchs cower,
And tremble in the proudest palace-tower:
   Fate seem'd his fiat, fortune as his guide;   510
And empire, held by suff'rance, was the dower
   Which, when he took unto himself a bride,
He spared an elder throne, with cool, contemptuous pride.

LXXXV.

What is he now? Ten years ago his death
   Had spread through Europe with a voice of thunder;   515
Fame's trump had blazon'd with her loudest breath
   The tale; and many a captive, groaning under
The conqueror's yoke, had snapt his chains asunder.

Stupid indifference now supplies the place,
In many minds, of that mute vacant wonder　　　　　　520
　　They then had known, what time they paus'd a space,
Before they deem'd him dead, with solemn doubtful face.

LXXXVI.
He dies upon a surf-surrounded rock!
　　Far from each court, and every courtly ring;
Far from the fields where once, in battle's shock,　　525
　　Death stalk'd around him, a familiar thing:
His "*eagle*" long before had furl'd his wing;
　　His "*star of honour*" set, to rise no more!
Nor could a hope remain that time might bring
　　Glory to either spell, as heretofore;　　　　　　530
Therefore to him the life of life itself was o'er.

LXXXVII.
And we, who of his death the tidings hear,
　　Receive them as a tale of times gone by,
Which wakes nor joy, nor grief, nor hope, nor fear:
　　And if in nobler hearts a passing sigh　　　　　　535
For *such* a lot reflection may supply,
　　Few follow up that feeling to its source:
The multitude, with undiscerning eye,
　　See all around pursue its usual course,
And care not for his death, nor thoughts it should enforce.　540

LXXXVIII.
But if such life, succeeded by such end,
　　Be void of interest like a thrice told tale;
If it have nought to "bless mankind, or mend,"
　　Ponder'd aright, and weigh'd in truth's just scale;
Sermons are useless! homilies must fail!　　　　　　545
　　And man be uninstructed still, because
He WILL NOT LEARN! May wiser thoughts prevail;
　　And may our better feelings, as we pause
To contemplate his course, teach wisdom's holier laws.

LXXXIX.

Nor could there be a fitter time than this 550
   For genuine friends of peace to vindicate
The truer policy, superior bliss,
   Of milder precepts; now when warfare's weight
Has left on each exhausted, weary state,
   Its natural burthen—debt; and deeper woes 555
Than statists can repair or calculate;
   While he, whose greatness from false glory rose,
Illustrates, by his lot, the boons which war bestows.

XC.

What can it give of glory, power, and fame,—
   And these are toys that make the heart-strings stir 560
Of those who wish to win a hero's name,—
   Which on Napoleon it did not confer?
It made him for a time the arbiter
   Of thrones and dynasties; and Fortune smil'd,
As she may do on some who follow her 565
   Believing her existence,—thus beguil'd,
Till in the end they know 'twas but a phantom wild.

THE CONTRAST

I.

I stood, in thought, on SHINAR's plain,
    And saw that tower arise,
Whose height so vast, by builders vain,
    Was meant to reach the skies:
It seem'd to stand before my sight,   5
Like phantoms which, in dreams of night,
    We see with wond'ring eyes;
Distrusted, when they meet our view,
But gazed at, till we think them true.

II.

I will not say that thought could cheat   10
    My judgment so to deem
Of this ideal counterfeit;
    Nor was it slumber's dream:
But in imagination's hour
The *past*, by her creative power,   15
    May like the present seem;
And make us for the time compeers
Of them who lived in distant years.

III.

And thus I thought before me stood
    That tower of early fame,   20
Rear'd by the erring multitude
    To make themselves a name:
Of lofty height, and ample base,
Though boasting little finished grace,
    Seem'd its gigantic frame;   25
Surpassing, in its wondrous size,
All Egypt's later prodigies.

IV.

It rose, until its massy form
    Far length'ning shadows cast;
Bidding defiance to the storm,   30
    And smiling at the blast:
And even to Euphrates' wave
Its lofty summit lustre gave,
    The loveliest, and the last
Which, borrow'd from the sun's last gleam,   35
It shed upon that distant stream.

V.

And SHINAR's plain was throng'd around
    With earth's primeval race,
Who all alike intent were found,
    Each lab'ring in his place,   40
To rear the tower, whose deathless fame
Should be their own enduring name,
    Their city's chiefest grace:
For to one common home they clung,
And spoke but in one common tongue.   45

VI.

But GOD came down to see the tower,
    And city they had made;
And by his overwhelming power
    Their policy gainsay'd;
Giving to each a tongue unknown,   50
Their plans and counsels were o'erthrown,
    His sovereignty display'd;
And what they eagerly had sought
To shun, their own presumption wrought.

VII.

O then, in that discordant crowd,   55
    What wild confusion rose!
As each, in accents fierce and loud,
    Attempted to disclose
The aid he proffer'd, help he sought;
Till they who were together brought   60
    As friends, were turn'd to foes;

Desirous but *apart* to roam,
And seek a *widely-sever'd home!*

VIII.
The vision pass'd! crowd, tower, and plain
   Fleeted in thought away: 65
Imagination's power again
   Resumed her dream-like sway;
And, as her magic spell prevail'd,
I stood amid the throng who hail'd
   The church's earlier day;   70
Nor greater contrast could be known
Than was by such transition shown.

IX.
Around me were the gather'd host
   Who came to seek their Lord;
Owning, that solemn PENTECOST,   75
   One place, with one accord:
And, for the time, I seem'd to stand
Spectator of that Christian band,
   By Gentile tribes abhorr'd,
Chosen to publish, far and wide,   80
The Gospel of THE CRUCIFIED!

X.
When, on a sudden, came a sound,
   As of a wind from heaven,
Which sweeps o'er ocean's depths profound,
   Or is through forests driven!   85
And on each head, in rev'rence bar'd,
Bright cloven tongues of fire declar'd
   The gift which God had given:
The power, in tongues unknown till then,
To make salvation known to men.   90

XI.
Well might that miracle then plead
   With hearts untouch'd before;
As Parthian, Elamite, and Mede,
   Crete, Arab, Roman, Moor,—

Each in his native tongue address'd 95
With deep surprise and awe confess'd
   That every doubt was o'er;
And eagerly preferr'd his claim
To be baptiz'd in JESUS' NAME.

XII.

This vision also pass'd away; 100
   Yet did it first disclose
How diff'rent is the scope and sway
   Of boons that God bestows.
The varying tongues which, heretofore,
On SHINAR's plain, with loud uproar, 105
   Converted friends to foes,
Here seem'd like manna to descend,
And made a foe far more than friend!

XIII.

Thus talents, gifts, and graces prove
   Of present good, or ill, 110
As given by GOD in wrath, or love,
   To work his gracious will:
Man cannot claim them as his own;
They come from God, and best are known
   His purpose to fulfil, 115
When the *Receiver's* humble aim
Would glorify the GIVER's NAME!

TO A ROBIN

I.

Mild melodist! whose artless note,
   At foggy eve, at chilly morn,
From nature's quiet haunts remote,
   Here seems a harmony forlorn;
Fain would I give thee, for thy song,   5
   A carol simple as thy own;
For thou, sweet bird! awak'st a throng
   Of thoughts which rise for thee alone.

II.

It is not that thy lay is fraught
   With music, like the sky-lark's strain,   10
Or nightingale's, so sweetly caught
   By listening ear, in midnight's reign;
Nor has thy note that deeper sound,
   Of which my heart has felt the thrall,
When I have heard, from groves profound,   15
   The lone wood-pigeon's frequent call.

III.

But these, each one, and all, give vent
   To song, where song is wont to flow;
Thou, thou art sweetly eloquent,
   With nothing near to wake that glow   20
Of music, in the haunts of men,
   Which, amid buildings cluster'd round,
From time to time arrests my pen,
   And makes me listen to its sound.

IV.

Oh! hearts that feel, and eyes that see
   All as it truly is, can find,
Ev'n in an object mean as thee,
   Food for the meditative mind:
But thus it is,—we close our hearts,
   Our ears, our eyes, to things which, view'd
With the keen sense that truth imparts,
   Might fill our souls with gratitude.

V.

And this absurd and frigid pride,
   By which our nature is disgrac'd,
Philosophy has dignified
   With the proud name of manly taste.
It seems a proof of childishness
   Thy song to love, thy praise to speak,
And he who should its power confess
   Must be the weakest of the weak.

VI.

Well! be it so:—if life have taught
   To me one truth distinctly clear,
'Tis this, that unto wakeful thought
   The humblest source of joy is dear.
The lowliest object that can wake
   Our better feelings by its power,
The minstrel for his theme may take,
   In contemplation's musing hour.

VII.

Canst thou not waken such, sweet bird?
   Yes; while I listen to thy lay,
Thought's hidden stream again seems stirr'd
   By breezes, which were wont to play
Over its current's dimpled course,
   As once it flow'd so sweetly wild,
In happy childhood, when its source
   Was by no worthless weeds defiled.

VIII.

For then thy song to me express'd
    All I conceiv'd of harmony;
And the red plumage of thy breast
    Was beautiful to childhood's eye.   60
While tales, by infancy held dear,
    Of funeral rites by thee perform'd,
Made, what was music to my ear,
    A spell that deeper feelings warm'd.

IX.

And since thou now bring'st back again   65
    The memory of such hours to me,
Shall I, beguil'd by that sweet strain,
    Blush for this tribute paid to thee?
No, never! if on wisdom's plan,
    (All worldly precepts far above,)   70
"The child be father of the man,"
    I justly owe thee praise and love.

X.

But not for me, alone, thy song
    Dost thou at eve and morn awake;
On other ears, amid this throng   75
    Of buildings, it may sweetly break:
Bed-ridden age, perchance, may hear
    Those soft and simple strains of thine;
And scenes, and hours long past, may cheer
    Its grief, as they have lighten'd mine.   80

XI.

One more reflection yet remains
    Or wise, or foolish, 'twill intrude;
I trace in thee, and in thy strains,
    My own, my song's similitude.
Like thee, in scenes adverse to song,   85
    I act the minstrel's humble part;
Like thine, my numbers, weak or strong,
    Nor seek, nor own the aid of art.

XII.

And I, methinks, were well content,
    Like thee, to be by most unheeded,   90
If with my artless strains there went,
    As with thy own, a charm that pleaded
For NATURE, TENDERNESS, and TRUTH,—
    Which childhood's innocence possesses,
Which beautify e'en blooming youth,   95
    And honour age's silver tresses.

VERSES ON THE DEATH OF BLOOMFIELD, THE SUFFOLK POET

Thou shouldst not to the grave descend
   Unmourn'd, unhonour'd, or unsung;—
Could harp of mine record thy end,
   For thee that rude harp should be strung,—
And plaintive sounds as ever rung   5
   Should all its simple notes employ,
Lamenting unto old, and young,
   The Bard who sang THE FARMER'S BOY.

Could Eastern Anglia boast a lyre
   Like that which gave thee modest fame,   10
How justly might its every wire
   Thy minstrel honours loud proclaim:
And many a stream of humble name,
   And village-green, and common wild—
Should witness tears that knew not shame,   15
   By Nature won for Nature's child.

The merry HORKEY's passing cup
   Should pause—when that sad note was heard;
The WIDOW turn HER HOUR-GLASS up,
   With tenderest feelings newly stirr'd;   20
And many a pity-waken'd word,
   And sighs that speak when language fails,
Should prove thy simple strains preferr'd
   To prouder Poet's lofty tales.

Circling the OLD OAK TABLE round,   25
   Whose moral worth thy measure owns,
Heroes and heroines yet are found

VERSES ON THE DEATH OF BLOOMFIELD

    Like ABNER AND THE WIDOW JONES;—
There GILBERT MELDRUM'S sterner tones
    In Virtue's cause are bold and free;   30
And e'en the patient suff'rer's moans,
    In pain, and sorrow—plead for thee.

Nor thus beneath the straw roof'd cot,
    Alone—should thoughts of thee pervade
Hearts which confess thee unforgot,   35
    On heathy hill, in grassy glade;
In many a spot by thee array'd
    With hues of thought, with fancy's gleam,
Thy memory lives!—in EUSTON's shade,
    By BARNHAM WATER's shadeless stream!   40

And long may guileless hearts preserve
    The memory of thy song, and thee:—
While Nature's healthful feelings nerve
    The arm of labour toiling free;
While Childhood's innocence and glee   45
    With green Old Age enjoyment share;—
RICHARDS and KATES shall tell of thee,
    WALTERS and JANES thy name declare.

On themes like these, if yet there breath'd
    A Doric Lay so sweet as thine,   50
Might artless flowers of verse be wreath'd
    Around thy modest name to twine:—
And though nor lute nor lyre be mine
    To bid thy minstrel honours live,
The praise my numbers can assign,   55
    It still is soothing thus to give.

There needs, in truth, no lofty lyre
    To yield thy Muse her homage due;
The praise her loveliest charms inspire
    Should be as artless, simple too;   60
Her eulogist should keep in view
    Thy meek and unassuming worth,
And inspiration should renew
    At springs which gave thine own its birth.

Those springs may boast no classic name 65
    To win the smile of letter'd pride,
Yet is their noblest charm the same
    As that by CASTALY supplied;
From AGANIPPE's chrystal tide
    No brighter, fairer waves can start, 70
Than Nature's quiet teachings guide
    From feeling's fountain o'er the heart.

'Tis to THE HEART Song's noblest power—
    Taste's purest precepts must refer;
And *Nature's tact*, not *Art's* proud dower, 75
    Remains its best interpreter:
He who shall trust, without demur,
    What his own better feelings teach,
Although unlearn'd, shall seldom err,
    But to the hearts of others reach. 80

It is not quaint and local terms
    Besprinkled o'er thy rustic lay,
Though well such dialect confirms
    Its power unletter'd minds to sway,
But 'tis not these that most display 85
    Thy sweetest charms, thy gentlest thrall,—
Words, phrases, fashions pass away,
    But TRUTH and NATURE live through all.

These, these have given thy rustic lyre
    Its truest, and its tenderest spell; 90
These amid Britain's tuneful choir
    Shall give thy honour'd name to dwell:
And when Death's shadowy curtain fell
    Upon thy toilsome earthly lot,
With grateful joy thy heart might swell 95
    To feel that these reproach'd thee not.

To feel that thou hadst not incurr'd
    The deep compunction, bitter shame,
Of prostituting gifts conferr'd
    To strengthen Virtue's hallow'd claim. 100
How much more glorious is the name,

The humble name which thou hast won,
Than—"damn'd with everlasting fame,"
   To be for fame itself undone.

Better, and nobler was thy choice   105
   To be the Bard of simple swains,—
In all their pleasures to rejoice,
   And soothe with sympathy their pains;
To paint with feeling in thy strains
   The themes their thoughts and tongues discuss,   110
And be, though free from classic chains,
   Our own more chaste THEOCRITUS.

For this should SUFFOLK proudly own
   Her grateful, and her lasting debt;—
How much more proudly—had she known   115
   That pining care, and keen regret,—
Thoughts which the fever'd spirits fret,
   And slow disease 'twas thine to bear;—
And, ere thy sun of life was set,
   Had won her Poet's grateful prayer.   120

'TIS NOW TOO LATE! the scene is clos'd,
   Thy conflicts borne,—thy trials o'er;—
And in the peaceful grave repos'd
   That frame which pain shall rack no more;—
Peace to the Bard whose artless store   125
   Was spread for Nature's lowliest child;
Whose song, well meet for peasant lore,
   Was lowly, simple, undefil'd.

Yet long may guileless hearts preserve
   The memory of thy Verse, and thee;—   130
While nature's healthful feelings nerve
   The arm of labour toiling free.
While SUFFOLK PEASANTRY may be
   Such as thy sweetest tales make known,—
By cottage-hearth, by greenwood tree,   135
   Be BLOOMFIELD call'd with pride *their own!*

BISHOP HUBERT

'Tis the hour of even now,
When, with pensive, thoughtful brow,
Seeking truths as yet unknown,
Bishop Hubert walks alone.

Fain would he, by lonely thought,   5
Nature's secret laws be taught,
Learn the destinies of man,
And creation's wonders scan.

From these data he would trace
Hidden mysteries of grace,   10
Dive into a deeper theme,
Solve redemption's glorious scheme.

So he flings aside to-day
Mitre's pomp, and crosier's sway—
Seeks the desert's silent scene,   15
And the marge of ocean green.

Far he has not roam'd, before,
On that solitary shore,
He has found a little child,
By its seeming play beguiled.   20

In the drifted barren sand
It has scoop'd with baby hand
Small recess, in which might float
Sportive fairy's tiny boat.

From a hollow shell, the while,   25
See, 'tis filling, with a smile,

BISHOP HUBERT

Pool as shallow as may be,
With the waters of THE SEA.

Hear the smiling Bishop ask—
"What can mean such infant task?" 30
Mark that infant's answer plain—
"'Tis to hold yon mighty main!"—

"Foolish trifler!" Hubert cries,
"Open, if thou canst, thine eyes;—
Can a shallow scoop'd by thee 35
Hope to hold yon boundless sea?

"Know'st thou not its space transcends
All thy fancy comprehends;—
Ope thy childish eyes, and know—
Fathomless its depths below." 40

Soon that child on ocean's brim
Opes its eyes, and turns to *Him!*
Well does Hubert read its look,
Glance of innocent rebuke!

While a voice is heard to say, 45
"If the pool, thus scoop'd in play,
Cannot hold yon mighty sea,
Vain must thy researches be.

"Canst thou hope to make thine own
Secrets known to GOD alone? 50
Can thy faculties confined
Fathom the ETERNAL MIND?"

Bishop Hubert turns away;—
He has learnt enough to-day—
Learnt how little man can know 55
On his pilgrimage below.

Reader, wouldst thou wiser be,
Let this truth suffice for thee;
Seek not what is sought in vain—
Knowledge by OBEDIENCE gain! 60

Be presumption's sin abhorr'd—
For the secrets of THE LORD,
If reveal'd to mortals here,
Dwell with those who LOVE!—and FEAR!

PITY FOR POOR LITTLE SWEEPS

The morn was dark, the wind was high
    With many a gusty swell;
And from the moonless, starless sky
    The rain in torrents fell:
An hour it was when sleep seem'd dear,   5
And wakefulness allied to fear.

'Tis pleasant, on a summer night,
    From tranquil rest to wake,
And see the moonbeams' silvery light
    In gentle glory break   10
Through opening clouds or leafy trees,
Whose whispers own the passing breeze.

And 'tis delightful, just as day
    Illumes the eastern skies,
To hear the first bird's matin lay,   15
    Or cock's shrill clarion rise;
To list, with unclos'd lids, and then
Gently to sink in sleep again.

But, on a stormy winter morn,
    When all is dark and drear;   20
When every sound, too, seems forlorn
    Which breaks upon the ear,—
If sleep be from the pillow gone,
The restless hours creep slowly on.

Such lot was mine not long ago;   25
    When to my ear was brought
A plaintive outcry, faint and low,

At first as faintly caught;
But soon the doleful whine of "*Sweep!*"
Betray'd its source, and "murder'd sleep."   30

For who *could* sleep, while such a strain,
    By *childish* accents pour'd,
Brought all its wretchedness and pain
    To be by thought explor'd,
And Fancy felt compell'd to range   35
Through sufferings varied, new, and strange?

The sea-boy, in the fearful din
    Of wild waves crested white,
Constrain'd the top-mast's height to win
    In some tempestuous night,—   40
His giddy, awful task may scan
With feelings worthy of a Man.

The winds may rock him to and fro,
    The thunder loudly rave,
The lightnings flash, the waves below   45
    May yawn,—an opening grave;
Yet with him to his post may climb
The germs of sentiments sublime;—

Of danger brav'd, of honour won
    By confidence and skill;   50
Memories of feats by others done;
    Proud hopes he may fulfil;
And cheering thoughts within may glow
Of messmates' watchful eyes below.

But thou, poor abject child! whose cry   55
    Still haunts my memory's ear,
What can thy weary lot supply
    The aching heart to cheer?
Poor outcast, what a doom is thine!
And nought save fruitless pity mine.   60

To brave the stormy winter's morn,
    Half naked, sparely fed;

PITY FOR POOR LITTLE SWEEPS

Dark, dangerous labyrinths forlorn,
   With limbs benumb'd, to thread;
To lead this life from day to day,   65
Of filth and misery the prey;—

To have been train'd to such a course
   By menaces and blows;
To follow it with pain, perforce,
   Through all its varied woes;—   70
A weary lot is thine, indeed,
Which, thus epitomiz'd, can plead.

Yet thou, poor Child! wast once, perchance,
   A widow's darling joy,
Whose speaking smile and sparkling glance   75
   Dwelt fondly on her boy;
Whose heart for thee fram'd schemes of bliss,
Whose lips press'd thine with many a kiss.

But she is dead! and thou art left
   To live thy weary day;   80
Of friends, of parents, hope bereft,
   With none to cheer thy way;
With none thy footsteps to reclaim
From ignorance, and vice, and shame.

What though to outward sight thou wear   85
   The human form divine,
How desolate thy scanty share
   Of what it should enshrine,—
Of all that is R<small>ELIGION</small>'s fruit,
And raises Man above the Brute!   90

Yet hast thou an immortal Soul,
   For which A S<small>AVIOUR</small> died;
And thou, at Judgment's awful goal,
   Thine audit must abide:—
A solemn thought *this*, sure, should be   95
To those who now might rescue Thee!

A MEMORIAL OF JOHN WOOLMAN; A MINISTER OF THE GOSPEL, AMONG THE QUAKERS

There is glory to me in thy Name,
   Meek follower of Bethlehem's Child!
More touching by far than the splendours of Fame,
   With which the vain world is beguil'd:—
'Tis the glory of goodness, the praise of the just,   5
Which outlives even death, and is fragrant in dust.

The warrior may win for his brow
   The proud victor chaplet of bay;—
But innocent blood sheds a stain on the bough,
   And steals all its verdure away: 10
While Humanity turns from the pageant aside,
By the sorrows and suff'rings of others supplied.

Success on the Bard may bestow
   The myrtle-wreath, meed of his lays;
And brightly and gaily that trophy may glow   15
   In the sunshine of popular praise:—
But if Virtue have turn'd from his page with disgust,
Soon, soon shall the trophy surrender its trust.

A king in his crown may rejoice;
   And Rank of its titles be proud;   20
The Singer exult in the charms of his voice;
   And Pomp in the gaze of a crowd;
And the martyr of Wealth, render'd poor by his store,
Be bow'd to by those who his Idol adore.

Yet the King must descend from his throne			25
    When the day of JEHOVAH shall come;
And titles be trustless, and Pomp stand alone,
    And the voice of the Singer be dumb;—
And Mammon, once worshipp'd, be loath'd and abhorr'd,
In the just and the terrible day of THE LORD!			30

Then who with acceptance shall stand
    In the presence of glory and light,
Having palm-branch, or censer, or harp in the hand,
    And array'd in apparel of white,—
While that volume its awful contents shall reveal,			35
Which THE LION OF JUDAH alone can unseal?

Even they who through great tribulation
    Have worship'd the holy I AM!
Whose spiritual garments are pure by lavation
    In the all-cleansing blood of THE LAMB!			40
'Tis these, and these only, by day and by night,
Shall kneel in his temple, and stand in his sight.

From them must the chorus ascend
    Which shall peal through the confines of space,
Of "Holy! thrice holy! and praise without end			45
    Unto GOD for the gift of HIS GRACE;—
And praise to THE LAMB, who for mortals was slain,
Yet liveth for ever and ever to reign!"

In that heavenly and heart-thrilling song,
    O Woolman! can silence be thine?			50
Or wilt thou not join with the jubilant throng
    In Hosannas to glory divine?—
Even such the fruition Faith whispers for Thee,
Nor happier nor holier could recompense be.

For, since those miraculous days			55
    When marvellous wonders were rife,
When the blind gaz'd with joy, and the dumb sang with praise,
    And the dead were restor'd unto life,—

I know not of one whom my heart could allow
More worthy the name of Apostle than Thou. 60

Though not upon thee were out-pour'd
   The gifts of that primitive age,
When wonders and signs spoke the power of The Lord,
   And baffled Priest, Monarch, and Sage,—
In the heart's secret temple an altar was thine, 65
And a Priesthood was given in the innermost shrine.

Not to outward and visible sense
   Did that Priesthood or Altar appeal;
Yet pure were the oracles utter'd from thence,
   And stamp'd with a questionless seal, 70
A seal which their spirits who felt them confest
By the power of thy Crucified Master imprest.

His glory alone was thy aim,
   His kingdom's advance was thy scope;
And The Cross which He bore, with its suff'ring and shame, 75
   The object and end of thy Hope!
By faith in this hope was thy spirit sustain'd,
Through that Cross was the Crown of Apostleship gain'd.

Then well may I think of thy Name,
   Meek follower of Bethlehem's Child! 80
As enwreath'd with a glory more touching than Fame,
   By which the vain world is beguil'd;
That glory by Christ and His Gospel made known,
Which proclaims not thy praise, but thy Master's alone!

A MEMORIAL OF JAMES NAYLER, THE REPROACH AND GLORY OF QUAKERISM

I know thy fall to some appears
    Our sect's reproach and shame;
That the dark clouds of distant years
    Still hover round thy name;
That not the sceptic's taunt alone,   5
And bigot's harsh upbraiding tone,
    Have been to thee unjust;
But some, who ought thy worth to feel,
Thy weakness gladly would conceal,
    And view thee with distrust.   10

These think that nothing can atone
    For such a lapse as thine,
And wish oblivion's curtain thrown
    O'er every word and line
Which tells of thy o'erclouded hour,   15
Of darkness' and delusion's power,
    The strange and fearful tale;
As if their silence could efface
Each humbling, yet instructive trace
    Of one who prov'd so frail.   20

Fruitless the wish, if such there be,
    Thy weakness to forget;
Though there be much combin'd with thee
    To waken keen regret;
Much to excite compassion's tear;   25
To prompt humility and fear,

    And vigilance to teach;—
Yet in thy penitence and shame
Not less might strictest Truth proclaim,
    Which every heart should reach.   30

Be it then known—though dire thy fall,
    And dark thy error's night,
Thy spirit rose from every thrall
    To liberty and light;—
That, through the Saviour's grace divine,   35
A peaceful, hopeful end was thine,
    His matchless power to tell;
And Gospel precepts, undefil'd,
From lips no more by doubt beguil'd,
    In dying accents fell.   40

"There is a spirit which I feel
    That would revenge no wrong,
Whose calm endurance can reveal
    The Hope that maketh strong;—
That Hope, which can all wrath outlive,   45
Contention's bitterness forgive,
    The scoffs of pride endure;
Can wear out cruelty; subdue
Whatever is oppos'd unto
    Its nature meek and pure.   50

"It sees to all temptation's end;
    And, while it suffers not
Aught evil with itself to blend,
    No brother's name would blot:
Betray'd, it bears it, for its ground   55
And spring is Mercy!—it is crown'd
    With meekness, love unfeign'd;
It takes its kingdom but by prayer,
Not strife,—and keeps with humble care
    What lowliness has gain'd: 60

"In GOD alone it can rejoice,
    Though none regard beside:
HE only owns its humble voice,

    Who first its life supplied:
In sorrow was it first conceiv'd,   65
Brought forth unpitied;—is it griev'd?
    Oppress'd?—no murmur flows;
Through suffering only comes its joy;
For worldly pleasures would destroy
    The hidden life it knows.   70

"I found this hope, when left alone,
    From man's communion hurl'd;
Therein sweet fellowship have known
    With outcasts of the world;
With them who lived in dens of earth,   75
Desolate places, far from mirth;
    But who, through death to sin,
A glorious resurrection gain'd,
And holy, steadfast hope obtain'd
    Eternal life to win!"   80

If such thy dying words—if such
    Thy parting spirit's tone—
Should not thy Memory waken much
    For Fellowship to own?
If few have ever fallen as Thou,   85
Yet few or none can Truth avow
    So gloriously restor'd;
And plac'd before the Christian's eye
A monument to testify
    The goodness of THE LORD!   90

So highly does my spirit prize
    Thy truly Christian fame,
OUR History boasts not, in my eyes,
    A more illustrious Name;—
Not one to which I oftener turn,   95
Afresh the excellence to learn
    Of watching unto prayer;
Of deep humility the worth;
Of Hope, which owes to Grace its birth,
    Where Nature would despair;—   100

Of shame and suffering, meekly crown'd
   With glory from above;
Of strength in conscious weakness found,
   And life in fervent love:
These may be lessons hard to learn 105
By those, who only will discern
   What outward sense can see;
But fools, in worldly wisdom's view,
Confess them excellent and true,
   Exemplified in Thee. 110

An ardent mind may be deceiv'd
   By wild enthusiast dreams,
Then doubt the light it once believ'd,
   Though brightly still it beams;
But from such visions to awake, 115
Their dark delusions to forsake,
   And see *The Light* yet shine;—
To own, to follow, love it still,
In self-abasedness of will,—
   Was worthy Faith like thine! 120

A MEMORIAL OF MARY DYER, ONE OF THE EARLY WORTHIES AND MARTYRS IN THE SOCIETY OF QUAKERS

We too have had our Martyrs. Such wert Thou,
    Illustrious Woman! though the starry crown
Of martyrdom have sate on many a brow,
    In the World's eye, of far more wide renown.

Yet the same spirit grac'd thy fameless end;   5
    Which shone in Latimer, and his compeers,
Upon whose hallow'd memories still attend
    Manhood's warm reverence, Childhood's guileless tears.

Well did *they* win them: may they keep them long!
    Their names require not praise obscure as mine;   10
Nor does my Muse their cherish'd memories wrong,
    By this imperfect aim to honour thine.

Heroic Martyr of a sect despis'd!
    Thy name and memory to my heart are dear:
Thy fearless zeal, in artless childhood priz'd,   15
    The lapse of years has taught me to revere.

Thy Christian worth demands no Poet's lay,
    Historian's pen, nor Sculptor's boasted art:
What could the proudest tribute these can pay
    To thy immortal spirit now impart?   20

Yet seems it like *a sacred debt* to give
    The brief memorial thou mayst well supply;
Whose life display'd how Christians ought to live;
    Whose death—how Christian Martyrs calmly die.

VERSES ON THE APPROACH OF SPRING, ADDRESSED TO MY LITTLE PLAY-FELLOW

Rejoice, my little merry mate!
   The blithesome Spring is coming,
When thou shalt roam, with heart elate,
   To hear the wild bee humming;
To hear the wild bee humming round,   5
   The primrose sweetly blowing,
And listen to each gentle sound
   Of gladsome music flowing.

The birds shall sing from many a bower,
   Joy like thy own obeying;   10
And, round full many a blooming flower,
   The butterfly be playing;—
Be playing, love! on wings as light
   As heart in thy young bosom,
And showing tints as fair and bright   15
   As does the opening blossom.

The snow-drops, by our garden-walk,
   Long since to life have started;
They wither now upon the stalk;
   Their beauty is departed: 20
Their beauty is departed,—but
   Flowers in the fields are springing,
Which by and by shall ope and shut,
   As to the glad birds' singing.

The robin, from the pear-tree bough,
    Gives us of song our ear-full;
The morns are getting lightsome now,
    The evenings growing cheerful:
And soon they'll be more long and light,
    With warm and pleasant weather;
And we, to see the sun-set bright,
    May go abroad together.

Then shall our summer haunts again
    Renew their former pleasures;
The poplar grove, the shady lane,
    For thee be full of treasures:
For flowers are treasures unto thee,
    And well thou lov'st to find them;
To gather them with childish glee,
    And then in posies bind them.

Spring is to me no merry time;
    Its smiles are touch'd with sadness;
For vanish'd, with Life's early prime,
    Is much that gave it gladness:
Yet, merry play-mate! for thy sake
    I will not sing of sorrow;
But since thou canst its joys partake,
    I would 'twere Spring to-morrow!

BEALINGS HOUSE

A modest Mansion, with its garden ground,
    Where the blithe bee pursues his gladsome chase;
    An undulating lawn, where Art's mild grace.
Is rustic Nature's willing handmaid found;
Fair slopes, and swelling uplands, cloth'd and crown'd   5
    With trees, whose young boughs fondly interlace
    Their varied foliage;—such the charms I trace
In the familiar landscape smiling round.—
Yet, fair as is the scene, its height'ning zest,
    To me, is not from outward features caught,   10
    But from bright hours with social converse fraught,
When oft, beneath that roof a well pleas'd guest,
Pleasure on winged moments has imprest
    The prouder stamp of fancy, feeling, thought.

TO A BUTTERFLY. TRANSLATED FROM THE FRENCH

I.
Born with the balmy breath of Spring,
   With fragrant roses dying,
With Zephyr's light and sportive wing
   In playful motion vying.

II.
Bright as the pure and cloudless blue   5
   Of heaven above,—or blossom
That opes its chalice, as to woo
   Thy beauty to its bosom.

III.
Intoxicated with perfume,
   With light and azure glowing;   10
From wings surcharg'd with youthful bloom
   Thy feathery glory throwing.

IV.
Then borne away, like thought or breath,
   To viewless, endless distance,
How lovely in thy life and death   15
   Appears thy brief existence!

V.
A gentle wish, a soft desire,
   To fancy, it resembles,
Which, ardent, restless, would aspire
   To bliss—at which it trembles:—   20

VI.

But still, unsatisfied below,
  Just glances o'er each treasure,
Then soars whence brighter splendours flow,
  To seek for purer pleasure.

ON A PORTRAIT OF BEATRICE CENCI

In the Collection at Bredfield House, the Residence of John FitzGerald, Esq.

I.
It haunts me still! that lovely face,
   With beauty's own undying power,
Whose pure, imaginative grace
   Exists beyond its mortal hour.

II.
That brow so thoughtful, yet so fair,   5
   Might tell of sorrow's chilling shade,
But patient gentleness is there
   Each mournful feeling to upbraid.

III.
Those features, moulded to delight
   In hours of mirth the gazer's eye,   10
Are more than beautifully bright
   With sorrow's calm sublimity.

IV.
'Tis not a face to charm awhile,
   By common art or outward spell,
Whose transient power of look or smile   15
   All who behold at once can tell.

V.
Nor is it one which, left behind,
   Can mingle with forgotten things;
Calm, energetic, full of mind,
   Round it the heart's fond memory clings—   20

VI.

Clings mournfully; while thought would shun
   The woes in which it was a sharer;
Joy may boast many a brighter one,
   But sorrow never own'd a fairer.

ON THE DEATH OF SAMUEL ALEXANDER, OF NEEDHAM-MARKET

"He whom the wretched and the poor knew best,
Whom, when the ear his footstep heard, it blest;
To whom the eye, with age or sorrow dim,
Gave witness, and whose works shall follow him:
Who silently his Saviour's steps pursued;
Whose creed was love, whose life was gratitude."
JOSIAH CONDER.

Belov'd, rever'd, and mourn'd,—Farewell!
   Though lost to every human eye,
Thy memory in our hearts shall dwell,
   'Till we, like thee, in earth shall lie:
Thy name, now utter'd with a sigh,   5
   As we thy recent loss deplore,
Hereafter shall a theme supply
   For fondest thoughts to linger o'er.

Though well we knew thy zenith past,
   And westward saw thy sun decline;—   10
So brightly, warmly—to the last
   That orb in glory seem'd to shine;
We can but mournfully resign
   A splendour which had known no chill,
Though, with a lustre more benign,   15
   In brighter skies 'tis glowing still.

There are who in advancing years
   Yet more and more our love engage,
In whom the worth that most endears
   Seems mellow'd, not impair'd, by age;   20

Who blend the wisdom of the Sage
    With Childhood's tenderness and truth,
And bear about to life's last stage
    The earlier greenness of its youth.

From such, although their locks be grey,   25
    Oh! who can feel prepared to part?
For them affection would delay
    By each procrastinating art
Life's certain close;—and tears will start
    When Death has snapt the vital chain   30
And sighs uncheck'd will rend the heart,
    Though sighs and tears alike are vain.

Thus have we mourn'd, thus mourn we yet;—
    And cold indeed that heart must be
Which owns no pensive, fond regret,   35
    When Death removes a friend like thee:
Oh! Spring may hang on many a tree
Green leaves by after Winter reft,
Ere we can hope on earth to see
    Fill'd up the void which thou hast left.   40

How deeply will thy loss be known
    In many a low and wretched cot,
Where oft thy kindness has been shown
    To cheer the inmates' joyless lot!
From many a sweet, secluded spot   45
    Whose beauties tell thy forming taste,
The eye which seeks, and finds thee not—
    Will turn—as from a dreary waste.

I dare not pause o'er every scene
    Where it was sweet with thee to share   50
Of social life each joy serene,
    For Thou wast oft the centre there!
Nor will I—in The House of Prayer—
    Dwell on that vacant seat—in thought,
Where thy deep meditative air   55
    With silent eloquence has taught.

ON THE DEATH OF SAMUEL ALEXANDER

Rather let thought and feeling turn—
   From themes that vain regret excite,
That PRINCIPLE's true worth to learn
   Which gave thy soul its inward light;   60
Which, far beyond the transient might
   Of aught that we can deem thine own,
Gave thee that influential right—
   More deeply lov'd—as longer known.

This last, this crowning gift of all   65
   Was GRACE DIVINE—belov'd, obey'd;
Follow'd, at Duty's secret call,
   With meek reliance on its aid:
Through life's bright sunshine or its shade
   Thy Spirit view'd with reverend awe   70
This inward guide, nor less display'd
   Obedience to God's written law.

Here shone the finish'd charm that lent
   Such brightness to thy lengthen'd days;
And—in the mortal instrument   75
   Proclaimed THY MASTER's power and praise:
The glory of the world decays,
   As added years its splendour dim;
Thine seem'd to borrow brighter rays
   As age but brought thee nearer HIM.   80

Therefore thy memory long shall live
   In hearts that truly knew thy worth,
Because *the light* it there may give
   Is not a meteor born of earth:
The flash of wit, the gleam of mirth,   85
   Death's shadowy clouds may veil in gloom;
But thine—immortal in its birth,
   Is unextinguish'd by the tomb!

BOW HILL

Cloudless and lovely is the night, the stars are bright on high,
The full-orb'd Moon in glorious light shines from the vaulted sky;
There's not a breath of wind to move the pine-tree's tufted crest;
But all around, and all above, seems hush'd in silent rest.
Methinks it were no vulgar bliss, could I my dream fulfil, 5
To climb in such an hour as this the summit of Bow Hill.

It was a lovely Summer's day, when last I wander'd there,
Nor has the picture pass'd away which then appear'd so fair;
On Memory's faithful tablet trac'd, its feature soft arise,
Perchance with added beauty graced by fancy's magic dyes: 10
Though when beheld, I thought no hue of Mind's creative skill
Could with a heighten'd charm imbue the landscape from Bow Hill.

The birds were singing sweetly round, the sun in heaven shone bright,
And there was music in the sound, and beauty in the light;
That glancing light on Ocean's breast diffus'd a richer glow, 15
That music rose with sweetest zest from Kingley's depths below:
And many a flow'ret's simple bloom there flourish'd wild at will,
Decking each ancient sea-king's tomb who fell on proud Bow Hill.

Fair was the landscape then! and now with fancy's aid I scale
At midnight's hour that summit's brow, and view that
    peaceful vale: 20
Though beautiful when I was there the prospect round might seem,
She paints it to my mind more fair by moonlight's silent gleam;
Its charms might then delight impart which woke a livelier thrill,
But, Oh! how soothing to the heart night's silence on Bow Hill.

How bright, in tints of moonlight drest, looks each fierce
    sea-king's tomb, 25

BOW HILL

While massy shadows darkly rest around the Yew-trees' gloom!
How does the distant glimm'ring light dance on the restless main,
Or clothe in splendour palely bright the wide extended plain!
While whispering leaves just faintly stirr'd, soft as a murm'ring rill,
At intervals alone, are heard, by night upon Bow Hill.   30

Past is my vision! lingers yet the charm that woke my lay,
And owns a more enduring debt than verse can ever pay:
The Danish tombs, the shadowy grove, the distant main I see,
But charms their beauty far above endear that scene to me;
And feelings absence cannot change, and distance cannot chill,   35
Must oft compel my thoughts to range with pleasure on Bow Hill.

1826–29: LITERARY FAME

A GRANDSIRE'S TALE

I.
   The tale I tell was told me long ago;
   Yet mirthful ones, since heard, have passed away,
   While this still wakens memory's fondest glow,
   And feelings fresh as those of yesterday:
   'Twas told me by a man whose hairs were grey,   5
   Whose brow bore token of the lapse of years,
   Yet o'er his heart affection's gentle sway
   Maintained that lingering spell which age endears,
And while he told his tale his eyes were dim with tears.

II.
   But not with tears of sorrow;—for the eye   10
   Is often wet with joy and gratitude;
   And well his faltering voice, and tear, and sigh,
   Declared a heart by thankfulness subdued:
   Brief feelings of regret might there intrude,
   Like clouds which shade awhile the moon's fair light;   15
   But meek submission soon her power renewed,
   And patient smiles, by tears but made more bright,
Confessed that God's decree was wise, and good, and right.

III.
   It was a winter's evening;—clear, but still:
   Bright was the fire, and bright the silvery beam   20
   Of the fair moon shone on the window-sill,
   And parlour-floor;—the softly mingled gleam
   Of fire and moonlight suited well a theme
   Of pensive converse, unallied to gloom;
   Ours varied like the subjects of a dream;   25
   And turned, at last, upon the silent tomb,
Earth's goal for hoary age, and beauty's smiling bloom.

IV.

We talked of life's last hour,—the varied forms
And features it assumes;—how some men die
As sets the sun when dark clouds threaten storms, 30
And starless night; others whose evening sky
Resembles those which to the outward eye
Seem full of promise:—and with softened tone,
At seasons checked by no ungrateful sigh,
The death of one sweet grand-child of his own 35
Was by that hoary man most tenderly made known.

V.

She was, he said, a fair and lovely child
As ever parent could desire to see,
Or seeing, fondly love; of manners mild,
Affections gentle,—even in her glee, 40
Her very mirth from levity was free;
But her more common mood of mind was one
Thoughtful beyond her early age, for she
In ten brief years her little course had run,—
Many more brief have known, but brighter surely none. 45

VI.

Though some might deem her pensive, if not sad,
Yet those who knew her better, best could tell
How calmly happy, and how meekly glad
Her quiet heart in its own depths did dwell:
Like to the waters of some crystal well, 50
In which the stars of heaven at noon are seen,
Fancy might deem on her young spirit fell
Glimpses of light more glorious and serene
Than that of life's brief day, so heavenly was her mien.

VII.

But, though no boist'rous playmate, her fond smile 55
Had sweetness in it passing that of mirth;
Loving and kind, her thoughts, words, deeds, the while
Betrayed of childish sympathies no dearth:
She loved the wild flowers scattered over earth,
Bright insects sporting in the light of day, 60
Blythe songsters giving joyous music birth

In groves impervious to the noontide ray;—
All these she loved as much as those who seemed more gay.

VIII.

Yet more she loved the word, the smile, the look,
Of those who reared her with religious care; 65
With fearful joy she conned that holy book,
At whose unfolded page full many a prayer,
In which her weal immortal had its share,
Recurred to memory; for she had been trained,
Young as she was, her early cross to bear; 70
And taught to love, with fervency unfeigned,
The record of His life whose death salvation gained.

IX.

I dare not linger, like my ancient friend,
On every charm and grace of this fair maid;
For in his narrative the story's end 75
Was long with fond prolixity delayed;
Though 'rightly fancy had its close portrayed
Before I heard it. Who but might have guessed
That one so ripe for heaven would early fade
In this brief state of trouble and unrest 80
Yet only wither here to bloom in life more blest.

X.

My theme is one of joy, and not of grief;
I would not loiter o'er such flower's decay,
Nor stop to paint it, slowly, leaf by leaf,
Fading, and sinking tow'rds its parent clay: 85
She sank, as sinks the glorious orb of day,
His glories bright'ning at his journey's close;
Yet with that chastened, soft, and gentle ray
In which no dazzling splendour fiercely glows,
But on whose mellowed light our eyes with joy repose. 90

XI.

Her strength was failing, but it seemed to sink
So calmly, tenderly, it woke no fear;
'Twas like a rippling wave on ocean's brink,
Which breaks in dying music on the ear,

    And placid beauty on the eye;—no tear, 95
    Except of quiet joy, in hers was known;
    Though some there were around her justly dear,
    Her love for whom in every look was shown,
Yet more and more she sought and loved to be alone.

XII.
    One summer morn they missed her:—she had been, 100
    As usual, to the garden arbour brought,
    After their morning meal; her placid mien
    Had worn no seeming shade of graver thought,
    Her voice, her smile, with cheerfulness was fraught;
    And she was left amid that peaceful scene 105
    A little space;—but when she there was sought,
    In her secluded oratory green,
Their arbour's sweetest flower had left its leafy screen!

XIII.
    They found her in her chamber, by the bed
    Whence she had risen, and on the bed-side chair, 110
    Before her, was an open bible spread;
    Herself upon her knees;—with tender care
    They stole on her devotions, when the air
    Of her meek countenance the truth made known:
    The child had died! died in the act of prayer! 115
    And her pure spirit, without sigh or groan,
To heaven and endless joy from earth and grief had flown.

STANZAS, COMPOSED DURING A TEMPEST

Dazzling may seem the noontide sky,
   Its arch of azure shewing;
And lovely to the gazer's eye
   The west, at sunset glowing.

Splendid the east—at morning bright,
   Soft moonlight on the ocean;—
But *glorious* is the hushed delight
   Born in the storm's commotion!

To see the dark and lowering cloud
   By vivid lightening riven,—
To hear the answer, stern and proud,
   By echoing thunders given;—

To *feel*, in such a scene and hour,
   —'Mid all that each discloses—
The presence of that viewless power
   On whom the world reposes;—

This, to the heart, is more than all
   Mere beauty can bring o'er it;
Thought—feeling—fancy own its thrall,
   And joy is hushed before it!

A PROPHET'S OLD AGE

"And Moses was an hundred and twenty years old when he died: his eye was not dim, nor his natural force abated."—Deuteronomy, xxxiv.7.

How lightly o'er thy guarded head
The lapse of silent years had sped,
   How poor the spoils of time,
To leave thee thus, in life's last stage,
A living greenness in old age   5
   So splendid and sublime.

Thy natural vigour unimpair'd,
An eye whose lustre still declar'd
   Age could not dim its ray,
How brightly must thy sun have set,   10
Which on the verge of night had yet
   The radiance of noon-day.

Had age so vigorous and serene
E'en in that distant era been
   A thing regarded not,   15
Not thus had history's page unroll'd
Thy triumph o'er decay, and told
   Thy proud, peculiar lot.

But thus conspicuously was shown
Vigour and brightness not thy own.   20
   To life's last parting hour,
That Israel in that wond'rous sign
Of might more glorious far than thine,
   Should own Jehovah's power.

A PROPHET'S OLD AGE

That we, who sooner reach life's close, 25
May in our weakness yet repose
   On his eternal truth,
Who, if to Him alone we live,
In age unto the soul can give
   Spring's renovated youth. 30

RUTH'S LOVE

"And they lifted up their voice, and wept again: and Orpah kissed her mother in law; but Ruth clave to her."—Ruth, i.14.

Though prouder names than thine may live
   In history's richly blazon'd page,
Adorn'd with all that fame can give
   To win the eye from age to age:

Yet by no sweeter, purer fame   5
   Hath joy been gladden'd, grief beguil'd,
Than that which brightly wreaths thy name,
   And speaks thy worth, Naomi's child!

Thy story, 'mid the stormier deeds
   The annals of thy time make known,   10
For humble truth and nature pleads
   With grace peculiarly their own.

And deep instruction yet is taught
   By thy delightful simple tale,
Disclosing to attentive thought   15
   The love which *can* and *cannot* fail.

There is a love, sincere, but weak,
   Which has no high, or heaven-ward stay;
Thus Orpah kiss'd her mother's cheek,
   Kiss'd her—and wept—yet turn'd away!   20

Thy own, heroic and sublime,
   Still to thy earthly parent clave,

RUTH'S LOVE

And lives, triumphant over time,
   For Heaven its holier courage gave.

And richly God vouchsaf'd to bless   25
   A love devoted, pure as thine,
By making thee the ancestress
   Of kingly David's royal line.

THE VANITY OF HUMAN KNOWLEDGE

"For we are but of yesterday, and know nothing, because our days upon earth are a shadow."—Job, viii.9.

   His birth of yesterday,
   To-morrow pass'd away;—
His life the shadow of a summer cloud;
   Shall mortal man be vain
   Of knowledge he may gain   5
In the brief span of time to earth allow'd?

   Not that we under-rate
   Or lightly estimate
The triumphs won by many an honour'd name
   Of those whose midnight oil,   10
   And unremitting toil,
In outward lore have won them worldly fame.

   Yet, oh! how poor, and brief,
   Like the frail Cistus' leaf
Must knowledge be—*confin'd* to things of time;   15
   Which, fetter'd by their thrall,
   Is ignorant of all
That renders an eternity sublime.

   What boots it to be vers'd
   In systems schools have nurs'd,—   20
If, gaining all the lore that these impart,
   That truth remain unknown,
   Whose teaching power, alone,
Convicts, converts, and sanctifies the heart?

A SOLILOQUY

"Unto thee, O Lord, do I lift up my soul."—Psalm, xxv.1.

Once more, lov'd solace of my lonely hours,
    Would I renew my intercourse with thee,
Suspended for a time—while Spring's gay flowers,
    Her bursting foliage, and her songs of glee
Allured me from my task to budding bowers,   5
    To shady lane, green copse, or blossom'd lea;—
In the fond hope, but not more fond than vain,
Their charms might lend fresh vigour to my strain.

Mistaken thought! To me shall come no more
    The once blithe impulse of a vernal day;   10
Nor can fair nature's countless charms restore
    Aught of congenial freshness to my lay;
The sanguine flush of youth's bright morn is o'er,
    The fairy dreams of fancy pass'd away;—
And were they still my own they could not lend   15
One living charm with thy deep truths to blend.

Not that I darkly view, or lightly prize,
    The beauties and the harmonies of Spring;
Yet is there what green earth, nor laughing skies,
    Nor blooming flowers, nor song of birds can bring   20
Over the spirit;—hid from human eyes
    Deep in the heart, like a far holier thing
Than outward nature's richest stores can yield,
The fount of thought and feeling is unseal'd.

And he who writes of themes which must endure   25
    When times and seasons shall have run their course,

Whose song is TRUTH, unchangeable and sure,
    If he aright would feel its truest force,
Must drink of streams unperishing and pure
    Which issue from a deeper, holier source;   30
Looking beyond the fading things of time,
To those which are eternal and sublime.

O! may I now, with no misgiving dread,
    Resume the task of many a winter night;
Nor deem devotion's purer influence fled   35
    Because no inly-answ'ring flood of light
From Spring's young glory on my soul is shed:
    The just shall walk by faith, and not by sight!
And he who seeks to frame a heavenly song
Through conscious weakness may be render'd strong.   40

Strong in the might and strength of Him, alone,
    Whose spirit down the vale of vision swept,
What time the seer beheld around him strown
    Bones dry and lifeless which in silence slept;
These, at the word divine, His power made known,   45
    And on their feet a living army leapt;
So may the spirit He vouchsafes to raise
Revive as from the dead to sing His praise.

A REFLECTION

Oh! were I borne in spirit to the time
    Which *now* the progress of my task hath won;
That era long foretold by seers sublime,
    When, born of woman, God's incarnate Son
Came to atone for folly, sin, and crime,   5
    And ransom man, without his aid undone;
Fulfilling in himself each sign and rite,
And making known his gospel's glorious light!

Who, plac'd on such ideal eminence,—
    But many a thoughtful glance must round him cast?   10
Viewing, as with an eye of faith intense,
    Now the more shadowy glories of the past,
Sublimely grand in dark magnificence,
    And splendidly imposing to the last;—
Then, turning from them, trembling, to survey   15
The gentler dawning of the gospel day.

In calm effulgence rises Bethlehem's Star
    Over the yet untravell'd holy ground;
There Calv'ry's hill uplifts its Cross afar,
    As with a diadem of brightness crown'd,   20
Majestic beauty with no cloud to mar,
    Like those which hover'd Sinai's heights around:—
And here the Mount of Olives to the sky
Uprears its leafy coronal on high.

How lovely, yet how solemn is the scene!   25
    Scene worthy of the truths which wait us there;
And hark the silent intervals between,

In silvery tones float on the midnight air,
Glad songs that hail the new-born Nazarene!
　　Songs in which angel hosts with transport share;　　　　30
Such as no more shall fall on mortal ears,
'Till heavenly music shall untune the spheres.

TEARS

"Jesus wept."—John, xi.35.

Not worthless are the tears,
    When pure their fountain-head,
Which human hopes and fears
    Compel us oft to shed.

In grief or joy they tell   5
    Far more than words can teach;
Their silence hath a spell
    Beyond the power of speech.

In joy, though bright and brief,
    Its essence they make known;   10
And how they soften grief
    The mourner's heart will own.

Yet tears there are which fall,
    Claiming a holier birth;
Which come not at the call   15
    Of time's brief woe or mirth.

Tears which are shed, alone,
    For God's all-pard'ning love;
But to the mourner known,
    And Him who dwells above.   20

Can there be drops more pure,
    More precious, holy yet;
Whose record shall endure
    'Till time's last sun be set!

Yes! Tears once fill'd His eye,   25
    Beside a mortal's grave,
Who left his throne on high,
    The lost to seek and save.

And fresh, from age to age,
    Their memory shall be kept;   30
While man shall bless the page
    Which tells that JESUS *wept*!

WALKING IN THE LIGHT

"But if we walk in the light, as he is in the light, we have fellowship one with another; and the blood of Jesus Christ his Son cleanseth us from all sin."—1 John, i.7.

Walk in the light! So shalt thou know
    That fellowship of love,
His Spirit only can bestow,
    Who reigns in light above.

Walk in the light!—and sin, abhorr'd,   5
    Shall ne'er defile again;
The blood of Jesus Christ, thy Lord,
    Shall cleanse from every stain.

Walk in the light!—and thou shalt find
    Thy heart made truly His,   10
Who dwells in cloudless light enshrin'd,
    In whom no darkness is.

Walk in the light!—and thou shalt own
    Thy darkness pass'd away,
Because that Light hath on thee shone   15
    In which is perfect day.

Walk in the light!—and e'en the tomb
    No fearful shade shall wear;
Glory shall chase away its gloom,
    For Christ hath conquer'd there!   20

Walk in the light!—and thine shalt be
    A path, though thorny, bright;
For God, by grace, shall dwell in Thee,
    And God himself is Light!

WHICH THINGS ARE A SHADOW

I saw a stream whose waves were bright
   With morning's dazzling sheen;
But gathering clouds, ere fall of night,
   Had darken'd o'er the scene:—
      "How like that tide,"   5
      My Spirit sighed,
   "This life to me hath been."

The clouds dispers'd:—the glorious West
   Was bright with closing day;
And on the river's peaceful breast   10
   Shone forth the sunset ray:—
      My Spirit caught
      The soothing thought—
   Thus life might pass away.

I saw a tree:—with ripening fruit   15
   And shady foliage crown'd;
But ah! an axe was at its root,
   And fell'd it to the ground:—
      Well might that tree
      Recal to me   20
   The doom my hopes had found.

The fire consum'd it:—but I saw
   Its smoke ascend on high!
A shadowy type, beheld with awe,
   Of that which cannot die,   25
      But, from the grave
      Shall rise to crave
   A home above the sky.

PREFATORY SONNET [TO *A WIDOW'S TALE, AND OTHER POEMS*]

The lamp will shed a feeble glimmering light,
   Until the oil which fed its flame be spent;
   The small stars twinkle in the firmament,
And the moon's pallid orb arise on night,
When day has waned;—the scath'd tree, in despite   5
   Of age look green, with ivy-wreaths besprent;
   And faded roses still retain their scent,
When death shall make them loveless to the sight.
So linger on, as seeming loth to die,
   Light, strength, and sweetness:—thus *unto the last*   10
   The poet o'er his lyre's lov'd strings will cast
A nerveless hand—and his fond labours ply;
Not unrewarded if its parting sigh
   Seem like the lingering echo of the past!

CARACTACUS

1.
Before proud Rome's imperial throne,
   In mind's unconquer'd mood,
As if the triumph were his own,
   The dauntless captive stood;
None, to have seen his freeborn air,   5
Had fancied him a prisoner there.

2.
Though through the crowded streets of Rome,
   With slow and stately tread,
Far from his own lov'd island-home
   That day in triumph led,—   10
Unbow'd his head, unbent his knee,
Undimm'd his eye, his aspect free.

3.
A free and fearless glance he cast
   On temple, arch, and tower,
By which the long procession pass'd   15
   Of Rome's victorious power;
And somewhat of a scornful smile
Upcurl'd his haughty lip the while.

4.
And now he stood with brow serene
   Where slaves might prostrate fall;   20
Bearing a Briton's manly mien
   In Caesar's palace hall;
Claiming, with kindling brow and cheek,
The privilege e'en there to speak.

5.

Nor could Rome's haughty Lord withstand
    The claim that look preferr'd;
But motion'd with uplifted hand
    The suppliant should be heard;
If he, indeed, a suppliant were,
Whose glance *demanded* audience there.

6.

Deep stillness fell on all the crowd;
    From Claudius on his throne
Down to the meanest slave that bow'd
    At his imperial tone;
Silent his fellow-captives' grief,
As fearless spoke the Island Chief.

7.

"Think not, thou Eagle-Lord of Rome,
    And master of the world,
Though vict'ry's banner o'er thy dome
    In triumph now be furl'd,
I would address thee as thy slave,—
But as the bold should greet the brave.

8.

"I might perchance, could I have deign'd
    To hold a Vassal's throne,
E'en now in Britain's isle have reign'd,
    A king, in name alone.—
Yet holding, as thy meek ally,
A monarch's mimic pageantry.

9.

"Then through Rome's crowded streets, this day,
    I might have rode with thee;
Not in a captive's base array,
    But fetterless, and free;—
If freedom he could hope to find
Whose bondage is of heart and mind.

10.

"But canst thou marvel that,—freeborn, 55
    With heart and hope unquell'd,
Throne, crown, and sceptre I should scorn,
    By thy permission held?
Or that I should retain my right,
'Till wrested by a conqueror's might? 60

11.

"Rome, with her palaces, and towers,
    By us un-wish'd, un-reft;
Her homely huts, and woodland bowers
    To Britain might have left;
Worthless to you their wealth must be, 65
But dear to us—for they were free!

12.

"I might have bow'd before;—but where
    Had been thy triumph now?
To my resolve no yoke to bear
    Thou ow'st thy laurell'd brow; 70
Inglorious victory had been thine,
And more inglorious bondage mine.

13.

"Now I have spoken—do thy will;
    Be life or death my lot,
Since Britain's throne no more I fill, 75
    To me it matters not:—
My fame is clear, but on my fate
Thy glory, or thy shame must wait."

14.

He ceased. From all around up-sprung
    A murmur of applause; 80
For well had truth's and freedom's tongue
    Maintain'd their holy cause:—
Nor could the conqueror's heart gainsay
Their nobler, and diviner sway.

SONNET; TO A GRANDMOTHER

"Old age is dark and unlovely."
OSSIAN.

O say not so! A bright old age is thine;
   Calm as the gentle light of summer eves,
   Ere twilight dim her dusky mantle weaves;
Because to thee is given, in strength's decline,
A heart that does not thanklessly repine   5
   At aught of which the hand of God bereaves,
   Yet all He sends with gratitude receives;—
May such a quiet, thankful close be mine.
And hence thy fire-side chair appears to me
   A peaceful throne—which thou wert form'd to fill;   10
   Thy children—ministers, who do thy will;
And those grand-children, sporting round thy knee,
Thy little subjects, looking up to thee,
   As one who claims their fond allegiance still.

STANZAS, WRITTEN FOR A BLANK LEAF IN SEWELL'S HISTORY OF THE QUAKERS

1.

Look back unto the morning of our day;—
   What does such retrospective glance afford?
Our Fathers' lot these pages shall display,
   A people scoff'd at, and a sect abhorr'd.

2.

Hist'ry describes them truly;—plac'd between
   Two persecuting fires, whose fury burn'd
For them with equal fierceness, by the spleen
   Alike of Church and Presbytery spurn'd.

3.

Whether a Stuart fill'd their country's throne,
   Or England bow'd to Cromwell's stern command,
Their lot remain'd the same, despis'd, unknown,
   The out-casts, and off-scow'ring of their land.

4.

Yet through that perilous and thorny path,
   Which they with meek submission humbly trod;
What was the world's contempt, the bigot's wrath
   To them whose hopes and fears were fix'd on God!

5.

They look'd on every suffering as a test
   Of their allegiance to the faith they lov'd,
And neither heights, nor depths had power to wrest
   Their confidence from HIM whose might they prov'd.

6.
Nor was that humble confidence misplaced;
   They did not vainly trust in God's right hand;
Through persecution's flames,—oppression's waste,
   It led them on to quiet's promis'd land!

7.
Oh! it is good for sects, with watchful eye,
   To look back to the rock whence they were hewn;
And when prosperity's bright sun is high,
   Compare their stormy morning to their noon.

8.
Although the early rise of such may be
   At times o'er-shadow'd by mistaken zeal;
Yet there, too, shines a brightness all may see,
   A simple dignity which all may feel.

9.
'Tis like the morning of the outward day,
   When chrystal dew-drops gem each trembling flower,
And through the low'ring clouds the sun's bright ray
   Flings its effulgence with triumphant power.

10.
For, as the outward sun advances through
   The clouds which compass him, earth's mists exhale,
The flowers put on their freshest, loveliest hue,
   Light robes the mountains, stillness soothes the vale.

11.
So when the Sun of Righteousness first flings
   His light on those who have in darkness sit,
And rises, as with healing on his wings,
   Pure life and love awake to welcome it.

12.
Then is the season of high-minded thought;
   High-minded, for its hopes are fix'd on high,
Yet humbled by a sense that God has brought
   This better dawn before their mental eye.

13.

The Saviour's yoke is felt no burthen then
    On shoulders which a grasshopper had bow'd;   50
To bear the cross which He once bore for men
    Appears a privilege to man allow'd.

14.

In this abandonment of all to HIM,
    Who claims it as His own undoubted right;
The glory of this world is render'd dim,   55
    Compar'd with that which makes their darkness light!

15.

They go forth in HIS name; they know no power,
    No wisdom of *their own*; they serve the Lord!
That duty is their spirits' richest dower,
    The coming of His kingdom their reward.   60

16.

Thus went our fathers forth; the seed they sow'd,
    In fear and faith, and saw its vast increase;
Conflict their lot upon life's narrow road,
    This they endur'd, and found its end was peace.

17.

Peace! which the world to worldlings cannot give,   65
    Nor, blessed be its Giver's name, destroy;
Peace which can all the ills of life out-live,
Promise and prelude of eternal joy.

THE VALE OF TEARS

1.
In visions which are not of night, a shadowy vale I see,
The path of pilgrim tribes who are, who have been, or shall be;
At either end are lowering clouds impervious to the sight,
And frequent shadows veil, throughout, each gleam of passing light;
A path it is of joys and griefs, of many hopes and fears;　　　　5
Gladden'd at times by sunny smiles, but oftener dimm'd by tears.

2.
Green leaves are there, they quickly fade, bright flowers,
　　but soon they die;
Its banks are lav'd by pleasant streams, but soon their bed is dry;
And some that roll on to the last with undiminish'd force,
Have lost that limpid purity which graced their early source,　　10
They seem to borrow in their flow the tinge of dark'ning years,
And e'en their mournful murmuring sound befits the vale of tears.

3.
Pleasant that valley's opening scenes appear to childhood's view,
The flowers are bright, the turf is green, the sky above is blue;
A blast may blight, a beam may scorch, a cloud may intervene,　　15
But lightly mark'd, and soon forgot, they mar not such a scene;
Fancy still paints the future bright, and hope the present cheers,
Nor can we deem the path we tread leads through a vale of tears.

4.
But soon, too soon the flowers that deck'd our early pathway-side
Have drooped and wither'd on their stalks, and one by one
　　have died;　　　　20
The turf by noon's fierce heat is sear'd, the sky is overcast,
There's thunder in the torrent's tone, and tempest in the blast;

Fancy is but a phantom found, and hope a dream appears,
And more and more our hearts confess this life a vale of tears.

5.

Darker and darker seems the path! how sad to journey on,   25
When hands and hearts which gladden'd our's appear for ever gone,
Some cold in death, and some, alas! we fancied could not chill,
Living to self, and to the world, to us seem colder still;
With mournful retrospective glance we look to brighter years,
And tread with solitary steps the thorny vale of tears.   30

6.

Then wasting pain and slow disease trace furrows on the brow,
The grasshopper, alighting down, is felt a burthen now,
The silver cord is loosening fast its feeble, slender hold,
The fountain's pitcher soon must break, and bowl of purer gold;—
Oh! were it not for that blest hope which even death endears,   35
How weary were our pilgrimage through this dark vale of tears!

CONCLUDING VERSES, TO A CHILD SEVEN YEARS OLD

1.

My opening numbers told of strength's decline;
    My last have painted life a vale of tears:—
Let me not mournfully my task resign,
    Like one whose dark existence nought endears;
Without are fightings, and within are fears!   5
    Be such awhile forgot; I turn to thee,
And to the promise of thy early years,
    As to the unfolding floweret flies the bee,
Or as I gaze in Spring on some young blooming tree.

2.

The gnarled oak, with ivy overgrown,   10
    Scath'd, blighted, blasted, when it meets the view
May well call forth thought's moralizing tone,
    Awakening meditations—sad, yet true:—
But objects may be found of brighter hue,
    To which it is delightful still to turn;   15
Heaven's cloudiest arch, at times, has spots of blue,
    Flowers bud and blossom round the funeral urn,
And gleams of sunshine break o'er Winter's landscape stern.

3.

Such hast thou been unto my spirit's eye,—
    A ray of sunshine on life's wintry scene,   20
"A spot of azure in a cloudy sky;"
    A wreath of ivy, with its glossy green,
Dark, wither'd leaves and mossy boughs between:
    A star in night's dim arch with brightness glowing,
A blooming lowly flower of modest mien   25

In unsunn'd depth of glade untrodden growing,
A solitary spring, in some bleak desert flowing.

4.

   These things derive their magic loveliness
      From contrast, and in darkness brighter shine,
   And such, amid the ceaseless throng and press   30
      Of ills which make the heart of manhood pine,
   The charm of guileless innocence like thine;
      Care-fretted hearts confess its soothing spell,
   The toil-worn spirits own its power benign,
      Feeling and thought ope memory's hidden cell,   35
And near life's fountain-head we briefly seem to dwell.

5.

   There is a holy, blest companionship
      In the sweet intercourse thus held with those
   Whose tear and smile are guileless; from whose lip
      The simple dictate of the heart yet flows;—   40
   Though even in the yet unfolded rose
      The worm may lurk, and sin blight blooming youth,
   The light born with us long so brightly glows,
      That childhood's first deceits seem almost truth,
To life's cold after lie, selfish, and void of ruth.   45

6.

   Oh! happy hours, when smile succeeds to tear,
      And tear to smile, each taintless, brief, and bright;
   When joy treads fast on sorrow, hope on fear;
      Yet all too fresh to sate the appetite:
   When peaceful slumbers seal the eyes at night,   50
      And happy dreams on tranquil rest attend;—
   Who but must mourn that age and sin should blight
      Young hearts on which celestial dews descend,
Or pain's deep rankling thorns with pleasure's blossoms blend?

7.

   Well spake our blessed Lord, while yet on earth,   55
      Suffer the little ones to come to me,
   And chide them not:—to those who know their worth
      Of such His heavenly kingdom seems to be;

CONCLUDING VERSES, TO A CHILD

   Nor can we hope its glories e'er to see,
      Or taste its blessedness, 'till reconcil'd   60
   To God, and through His holy grace set free
      From every sin whose thraldom has defil'd,
The spirit enter there e'en as a little child.

8.

   Then when we meet with such, whose very glee
      Is ting'd with thoughtfulness beyond their years,   65
   Each thought and feeling now inspir'd by Thee
      The natural homage of the heart appears:
Object of fondest wishes, hopes, and fears,
      Might prayer of mine, dear child, a blessing claim,
Bright be thy smiles, and pangless be thy tears   70
      As now they are, and ne'er may guilt or shame
Corrode thy guileless heart, or taint thy spotless name.

SONNET TO WILLIAM AND MARY HOWITT

The breath of Spring is stirring in the wood,
   Whose budding boughs confess the genial gale;
   And thrush and blackbird tell their tender tale;
The hawthorn tree, that leafless long has stood,
Shows signs of blossoming; the streamlet's flood   5
   Hath shrunk into its banks, and in each vale
   The lowly violet, and the primrose pale,
Have lured the bee to seek his wonted food.
Then up! and to your forest haunts repair,
   Where Robin Hood once held his revels gay;   10
   Yours is the greensward smooth, and vocal spray;
And I, as on your pilgrimage ye fare,
In all your sylvan luxuries shall share
   When I peruse them in your minstrel lay.

SONNET TO THE SAME

Winter hath bound the brooks in icy chains;
    The bee that murmured in the cowslip bell
    Now feasts securely in his honied cell;
Silence is on the woods and on the plains,
And darkening clouds and desolating rains   5
    Have marred your forest fountain's quiet spell;
    Yet, though retired from these awhile ye dwell,
Your hearts' best hoard of poesy remains.
The sports of childhood, the exhaustless store
    Of home-born thoughts and feelings dear to each,   10
    Converse, or silence eloquent as speech;
History's rich page, tradition's richer lore,
Of tale and legend prized in days of yore;—
    These, worthy of the Muse, are in your reach.

THE DAUGHTER OF HERODIAS

On his royal throne of state,
Herod sits, in power elate;
Rank and splendour round him wait,
      Kingly pride enhancing;
He suspecting not the while   5
Hatred's cruelty and guile,
Gazes with approving smile
      On that maiden dancing.

Lovely as the graceful play
Of a fount in moonlight's ray,   10
Or a proud swan on its way
      Ripling waves dividing;
Airy as a sweet bird's flight
Through the azure realms of light,
Seems that form of beauty bright   15
      Now before him gliding.

Ceased the music's festive sound!
Ceased the dancer's sportive bound!
When the monarch, looking round,
      Craved the syren's pleasure:—   20
"Ask whate'er thou wilt," said he,
"And my oath I plight to thee
Thou shalt have it, though it be
      Half my kingly treasure!"

"Give me here," the maiden said,   25
"John the Baptist's forfeit head!"
Herod heard with shame and dread,
      And too late repented;

THE DAUGHTER OF HERODIAS

But false honour's specious tie,
Plighted oath,—his courtiers by 30
Doomed the martyr saint to die
      Death revenge invented.

Heartless damsel! though the blame
Of this act of fraud and shame
Render odious Herod's name, 35
      Thou that odium sharest :
More revolting was *thy* part,
Blending cruelty with art;—
Girl-hood's grace without its heart,
      Hateful makes the fairest. 40

Bard or painter, who would dress,
"Beauty in unloveliness,"
Draw from thee: and thus express
      All thy charms have brought thee;—
Sterner tone and deeper hue 45
Best may body forth to view
That relentless mother—who
      Thy foul lesson taught thee!

GODIVA

The spacious streets were silent as the grave!
   As though the place were uninhabited,
   Or some deserted city of the dead,
With doors and windows closed:—when, meekly brave,
From feudal tyranny's stern law to save,   5
   GODIVA from her palace forth was led,
   In bashful boldness, of true Virtue bred;
While tears and prayers her only welcome gave
   From thousands—LISTENING FOR HER COURSER'S TREAD!
So on she rode in unblenched majesty;   10
   "Naked, yet not ashamed!"—her tresses pale
   At once her modesty's and beauty's veil
From every wanton or unhallowed eye;
More proudly clothed in thoughts and feelings high
   Than warrior panoplied in triple mail!   15

Figure 1. Jusepe de Ribera [Lo Spagnoletto], *Man, Wine Bottle and Tambourine* (1631). Oil on canvas. Gösta Serlachius Fine Arts Foundation, Mänttä, Finland. Photographer: Yehia Eweis. Reproduced with the kind permission of the Gösta Serlachius Fine Arts Foundation

ON A PORTRAIT BY SPAGNOLETTO

I.
'Tis not the subject!—More than this
   My eye had loved to greet
Some quiet scene of past'ral bliss,
   The Muses' calm retreat:
Or watch-tower, beetling o'er the sea: 5
Or broken bank, with scathed tree:
   Or, yet more mildly sweet,
The matron majesty and grace
Of some Madonna's lovely face.

II.
Such is the beauty whose soft spell   10
   Is dearest to my heart:
On which thought most delights to dwell
   In Nature or in Art;
Its gentle, fascinating power
To Sorrow's darker, colder hour   15
   Brief sunshine can impart,
Wakening calm thoughts and feelings high
Which soar beyond mortality.

III.
Yet much the genius would I prize
   In nobler form displayed,   20
Whose sterner, stronger energies
   Are deeply here pourtrayed:
Whose power, like Rembrandt's, has imbued
With solemn grandeur, bold and rude,
   And magic light and shade,   25
This portrait of the olden time,
Dim, sombre, shadowy, and sublime!

IV.

Not brightening tint, not mellowing tone,
    Thy mastery supply:
A higher charm is round thee thrown   30
    By hoar antiquity;
In thee my musing thought reveres
The memory of revolving years,
    Now passed for ever by!
Of them, of thee, how many a thought   35
With vague conjecture might be fraught.

V.

Thrice fifty years, and more, hast thou
    Time's devastations dared,
And still that hand, and arm, and brow,
    By age are unimpaired;   40
While he, whose master-hand first drew,
And gave to each its living hue,
    Man's common lot hath shared:
His life a scanty span appears
Compared with thy protracted years.   45

VI.

But WHO wast thou?—that flask of wine,
    The uplifted tambourine,
Should speak a mood of joyaunce thine
    Which loved the festive scene:
Yet no glad smile of humour gay   50
Is seen in sunny light to play
    O'er thy stern, fearless mien,—
Projecting from its mass of shade
Laughter to chill, and mirth upbraid.

VII.

A bandit, at his lonely feast?   55
    A monk within his cell,
From cloistered solitude released—
    Art thou?—or, truth to tell,
Did Spagnoletto here design
To paint *himself?*—face, form like thine   60
    Befit the artist well,

If in his works we rightly scan
The moods and passions of the man.

VIII.

But, be thou who thou may'st, declare,
   If thou canst find a tongue,　　　　　　　　　　65
How time has passed with thee, and *where*?
   In what far homes up-hung?
Hast thou e'er graced the trophied hall
Of wealth and grandeur, on whose wall
   Bright lamps their lustre flung;　　　　　　　　　70
While thronged beneath, in rich array,
The young, the thoughtless, and the gay.

IX.

Thus Fancy chronicles thy lot;
   Then thy sad fall pourtrays,
Borne from the castle to the cot;　　　　　　　　　　75
   There, by the wood-fire's blaze,
Now pale and dim, now proud and bright,
Striking some simple urchin's sight
   With awe and mute amaze:—
And thence by Taste or Traffic's wile　　　　　　　　80
Transplanted to our northern isle.

X.

Yet why should Fancy more make known
   The history of thy lot?
Or in an exhibition shown,
   Or broker's stores forgot?　　　　　　　　　　　85
Who sold, who bought thee, unto me
Is but a vision, and to thee
   I ween it matters not:—
Enough for me to feel thy power,
For thee to soothe my lonely hour.　　　　　　　　　90

FIRESIDE QUATRAINS, TO CHARLES LAMB

It is a mild and lovely winter night,
    The breeze without is scarcely heard to sigh;
The crescent moon, and stars with twinkling light,
    Are shining calmly in a cloudless sky.

Within the fire burns clearly; in its rays   5
    My old oak book-case wears a cheerful smile,
Its antique mouldings brightened by the blaze
    Might vie with any of more modern style.

That rural sketch; that scene in Norway's land
    Of rocks and pine-trees by the torrent's foam;   10
That landscape traced by Gainsborough's youthful hand;
    Which shows how lovely is a peasant's home;—

That virgin and her child, with those sweet boys;
    All of the fire-light own the genial gleam,
And lovelier far than in day's light and noise   15
    To me at this still hour their beauties seem.

One more there is, which should not pass by me
    Unhonoured or unsung, because it bears
In many a lonely hour my thoughts to thee,
    Heightening to fancy every charm it wears.   20

How beautiful that group! A mother mild,
    And young, and fair, who fain would teach to read
That urchin by her patience unbeguiled,
    The open volume on her lap to heed.

With fingers thrust into his ears he looks							25
   As though he wished his weary task were done;
And more the love of pastime than of books
   Lurks in that arch dark eye so full of fun.

Graver, or in the pouts, 'twere hard to tell
   Which of the twain, his elder sister plies				30
Her sempstress labours, none can read so well
   The mute expression of her downcast eyes.

Dear Charles, if thou shouldst haply chance to know
   Where such a print once hung in days of yore,
Its highest worth, its deepest charm to show,						35
   I need not tax my rhymes or fancy more.

It is not womanhood in all its grace,
   And boyhood in its beauty—only plead;
Though these each stranger eye delights to trace,
   And many a plaudit oft has been their meed.			40

With them my thoughts and feelings fondly blend
   A hidden charm, unborrowed from the eye,
Claimed by each object that recalls a friend,
   And chronicles the pleasant hours gone by.

ENGLAND'S OAK

Let India boast its spicy trees,
   Whose fruit and gorgeous bloom
Give to each faint and languid breeze
   Its rich and rare perfume.

Let Portugal and haughty Spain   5
   Display their orange groves;
And France exult her vines to train
   Around her trim alcoves.

Let Norway vaunt its hardy pine,
   And Araby its palm,   10
Libanus for its cedars shine,
   And Gilead for its balm.

Old England has a tree as strong,
   As stately as them all,
As worthy of a minstrel's song   15
   In cottage, or in hall.

'Tis not the yew-tree, though it lends
   Its greenness to the grave;
Nor willow, though it fondly bends
   Its branches o'er the wave: 20

Nor birch, although its slender tress
   Be beautifully fair,
As graceful in its loveliness
   As maiden's flowing hair.

'Tis not the poplar, though its height
    May from afar be seen;
Nor beech, although its boughs be dight
    With leaves of glossy green.

All these are fair, but they may fling
    Their shade unsung by me;
My favourite, and the forest's king,
    The British Oak shall be!

Its stem though rough is stout and sound,
    Its giant branches throw
Their arms in shady blessings round
    O'er man and beast below;

Its leaf, though late in spring it shares
    The zephyr's gentle sigh,
As late and long in Autumn wears
    A deeper, richer dye.

Type of an honest English heart,
    It opes not at a breath,
But having opened, plays its part,
    Until it sinks in death:

Not early won by gleam of sun
    Its beauties to unfold;
One of the last in skies o'ercast
    To lose its faithful hold.

Its acorns, graceful to the sight,
    Are toys to childhood dear;
Its misletoe, with berries white,
    Adds mirth to Christmas cheer.

And when we reach life's closing stage,
    Worn out with care or ill,
For childhood, youth, or hoary age,
    Its arms are open still.

ENGLAND'S OAK

But prouder yet its glories shine,
    When, in a nobler form,
It floats upon the heaving brine,
    And braves the bursting storm.   60

Or when, to aid the work of love,
    To some benighted clime
It bears glad tidings from above,
    Of gospel truths sublime;

Oh! then, triumphant in its might,   65
    O'er waters dim and dark,
It seems, in heaven's approving sight,
    A *second* glorious ARK!

On earth the forest's honoured king!
    Man's castle on the sea!   70
Who will another tree may sing,
    Old England's oak for me!

SUMMER MUSINGS

A cloudless sky once more is ours,
    With all its depth of blue,
Bright as the tint of sapphire flowers
    When bathed in morning dew;
And verdant leaves and blossoms fair   5
Live in the balmy summer air.

On hill, in valley, field and grove,
    From thousand trembling sprays,
In notes of happiness and love
    Blythe warblers pour their lays;   10
And glad bees round the flowrets hum
For joy that summer's reign is come.

But not the glorious azure sky,
    Gay flowers, nor foliage green,
Nor happy songster's melody,   15
    Which animates the scene,
Nor all I hear, nor all I see
Can bring life's summer back to me.

The mists of autumn gather round,
    My leaf is wan and sere,   20
My spirit hears the hollow sound
    Of wintry winds draw near;
Those winds which, while they loudest rave,
Portend the silence of the grave.

Yet sometimes, e'en amid the gloom   25
    Of autumn's later days,
Some ling'ring flowers burst forth in bloom,

SUMMER MUSINGS

    To greet its parting rays,
Like smiles that break through glistening tears,
Or cherish'd hopes through chilling fears.   30

Such the reflected lustre flung
    By memory o'er my soul,
Borrow'd from hours when life was young,
    And knew not grief's control;
When all without, whose charms might win,   35
Its brightest mirror found within.

And such, I fain would hope, the gleams
    Which greet my mental eye,
Whose splendour far outshines the beams
    Which gild the eastern sky;   40
Bright gleams of hope, whose heavenward ray
Leads on to faith's more perfect day.

While memory thus, in visions fond,
    Can call back former years;
While Hope's meek glance can look beyond   45
    This transient vale of tears,
THE PAST, THE FUTURE may atone
For all THE PRESENT can make known.

And e'en in autumn's pensive mood,
    With winter's clouds in sight,   50
My quiet thoughts may calmly brood
    O'er hours more blest and bright,
When heaven's unclouded spring may shine,
And more than summer's light be mine.

EPISTLE TO THE EDITOR OF FRIENDSHIP'S OFFERING

 Honoured and gifted Friend,
Why ask of me, a votary of the Nine,
 My bootless aid to lend
E'en to one page of such a tome as thine?

 Hast thou not heard the news,   5
That BARDS and POESY are "out of date?"
 And that the only MEWS,
Now cared for, is of *quadrupedal* state?

 "Cui bono?" is the cry:—
Mechanics' Institutes, Steam-engines, Shares   10
 In some New Company,—
Omnium, and Scrip, the talk of Bulls and Bears.

 Some new and vulgar wonder
Far more than Poetry may hope to please;—
 Thames and its Tunnel under,   15
Or else Don Miguel and the Portuguese!

 Or Wright, and his Champagne,
So much per dozen, counting in the packing;
 The price of hides and grain,
Or peerless qualities of Warren's Blacking!   20

 Such are the themes and things
Which now are popular: but who for such
 Could tune the lyre's sweet strings,
Nor feel that he profaned them by his touch?

TO THE EDITOR OF FRIENDSHIP'S OFFERING

    Then be the harp unstrung 25
'Till simple Nature re-assert her reign;
    And hearts, once more grown young,
Respond with feeling to its gentlest strain.

    'Till then, alas! I fear
Whoe'er may sing the world will heed them not; 30
    But just as soon would hear
Sir William Curtis as Sir Walter Scott!

1830–49: LATE BARTON

THE CORONATION OF INES DE CASTRO

Through windows richly dight
   The mellow sunbeams shine,
But sadly falls their light
   On Sancta Clara's shrine.

The King and Court are there,　　　　　　　　　5
   Robed Priests and Knights in mail;
But every head is bare,
   And every cheek is pale.

The young and fair are met,
   The brave and haughty come,　　　　　　　10
But eyes with tears are wet,
   And lips with awe are dumb.

In pomp of regal pride
   There sits enthron'd a Queen;
Don Pedro at her side　　　　　　　　　　　　15
   Surveys the solemn scene.

Though grief be on his brow,
   Yet tearless is his eye,
He hears each plighted vow
   With spirit stern and high.　　　　　　　　20

Yet even He must feel
   Far more than tongue could own,
As one by one they kneel
   Before that silent throne.

As one by one they take 25
   That passive hand to kiss,
His thoughts and feelings wake
   Dreams of departed bliss.

For oh! no life-blood warm
   That frame may animate, 30
But wasted is the form
   Thus thron'd in splendid state;

Its glittering crown of gold
   Rests on a lifeless head;
Its broider'd robes enfold 35
   The reliques of the dead!

Those robes are but a pall,
   However bright their sheen;
She sits before them all
   The spectre of a Queen. 40

They bear her back to earth,
   And close the fearful rite,
But not one thought of mirth
   The pageant should excite:

For by it may be seen, 45
   In its glory and its gloom,
How brief the space between
   The proud throne and silent tomb.

TO THE WHITE JASMINE

Jasmine! thy fair and star-like flower with honours should be crown'd:
In day's rude din and sunny hour, it sheds faint sweetness round;
But still, at eve, its rich perfume with fragrance fills the air,
As if to cheer the hours of gloom, and soothe the brow of care.

Oh! thus, in Fortune's sunny ray, the light of Love seems pale, 5
Till dark clouds o'er the glare of day have cast their shadowy veil;
Then, like thy odours, it bursts forth, a guide to Joy's glad goal,
Blest beacon of surpassing worth, and pole-star of the soul!

TO WM. KIRBY, RECTOR OF BARHAM, SUFFOLK

One of the Authors of the "Introduction to Entomology."

I know not which to envy most,
Thy knowledge of the insect host,
   Tenants of earth, or air;
Or thy acquaintance with each scene
Of barren heath, or meadow green,   5
   To which their tribes repair.

The first hath cast around thy name
A purer, and a happier fame
   Than e'er was won by arms;
While both have surely taught thy heart   10
Somewhat of wisdom's better part,
   Through nature's hidden charms.

For well I ween, a heart like thine
Contemplating the Hand Divine
   Thy favorite science shows,   15
Taught by each proof of power and love,
To Him who dwells and reigns above
   With grateful feeling glows.

And, such a feeling to extend,
To show how skill and goodness blend   20
   Throughout creation's plan,
Must rank amongst those wise pursuits,
Whose genuine, and whose grateful fruits
   Are blessed of God, and man!

TO WM. KIRBY, RECTOR OF BARHAM, SUFFOLK

Yes, every science, lore, or art,   25
Which tends to foster in the heart
   Knowledge of nature's laws,
Must, sanctified by grace divine,
"Precept on precept, line on line,"
   Exalt their First Great Cause!   30

Pursue, then, my ingenious friend,
Thy search; and mayst thou, in the end,
   Partake a prouder change,
Than e'er thy insect tribes can know,
Despite the beauty these may show,   35
   In transformations strange.

For these, though plumed with splendid wings,
Are still but fair and fragile things,
   Which seem but born, to die;
Whilst thou, thy web of knowledge spun,   40
Thy daily task of duty done,
Shalt soar above yon glorious sun,
   To immortality!

THE SEA-SHELL

Hast thou heard of a shell on the margin of ocean,
    Whose pearly recesses the echoes still keep,
Of the music it caught when, with tremulous motion,
    It join'd in the concert pour'd forth by the deep?

And fables have told us, when far inland carried   5
    To the waste sandy desert, or dark ivied cave,
In its musical chambers some murmurs have tarried
    It learn'd long before of the wind and the wave.

Oh! thus should our spirits, which bear many a token
    They are not of earth, but are exiles while here,   10
Preserve in their banishment, pure and unbroken,
    Some sweet treasur'd notes of their own native sphere.

Though the dark clouds of sin may at times hover o'er us,
    And the discords of earth may their melody mar,
Yet to spirits redeem'd some faint notes of that chorus,   15
    Which is borne by the bless'd, will be brought from afar!

A NEGRO MOTHER'S CRADLE-SONG

Sleep, my child! and might the prayer
Of thy mother's dark despair
Be accepted for thy sake,—
'Twere that thou no more shouldst wake.

Though a mother's love be mine,										5
And a daughter's fondness thine,
Yet, for thee, a parent's breath
Craves the boon of early death.

Worse to live a helpless slave,
Than to fill an early grave;										10
Better far the silent tomb,
Than the captive's hopeless doom.

White man's cruelty and lust
Cannot harm the lifeless dust;
Powerless the oppressor's rod,										15
Brandish'd o'er a senseless clod.

Ruthless lash, and galling chain,
Countless tasks—performed with pain,
Nights of sorrow, days of toil—
These have made my life their spoil.									20

Such, with life, must be thy lot;
Dying—thou shalt know them not;—
O, be thine, all fetters breaking,
Sleep that knows on earth no waking!

Woodbridge, 4th of 5th Mo. 1826.

THE BIBLE ['LAMP OF OUR FEET!']

Lamp of our feet! whereby we trace
   Our path, when wont to stray;
Stream from the fount of heavenly grace!
   Brook by the traveller's way!

Bread of our souls! whereon we feed;   5
   True Manna from on high!
Our guide, and chart! wherein we read
   Of realms beyond the sky!

Pillar of fire—through watches dark!
   Or radiant cloud by day!   10
When waves would whelm our tossing bark—
   Our anchor and our stay!

Pole-star on life's tempestuous deep!
   Beacon! when doubts surround;
Compass! by which our course we keep;   15
   Our deep-sea lead—to sound!

Riches in poverty! Our aid
   In every needful hour!
Unshaken rock! the pilgrim's shade,
   The soldier's fortress-tower!   20

Our shield and buckler in the fight!
   Victory's triumphant palm!
Comfort in grief! in weakness, might!
   In sickness—Gilead's balm!

Childhood's preceptor! manhood's trust!   25
    Old age's firm ally!
Our hope—when we go down to dust—
    Of immortality!

Pure oracles of Truth Divine!
    Unlike each fabled dream   30
Given forth from Delphos' mystic shrine,
    Or groves of Academe!

W̲ord of T̲he ever-living G̲od!
    W̲ill of H̲is G̲lorious S̲on!
Without Thee how could earth be trod?   35
    Or heaven itself be won?

Yet to unfold thy hidden worth,
    Thy mysteries to reveal,
That S̲pirit which first gave thee forth
    Thy volume must u̲nseal!   40

And we, if we aright would learn
    The wisdom it imparts,
Must to its heavenly teaching turn
    With simple, child-like hearts!

A CLERICO-POLITICO PORTRAIT

Inscribed, with all Due Respect, to Dr. Etough, of Claydon

"Mr. Bell is a Christian man. I have all proper reverence for God's corbies; but for the carnality that is in the Priesthood, I have as little respect as for the insolence of other men."—(*Galt's Laurie Todd*.)

    A bullying, brawling Champion of the Church,
Pert as a Parrot, screaming on his perch;
And, like that Parrot, mouthing out by rote,
The same "stale, flat, unprofitable" note;
A Tavern Orator, worse taught than fed,   5
With but one stock-idea in his head;
To him Religion, Reason, every thing—
The senseless, worn-out war-cry, "Church and King;"
Twist it and turn it howso'er you will,
This is the cuckoo-note he harps on still: 10
A railer at each Radical and Whig;
A sturdy stickler for his own Tithe Pig!
Without one liberal sentiment enshrined,
In the dull vacuum of his barren mind,
Or one bright ray of information brought   15
From the vast regions of expanded thought:
With a High Tory's party zeal—increased
By all the arrogance that marks the Priest;
With a true Bigot's blindness—and without
The sense to reason, self-distrust to doubt: 20
A pompous, superficial, empty prater;
A tedious, dull, dogmatic debater;
One who declares, *upon* his solemn word,
The "*Voluntary System*" is absurd:

A CLERICO-POLITICO PORTRAIT

He may well say so—for 'twere hard to tell 25
Who would support him, did not law *compel!*

   Episcopacy must be in the lurch,
Ere such a Doctor could disgrace the Church:
Who but must smile, if such an one there be?
Who but must laugh, were Dr. Etough he? 30

Figure 2. *Philip Doddridge as a child being taught the Old and New Testaments by his mother using ceramic tiles around the fireplace.* Engraving by G. Presbury after J. Franklin. Wellcome Collection. Reproduced under the terms and conditions of the Creative Commons Attribution licence (CC BY 4.0). https://wellcomecollection.org/works/a62hdt7g. This image was used as the accompanying illustration to 'First Scripture Lessons' in *Fisher's Juvenile Scrap-Book* (1839)

FIRST SCRIPTURE LESSONS

'Tis winter, and the fire burns bright,
   And by its gleams the while,
Looking the lovelier for its blaze,
   Shines forth each storied tile.

A Mother, and her darling Boy,   5
   Are placed the fire beside;
She is his kindest, truest friend,
   And he her hope and pride.

The Bible, open on her knee,
   Her narrative supplies;   10
And much those story-pictur'd tiles
   Delight his wondering eyes.

She reads, and points, and leads him on
   With love which cannot fail;
'Till deep into his heart hath sunk   15
   The moral of each tale.

Thus is the Book of books to him,
   By blameless art like this,
Made, even to his boyish heart,
   A source of sweetest bliss.   20

And who shall doubt, in after life,
   The knowledge thus acquired
Tended to make him, when a man,
   What she at heart desired?

Those old Dutch tiles! those old Dutch tiles!   25
    It was a happy thought
Which scripture lore by graphic aid
    Thus to the fire-side brought.

I well remember, when a child,
    The wonder and delight   30
It gave, to see what I had read
    Depicted to my sight.

Though quaint and rude was each design
    The artist there had traced,
Perspective at defiance set,   35
    And groups but oddly placed;

Still every tinted tablet told
    Of some familiar tale:—
Of David, with the sling and stone
    Goliath, clad in mail.   40

Of Joseph, when a stripling youth,
    By cruel brethren sold,
To be a slave in Egypt's land,
    The story there was told.

And that of gentle Ruth, who went   45
    In Boaz' fields to glean;
And Naaman, by the prophet bade
    To wash—and so be clean!

There, too, the Saviour, when a boy,
    With learn'd doctors talk'd;   50
And here, upon the tossing sea,
    At midnight's hour He walk'd.

Here through Jerusalem He rode,
    In meek, though kingly pride;
At Calvary, there, upon the Cross,   55
    He bowed his head and died!

FIRST SCRIPTURE LESSONS

The Bible is a blessed book;
   And they were not unwise,
Who thus familiar made its truths
   To childhood's eager eyes.   60

But fashion now has banish'd quite
   Those tomes of touching lore;
And by the fire, when blazing bright,
   We read Dutch tiles no more!

ON A DRAWING OF THE COTTAGE AT ALDBOROUGH, WHERE CRABBE LIVED IN BOYHOOD

"Fame asks not where was sown the seed,
Or where was nursed the root;
But victory's palm and honour's meed
Adjudges to the fruit!"

It stood beside the broad and billowy deep,
    A humble dwelling, in its better day;
Over its thatch the winter winds would sweep,
    And on its walls oft beat the ocean spray:
    As years rolled on it fell into decay,   5
Sharing the doom that prouder piles must share,
    And now its very form hath passed away,
Buried amidst the wreck of things which *were*;
Yet still its memory lives, cherished with grateful care.

For Genius hath immortalized the spot!   10
    Blending it with the Poet's deathless name,
And casting round the memory of that cot
    The potent charm of his enduring fame;
    Potent—because not won by numbers tame
And common-place, in flowers of fiction drest,   15
    But by the TRUTH, which formed his proudest claim,
"Though Nature's sternest painter, yet the best!"
This was his highest charm, his verses' truest test.

It was not his to sing of rural swains,
    In strains Arcadian, caught from days of yore;   20
Painting their hopes and fears, their joys and pains,

ON A DRAWING OF THE COTTAGE AT ALDBOROUGH

    To classic models true—and nothing more;
      He sang them, as he found them on the shore
  Of the wild ocean, "an amphibious race;"
      Yet not unmindful, in their varied store   25
  Of good and ill, of each redeeming grace,
Though few and far between, which truth allowed to trace.

    'Tis in the sterling truth and sober sense
      Legible in his deeply moral lay,
  Are found "the head and front of the offence,"   30
      For which some still his graphic page gainsay:
    Poetry was, with him, no artist's play!
  But Nature's voice, the heart's interpreter;
      And by this standard tested, even they
  Who at his darker touches most demur,   35
Must own him of his themes a faithful chronicler.

    Sailors and smugglers, gipsies, poachers, boors,
      Fishers, and publicans; a motley throng!
  The life these led, or in or out of doors,
      Such, chiefly, formed the staple of his song;   40
    His lot was cast, by circumstance, among
  Those samples of our kind; and are they not
      All human beings? marred by much of wrong,
  And stained by many a foul and flagrant blot,
They are—yet from our race, all these, divorce them not!   45

    And this is the redeeming charm that lends
      Its lustre to our Suffolk Poet's page;
  A spirit of humanity, which blends
      Our lighter lot on life's eventful stage,
    With their's whose hardships seem their heritage;   50
  Instructing us, ere harshly we condemn,
    To bear in mind the warfare they must wage,
  The rougher tide which they perforce must stem!
A lesson, taught aright, that well may plead for them!

    Then turn not from his pages—though they bear   55
      The brand of much that virtue must reprove;
  Much is there truest sympathy to share;
      Much to be pitied; somewhat, too, to love!

  It is the part of wisdom from above
To sever, as by alchymy sublime,   60
  Feelings and impulses to vice which move,
 From those which bid our spirits upward climb;
The criminal to mourn, e'en while we loathe the crime.

 Hence those who know and feel our Poet's worth,
  This frail memorial of his boyish years   65
 Will love and cherish: here, perchance, had birth
  That mastery o'er the source of smiles and tears,
  Which still his minstrel memory endears;
 And e'en this humble room becomes a shrine,
  Where all who justly rate the hopes and fears   70
 That round our human hearts must ever twine,
Must to his well-earned fame their grateful praise assign.

AN EPISTLE TO A PHONOGRAPHIC FRIEND; OR A FEW WORDS ON PHONOGRAPHY

"A thing of sound (not fury)
Signifying nothing."

When I am weary of my Mother-tongue,
In which I learn'd to read and spell, when young;
Or *speak*, and *write*, and am not understood,
As heretofore, by my own flesh and blood;
When Chaucer's Tales, and Spenser's Fairy Lay,   5
As worn-out legends shall have pass'd away;
When universal Shakespeare's page profound
Shall be a thing to criticise by sound;
And Milton's Song, caught from a higher sphere,
Hath lost its music to my palsied ear;   10
When they who, by new crotchets unbeguil'd,
Drank from the well of English undefil'd,
Bards, Statesmen, Orators, and grave Divines,
Whose memories live in their immortal lines;
When THESE, by some new-fangled strange conceit,   15
Shall, with their works be counted obsolete,
Then, not before, I may for truth receive
All modern babblers ask me to believe!

Nor can I look upon as more inviting,
The novel characters you give for writing;   20
I'm child enough, and hope such long to be,
To have a *liking* for my A B C;
And to our antiquated Alphabet
Owe a long-standing and long-cherished debt.

Its old familiar aspect, to mine eye, 25
No hieroglyphic symbols can supply;
Sprawls, scratches, dashes, spider-legs, and lines,
To me are unintelligible signs;
Upright or sloping, this or that way leaning,
They speak no language, and convey no meaning. 30

But the New System saves much time. Indeed!
Must we then write, read, spell, by rail-road speed
'Tis bad enough, whene'er we go abroad,
That fire and smoke must urge us on our road,
And, for the music of the birds and spheres, 35
To have that horrid whistle din our ears;
Must we not *ride*, alone, as if we flew,
But the same haste adopt in all we do?
"*More haste worse speed*,"—the proverb still holds true!

I wish that Pitman, Reid, and all their crew, 40
Or better taste, or better manners knew;
To one accustomed to the olden lore
Their boasted *System* is a dreadful bore,
Through trumpeted with empty acclamation
A READING, *Writing, Printing,* REFORMATION! 45
Misses and masters in six lessons taught
What a life's labour to our fathers brought;
Can write in short-hand, or like parrots speak,
Chaldee or Coptic, Sanscrit, Hebrew, Greek;
But the sum total of this parrot lore 50
Appeals to sight and sound, and little more.

Alas! for honest, credulous John Bull!
Of every novelty the veriest gull!
His sconce he yield to the Phrenologist;
His faith and feelings to the Mesmerist; 55
His Constitution to the puffing Quack;
To bubbles—e'en the coat upon his back;
And last, not least, true to his character,
To read, write, spell, pronounce, needs a Phonographer.

TO THE B.B SCHOONER, ON SEEING HER SAIL DOWN THE DEBEN FOR LIVERPOOL

Glide gently down thy native stream,
    And give thy swelling sail
To April's bright and sunny beam,
    And to its favouring gale.

In safety speed thine onward way,   5
    By prosperous breezes fanned;
Breasting old Ocean's briny spray,
    To Mersey's distant strand.

Thou bear'st no proud or lofty name,
    Which all who read must know;   10
Yet for *its* sake thou well mayest claim
    The verse I now bestow.

That name was given to honour me,
    By those 'mid whom I dwell,
And cold indeed my heart must be,   15
    Could I disown its spell.

For all the homage fame can give
    To those who for it roam,
That lowlier tribute should outlive,
    Which comes, unasked, at home!   20

1843.

SONNET, TO A FRIEND NEVER YET SEEN, BUT CORRESPONDED WITH FOR ABOVE TWENTY YEARS

Unknown to sight! for more than twenty years
Have we, by written interchange of thought
And feeling—been into communion brought
Which friend to friend insensibly endears!
In various joys and sorrows, hopes and fears, 5
Befalling each; and serious subjects—fraught
With wider interest, we at times have sought
To *gladden this*—yet look to *brighter spheres*!
We never yet have met! and never may,
Perchance, while pilgrims upon earth we fare: 10
Yet as we seek each other's load to *bear*,
Or *lighten*, and that law of love obey,
May we not hope in heaven's eternal day
To meet, and happier intercourse to share?

A POSTSCRIPT TO 'TO THE DEAD IN CHRIST'

Sweet is it thus at times to feel
   Of blessed spirits, gone before us;
And deem, in hours of woe or weal,
   That such, unseen, are hovering o'er us.

Still scattering, as from angel-wings,   5
   Those amaranth wreaths that ne'er can wither;
While strains from harps of golden strings
   More sweetly whisper—"Come up hither!"

THE YELLOW-HAMMER; A SONG, BY A SUFFOLK VILLAGER

O sad yellow-hammer! that singest to me,
While blows by my window the swinging birch tree;
That sorrowful cadence is sweet to mine ear,
For it seeks the forgotten, and summons them here.

O sad yellow-hammer! what long years ago 5
Through the old woody places we two used to go;
Just that very note falling from bough after bough,
It seemed the same bird that sits singing here now.

O sad yellow-hammer! there was a dun cow
Used to be always grazing, where space would allow 10
The tall grass to shoot up, and primrose leaves green,
Beside the park palings the tree stems between.

O sad yellow-hammer! a little black dog
Used to flit like a spirit through brier and bog;
The violets all purple bent under its tread, 15
And the rose-leaves fell down on its beautiful head.

You may go to those woody lanes day after day,
But the cow and the dog they are always away;
I hear in the dim shade, un-life-lighted now,
But the sad yellow-hammer that sings on the bough. 20

When Summer *was* Summer, beneath those green trees,
A musical voice used to blend with the breeze;
I never went roaming the hazel-wood's side,
But a dark eye flashed by me, a step at my side.

THE YELLOW-HAMMER; A SONG

I've outgrown the childhood when we wandered so, 25
And for hazel-nuts caring have left long ago;
But, sad yellow-hammer, within the birch bough,
I care for the tones thou art bringing back now!

O sad yellow-hammer! while thou sing'st to me,
A carol comes floating far over the sea; 30
A light laugh is ringing where billows gleam pale,
And a distant voice singing to dare the wild gale.

O sweet yellow-hammer! that singest to me,
An anxious heart's blessing thy recompence be;
Ay, shake the light birch bough, and cheerly sing on, 35
For cheerly thou bringest back them that are gone!

TO E.F. [ELIZABETH FRY], ON HER REAPPEARANCE AMONG HER FRIENDS AT THE YEARLY MEETING, 1845

Once more thy well-known voice lift up,
    A Saviour's goodness to proclaim;
Take in thy hand salvation's cup,
    Call on thy God, and bless His name!
It harmonizes with the past   5
    Of a devoted life, like thine,
That thus serenely to the last
    Thy setting sun should brightly shine.
Long since first shone its morning rays,
    Its noon-tide splendour may be spent;—   10
Can coming night avert our gaze,
    While stars are in the firmament?
Faith, hope, and love, as stars come forth,
    Making a more than noon of night!
And bear this witness to thy worth,   15
    'Tis eventide, and round thee—light!

SONNET, TO JOB'S THREE FRIENDS

However ye might err in after speech,
The mute expression of that voiceless woe
Whereby ye sought your sympathy to show
With him of Uz—doth eloquently preach!
Teaching a lesson it were well to teach   5
Some comforters—of utterance less slow,
Prone to believe that they more promptly know
Grief's mighty depths, and by their words can reach.
"*Seven days and nights,*" in stillness as profound
As that of Chaos, patiently ye sate   10
By the heart-stricken and the desolate!
And though your sympathy might fail to sound
The fathomless depth of his dark spirit's wound,
Not less *your silence* was *sublimely great!*

SONNETS, WRITTEN AT BURSTAL

Sonnet I. Berry's Hill

Who gave this spot the name of Berry's Hill
I know not, and in sooth care not to know,
For names, like fashions, ofttimes come and go,
By mere caprice of arbitrary will:
But 'tis a lovely spot! enough of skill   5
Hath been employed to make it lovelier show,
Yet not enough for Art to overthrow
What Nature meant should wear her livery still.
That gleaming lakelet, sparkling in the ray
Of summer sunshine; these embowering trees,   10
Rustled each moment by the passing breeze;
And those which clothe with many-tinted spray
Yon wooded heights; green meads with flowrets gay;
Each gives to each yet added powers to please.

Sonnet II. The Seat at Berry's Hill

It was a happy thought—upon the brow
Of this slight eminence, abrupt and sheer,
This artless seat and straw-thatched roof to rear;
Where one may watch the labourer at his plough;
Or hear, well-pleased, as I am listening now,   5
The song of wild birds falling on the ear,
Blended with hum of bees, or sound more drear,
The solemn murmur of the wind-swept bough.
Tent-like the fabric! in its centre stands
The sturdy oak, that spreads its boughs on high   10
Above its roof; while to the unsated eye
Beauteous the landscape which below expands!

Where grassy meadows, richly cultured lands,
With leafy woods and hedge-row graces vie.

Sonnet III. The Same Scene, Continued

It were, methinks, no very daring flight
Unto a poet's fond imagination,
To make this tent a prouder habitation;
Where Nature's worshipper and votary might,
With each appropriate and simple rite,   5
Bow to her charms, in quiet adoration
Of Him who meant his visible creation
Should minister to more than sense or sight!
Oh, then, this tent-like seat might well become
A temple—more befitting prayer or praise,   10
Than the mere listless loiterer's idle gaze;
And if it struck the sordid worldling dumb,
Proving of Nature's charms the countless sum,
'Twere not less worthy of the poet's lays!

Sonnet IV. In the Shrubbery, Near the Cottage

Fair Earth! thou surely wert not meant to be
Time's show-room! but the glorious vestibule
Of scenes that stretch beyond his sway and rule,
Or that of aught we now can hear or see!
For he who most intently looks on thee,   5
Must be a novice e'en in Nature's school,
In one far higher a more hopeless fool,
To go no further with her master-key!
Beautiful as thou art, thou art no more
Than a faint shadow, or a glimmering ray,   10
Of beauty, glory, ne'er to pass away;
Nor thankless is thy minstrel, at threescore,
While he can revel in thy bounteous store,
To look beyond thy transitory day.

Sonnet V. The Burstal Lakelet

The dweller on *Ullswater's* grander shore,
Or *Keswick's*, would deny thee any claim

Even to hear a lakelet's borrowed name,
Of thy small urn so scanty seems the store!
And such would, doubtless, scout the poet's lore, 5
Who one poor Sonnet should presume to frame
In celebration of thy humble fame,
Although to their's he could award no more!
Yet all the pomp and plenitude of space
They boast, can but reflect the wider scene 10
Of beauty round: as lovely is the sheen
Of thy clear mirror, in which now I trace
The softened impress and the heightened grace
Of earth and sky, both silent and serene!

SONNET VI. THE TWO OAKS

There are, among the leafy monarchs round,
Trees loftier far than you, of ampler size,
And likelier to attract a stranger's eyes,
With sylvan honours more superbly crowned:
And yet in you a higher charm is found, 5
And purer—to *our* sweetest sympathies,
Than all that Nature's lavish hand supplies
To others—growing on this fairy ground.
Ye are mementos of a wedded pair,
Once wont this loved, familiar scene to tread! 10
Death, which has lowly laid *one* honoured head,
Has but conferred on you an added share
Of love and interest; since to us ye are
Memorials of the living! and the dead!

SONNET VII. EVENING EFFECT ON THE VALLEY

"Earth has not any thing to show more fair!"
So Wordsworth sang, what time he made his theme
The bridge that arches Westminster's proud stream:
Yet had he seen this lovely valley wear
The lingering brightness day hath yet to spare, 5
Each lengthening shadow, and each sunny gleam,
Silent in all their changes as a dream!
He might have doubted which the palm should bear.
And now calm eve would draw her curtain grey

Over the melting landscape's mellower flush!   10
But for the brightly-glowing roseate blush
That tinges still the west:—it fades away!
And Nature owns the meek and gentle sway
Of pensive Twilight's universal hush!

Sonnet VIII. Burstal, in the Four Seasons

How sweet it were, methinks, to sojourn here,
And watch the seasons in their changeful flight;
To see the Spring bedeck, with wild flowers bright,
The valley and those swelling uplands near;
To mark the Summer, in her blithe career,   5
Bursting in rich luxuriance on the sight;
And matron Autumn reassert her right
To crown with harvest boons the circling year!
Nor undelightful would it be, I ween,
At Christmas, here to trim the cottage fire,   10
Pore o'er the lay, or tune the Muses' lyre,
What time rude Winter, with his sterner mien,
In spotless snow arrayed the altered scene,
And hushed in stillness all the woodland choir.

POETICAL ILLUSTRATIONS FROM *NATURAL HISTORY OF THE HOLY LAND*

THE ELK

Thou bear'st thy branchy Antlers well,
Which almost seem to me, 2
Like Coral fans that grow and dwell
Beneath the briny sea. 4

THE HERON

Bird of the lonely lake,
And solitary stream; 2
Patient for plunder's sake,
And silent as a dream! 4

BUTTERFLIES

The Butterfly from hour to hour,
Flutters about from flower to flower, 2
And glistening in the sun's bright beams,
Almost a *winged flowret* seems. 4

SERPENT OF THE ISLE OF CELEBES

Sinuous monster! long and lithe,
In thy fearful coil. 2
Man, though he may briefly writhe,
Soon becomes thy spoil. 4

Barbary Ape & Ouran Outang

Barbary Ape! Ouran Outang!
Enough you Man resemble 2
To give his Pride a moment's pang,
And make his self-love tremble. 4

Thou bear'st thy branchy Antlers well,
Which almost seem to me,
Like Coral fans that grow and dwell
Beneath the briny sea.

Figure 3. *The Elk*, engraved by T.[homas?] Dixon. Plate from Lucy Barton, *Natural History of the Holy Land* (1856). Reproduced from editor's own copy, with the kind assistance of the University of Exeter's Digital Humanities Lab. Photographer: Emma Sherriff

Bird of the lonely lake,
And solitary stream;
Patient for plunder's sake,
And silent as a dream!

Figure 4. *The Heron*, engraved by T.[homas?] Dixon. Plate from Lucy Barton, *Natural History of the Holy Land* (1856). Reproduced from editor's own copy, with the kind assistance of the University of Exeter's Digital Humanities Lab. Photographer: Emma Sherriff

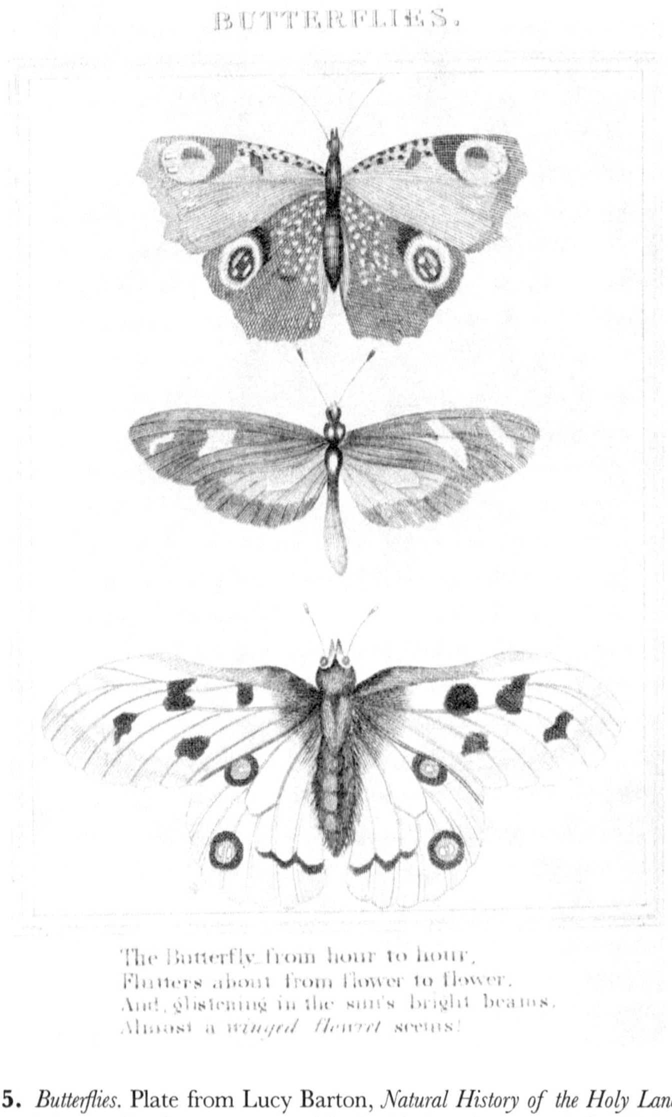
BUTTERFLIES.
The Butterfly from hour to hour,
Flutters about from flower to flower,
And, glistening in the sun's bright beams,
Almost a *winged flower* seems!

Figure 5. *Butterflies.* Plate from Lucy Barton, *Natural History of the Holy Land* (1856). Reproduced from editor's own copy, with the kind assistance of the University of Exeter's Digital Humanities Lab. Photographer: Emma Sherriff

Figure 6. *The Serpent of the Isle of Celebes*, engraved by T.[homas?] Dixon. Plate from Lucy Barton, *Natural History of the Holy Land* (1856). Reproduced from editor's own copy, with the kind assistance of the University of Exeter's Digital Humanities Lab. Photographer: Emma Sherriff

Figure 7. *Barbary Ape & Ouran Outang*, engraved by T.[homas?] Dixon. Plate from Lucy Barton, *Natural History of the Holy Land* (1856). Reproduced from editor's own copy, with the kind assistance of the University of Exeter's Digital Humanities Lab. Photographer: Emma Sherriff

A PREFATORY APPEAL FOR POETRY AND POETS

A long Preface to a very small volume of Poems may, at first sight, appear a superfluity, if not an impertinence: the first would imply a waste of time, for which I should be sorry; and of the last I should still more regret being wilfully culpable. But when I state that my only reason for prefixing to these few pages any preface at all, arises from a desire to plead the cause of Poetry, in the abstract, without any especial reference to my own, I hope I have stated enough to obtain a patient, if not an indulgent, perusal, from all interested in the subject: and by those, if such there be, who care little or nothing about Poetry, or Poets, I am not so unreasonable as to expect either this prefatory essay to be read, or the volume which it accompanies.

But can it be possible, in an age which is styled liberal, enlightened, and philosophical, that any, whose enlarged views and cultivated intellect have done aught justly to entitle it to such epithets, will avow themselves indifferent to Poetry, and uninterested on behalf of those who labour in their vocation as its professed votaries? I own myself unwilling to admit, unable to believe the fact. Fewer volumes of Poems may issue from the press, and Poetry may not be so fashionable as it was fifteen or twenty years ago; but I have never met with even one instance of a person of refined taste, pure and correct feeling, and a cultivated mind, to whom Poetry was an object of indifference, or by whom a genuine Poet, however humble, was regarded with apathy.

That for one volume of Poetry, published at the present time, a dozen or a score might be put forth a few years since, is no positive proof of that general distaste for Poetry, which has been, is perhaps too hastily, assumed to exist, by superficial or unreflecting observers. The very popularity which this department of literature, at no remote period, seemed to obtain for its votaries, was almost sure to be followed, and this at no distant era, by an apparent re-action. When, owing to the almost unceasing demand for novelty in this branch of the Belles Lettres, candidates for fame and favour became numerous beyond all precedent; and the demand, however great, was met by a supply still more ample, it was almost impossible, certainly very improbable, that for any long-protracted period, "increase of appetite could grow by what it fed on." Perhaps, too, some of those who then catered for the public taste, might not play their parts well or wisely for the permanence of their own fame, or the continuance of the public favour. Popularity is proverbially fickle; but it may be, and generally is, more or less ephemeral, in proportion to the taste, discretion, and judgment of those who are its objects, and who, for the time, influence the public taste.

In throwing off the artificial trammels and technical phraseology by which Poetry had been too long encumbered and enfeebled; in looking abroad on Nature with a less fastidious eye; and in analyzing more deeply, and appealing more directly to stronger passions, and more hidden springs of thought and feeling; the Master Spirits of that day did much, which could scarcely fail to magnify their calling, and make it more widely popular. But in the ardour of excitement thus called into action, passions were appealed to, thoughts and feelings wrought upon, and principles brought into operation, of a mingled and conflicting nature and tendency. To use such means as not abusing them, required more than genius alone can give to its proudest and most gifted possessor; and far more than could be hoped for from those who were but Copyists and imitators of the style and manner which became, to a certain extent, the fashion of the day. These only saw the effect produced by the potency of stronger spells than Poets of a later age had dared to use: they saw, too,—for the frailties and errors of genius are more perceptible to the multitude than the secret of its faculty divine,—that some of those who invoked such accessaries [*sic*], could not always command them, but were sometimes carried away by them; and without scruple availing themselves of appliances they were every way incompetent to manage, they contrived to copy the faults of those whom they admired, without exemplifying the talent by which those faults were partially redeemed.

Owing, in part, to these causes, a moody, morbid, and exaggerated style, an unhealthily excited tone of feeling became, in some degree at least, the mannerism of much of our modern Poetry,—a mannerism, if possible, more offensive to pure taste and right feeling, than even the sentimentalism and stately formality which it supplanted. It was one, too, likely sooner to end in satiety; for milk and water, and even a dry crust, are more wholesome viands, however unsatisfactory, than highly seasoned ragouts or exciting liqueurs, and the mental appetite can no more be kept in a healthful state, by the constant use of stimulants, than the bodily.

In the silent, imperceptible, yet natural operation of the causes thus briefly adverted to, quite as much, if not more than in any important change of public opinion, may be traced the effect generally admitted in a greater or less degree, that Poetry is become less popular. But to those who have loved, read, and studied our better Poets; whose attachment to Poetry is pure and unworldly, founded on a discriminating taste, and associated with a true feeling of its legitimate aim and end, to such its seeming neglect, for a time, need bring no despondency, and can excite no surprise. Taste may fluctuate, fashion, in literature, as well as in everything else, may change; but while aught of a child-like heart is left to our human nature, giving freshness to the earlier portion of existence, and lingering greenness to its latest, so long will Poets find readers. The elements of Poetry are in their very nature ineradicable and indestructible; and to suppose that Science, even by its proudest achievements, can furnish a fitting substitute to supply its place, would almost imply, in the estimation of those who have known and felt its worth, the creation of a new race of human beings, if human they might be called,—endowed with heads, indeed, but destitute of hearts; automata, set in motion by steam, and made only to travel on in monotonous and interminable rail-roads.

For what is poetry, rightly understood, in its most enlarged and comprehensive acceptation? It is not verse, alone. Thought, feeling, fancy, imagination, the gentler affections, the deeper passions of our nature, when they seek and find utterance, must, in their spirit and essence, be poetical; and, if unchecked by artificial restraints, unawed by the fear of "the world's dread laugh," their language would be Poetry. In the conventional phraseology of the world, and in our intercourse with the worldly-minded, the heart can scarce give vent to many of its best and purest feelings; nor can thought find a language to express many of its highest and holiest aspirations, without hazarding the imputation of enthusiasm or affectation; or exciting distrust, if haply it may escape scorn and derision. To childhood the privilege of expressing its emotions, unfettered by those chains which hold adults in bondage, is allowed as its artless right, and simple prerogative. But, in after-life, how much is there in every susceptible heart, how much in every thoughtful mind, untranslateable into the technical idiom, and common-place Prose of every-day existence? Can it be for the interest or happiness of mankind that all such thoughts and feelings should find no vent? Comprising, as they do, much that tends to soften and humanize, and not less to elevate and spiritualize, our imperfect and fallen nature, much to check and counteract the deadening influence of a worldly spirit, we may thankfully rejoice that there is a language, if I may so speak, confined to no tongue, but universal as the emotions and wants, the hopes and fears, the joys and sorrows, of our common nature, in which these thoughts and feelings may be poured forth. That language is Poetry!

It is the privilege of the Poet, if he will but use it well and wisely, freely to give utterance to that which, in no other form, perhaps, he would have courage to express, or a great portion of his fellow-creatures toleration enough to listen to. In the form, and under the name of Poetry, he may unburden every feeling of his heart which claims alliance with whatsoever is pure, lovely, and of good report; he may follow up, and put on record, every train of thought, and mood of meditation, which in moments of retirement have been fraught with joy, peace, solace, or instruction to his own mind. He may do all this, too, if he exercise his faculty with meekness, and labour in his vocation with love, not only without fear of heartless ridicule, but with a rational hope of appealing, more or less successfully, to the sympathies of many a heart, and wakening in many a mind a tone of thought analogous to that which has soothed or gladdened his own. Nor is this all which the Poet may fairly plead for his art. If it be true, as we are perpetually reminded by Utilitarians, that knowledge is power, a truth no one can dispute; it is not less true that feeling, fancy, imagination, were all designed, by proper culture, and due regulation, to be accessary to happiness. The love and admiration of the beautiful, the approbation of the noble and the lofty, the consciousness of the sublime, are as worthy to be cherished by an immortal spirit, as an attachment to the merely useful; more so, if that attachment be exclusive—for then there is much danger of its confining our views too much to what are objects of sense alone. Knowledge is power! but the phrase, as often used by political economists, implies no more than power over the material and the tangible; things which are of the earth, earthy; useful as the means, unworthy as the end, of our existence; and adding little to our truest happiness. Compared to knowledge thus limited and selfish, Poetry is power of a higher order; and possessing a wider range, for its empire is the ethereal, the intellectual, the eternal.

Such is my view of the nature, aim, and end of Poetry, and of the province and privilege of the genuine poet; and, however imperfectly this hasty and feeble estimate of both may express that view, I trust it may be intelligible to some. Regarded in this light, the idea that Poetry is an evil requiring to be suppressed; a superfluity, even, which can very well be spared; or Poets an encumbrance of which Society would be well rid, appears to me to imply the extinction, the annihilation, of many of our best feelings, and loftiest thoughts; the quenching of many an aspiration which, by "making the past and the future predominate over the present, raises us in the dignity of thinking beings."

In the world, and its countless cares and encumbrances; in the struggle for mere subsistence on the part of the many; in the pursuit after pleasure of those who are regarded as the more fortunate few;—there is quite enough to fetter our spirits to the objects immediately around us; to give a preponderance to the positive and the real, over the ideal and the imaginative. We have abundant need of every counteracting impulse of which we can avail ourselves to keep in check the worldliness of our own hearts: we require the aid of every lever on which we can lay our hands to lift us out of ourselves; of every incentive which may lead us to live and look beyond ourselves; of every connecting link which binds us to the great family of human beings, to the beautiful and bountiful earth on which we dwell, which would lead us to the heaven we hope for, and an Almighty and Beneficent Creator, their and our common Parent and Benefactor. Can Poetry do nothing to cherish and foster feelings and thoughts of this kind? Have its countless appeals to the human heart found no echo there? produced no fruits on earth? sown no seed, which through the blessing of Him who is the giver of every good and perfect gift, may contribute to a yet more glorious harvest in heaven? If it be said it is the province of Religion to do all this,—I would ask are Religion and Poetry, taking the view I entertain of the latter, incompatible? Or is not Poetry, rather, when used and not abused, when honoured and not degraded, one of the most natural allies, one of the most potent and persuasive advocates of Religion? I speak, of course, of the subordinate and human means,—the auxiliaries which God has given to His creatures; which they may prostitute and profane, but which were assuredly given for nobler ends and holier purposes. There may have been irreligious Poets; but we may also remember there was an apostate among the Apostles; and we have no more right to denounce Poetry for the desecration of its legitimate functions on the part of its unworthy votaries, than we have to cavil at Christianity for the base desertion and foul betrayal of his Divine Master by Judas.

But for the alliance which may and ought to exist between Religion and Poetry, though I need only refer to The Bible, as containing much, which for its tenderness and beauty, its simplicity and pathos, is most deserving of that epithet; though I might do this, and challenge any one to disprove the soundness of the argument; I will take my stand on humbler ground, and illustrate my position by a less aspiring exemplification. Let me appeal to the simple unelaborate, and comparatively unadorned productions of many Poets of a later age, and not a few of our own country. Men preferring no claim to supernatural inspiration, some of whose performances the critical and the fastidious would hardly call poetry: but who, by the artless expression of pure thoughts and devotional feelings in unpretending verse, have soothed, and comforted, and gladdened, in sorrow, in sickness, and in death, the hearts of many an humble believer.

Let the Poet, then, but worthily use his gift, and exercise his calling; and he may safely commit his fame among men, his favour with God, to the sympathies of our common nature, and the yet more boundless mercies of One infinitely purer, higher, and holier. Even in this world he will find no want of fitting auditors, to repay his toil. Childhood with its tenderness of thought, and guilelessness of feeling, will ever furnish him with numerous readers who will gladly turn to his pages. Youth, with its ardent and generous susceptibility, will there find a chord responsive to its own kindling and spirit-stirring aspirations. Manhood will ever muster, even from among those who are engaged in its toils, its cares, its pursuits, and its pleasures, some glad for a while to escape from these, and from themselves, to breathe in a purer atmosphere, to live amid calmer and brighter scenes, and to hold fellowship with gentler beings than those by whom they are daily surrounded. Womanhood, while true to itself, and to every thought and feeling by which its best influence over man can be strengthened and sustained, will supply a yet greater portion of the Poet's adherents and advocates: their sway is that of the affections; the domestic virtues are their penates; the household hearth their earthly altar, and themselves its ministering attendants: and of all these the poet, if worthy of his vocation, will ever speak, and think, and feel, as one who knows them to be his strong-hold and citadel. Even old age, amid its decrepitude and infirmity, will find some among its veterans, who will lend no unwilling ear to strains which bring back the occasional gush of youthful emotion to the heart; and a yet more joyful one to the song which tells of a glorious and blissful immortality.

With such to listen to his lays, the Poet can have no just cause to doubt or to distrust his finding an auditory on earth; and in the brief span of time allotted him as a sojourner thereon: while for Heaven, and through the countless ages of Eternity, he may humbly cling to the hope set before him, that hope which is as an anchor to the soul, sure and stedfast, in which, if he be a Christian Poet, he has a common interest with all his fellow-believers in the mercies of God through Christ Jesus; trusting that by occupying diligently with *the one talent intrusted to him*, he may not, at the last day, be numbered with the slothful and the negligent; but rather with those who have endeavoured to honour The Giver in the use of His own gift, by exercising it for the happiness of His creatures.

Bernard Barton
Woodbridge, 4th Month, 26th, 1836.

CONTEXTUAL MATERIAL

Edward FitzGerald, 'Memoir of Bernard Barton'
Quoting Barton on his childhood memories.

My most delightful recollections of boyhood are connected with the fine old country-house in a green lane diverging from the high road which runs through Tottenham. I would give seven years of life as it now is, for a week of that which I then led. It was a large old house, with an iron palisade and a pair of iron gates in front, and a huge stone eagle on each pier. Leading up to the steps by which you went up to the hall door, was a wide gravel walk, bordered in summer time by huge tubs, in which were orange and lemon trees, and in the centre of the grass-plot stood a tub yet huger, holding an enormous aloe. The hall itself, to my fancy then lofty and wide as a cathedral would seem now, was a famous place for battledore and shuttlecock; and behind was a garden, equal to that of old Alcinous himself. My favourite walk was one of turf by a long strait pond, bordered with lime-trees. But the whole demesne was the fairy ground of my childhood; and its presiding genius was grandpapa.

Lord Byron, Letter to Bernard Barton, 1 June 1812
On Barton's early work.

Some weeks ago my friend Mr. Rogers showed me some of the Stanzas in MS., and I then expressed my opinion of their merit, which a further perusal of the printed volume has given me no reason to revoke. I mention this as it may not be disagreeable to you to learn that I entertained a very favourable opinion of your power before I was aware that such sentiments were reciprocal.

B.B. [Bernard Barton?], 'The Friends: To the Editor of the Examiner'
A response to William Hazlitt's account of Quaker culture.

I can assure W.H. that he is altogether mistaken in us; that we are not the automatons he takes us for; and that if he will but take the trouble of becoming better acquainted with us, he will find, notwithstanding the demureness of our drab, and the amplitude of our beaver, we have an intimate "consciousness of human follies, human pursuits, and human pleasures"; that although we have not produced either a Handel, or an Apelles, we are not systematic despisers of the Fine Arts; and that to the useful arts we are warm friends.—W.H. says, that "a Quaker poet would be a phenomenon"; perhaps so; the Sage in Rasselas drew so brilliant a picture of the necessary qualifications of a poet, that his auditor was convinced the attainment of the proud title was utterly impossible, and W.H. may be as fastidious; yet it does happen that the poetical works of a Quaker may be found in, I believe, more than one edition of our British Bards; and I believe I may safely assert, that a taste for poetry is by no means either extraordinary or unusual among us.

In short, I hope, if W.H. will come a little more among us, he will find that we have both heads and hearts; and that we are not entirely destitute either of fancy, or of feeling, or of imagination.

Robert Southey, Letter to Bernard Barton, 21 January 1820

On the propriety of Quakers as poets.

You propose a question to me which I can no more answer with any grounds for an opinion than if you were to ask me whether a lottery ticket should be drawn a blank or a prize; or if a ship should make a prosperous voyage to the East Indies. If I recollect rightly, poor Scott, of Amwell, was disturbed in his last illness by some hard-hearted and sour-blooded bigots who wanted him to repent of his poetry as a sin. The Quakers are much altered since that time. I know one, a man deservedly respected by all who know him, (Charles Lloyd the elder, of Birmingham,) who has amused his old age by translating Horace and Homer; and he is looked up to in the Society, and would not have printed the translations if he had thought it likely to give offence.

Judging, however, from the spirit of the age as affecting your Society, like everything else, I should think they would be gratified by the appearance of a poet among them who confined himself within the limits of their general principles. They have been reproached with being the most illiterate sect that has ever arisen in the Christian world, and they ought to be thankful to any of their members who should assist in vindicating them from that opprobrium. [...] If poetry in itself were unlawful, the Bible must be a prohibited book.

Review of *Poems* (1820) in the *London Magazine*

On the Quaker muse, and expression versus feeling.

We have felt a good deal interested in this volume, in consequence of hearing that its author is one of the Society of Friends; but certainly it cannot be said of him, that he sees creation clothed in a drab-coloured suit. He writes stanzas to ladies, versies [*sic*] to valleys, and a lyrical address to the Gallic eagle;—and all this he does in as quick, free, and lively a spirit, as any worldling poet that can be named. The only peculiarity we can discover about the pieces, indicative of their writer's sect, is their extreme benevolence, and spotless innocence. In these respects, indeed, his muse may be said to possess a lovely Quaker countenance,—such as we have sometimes had the good fortune to see in stage coaches, and have invariably fallen in love with, whenever we have seen it. The eye sparkling, but quiet in self-possession and modesty; the delicate complexion reflecting health of body and mind; the regular features, ever undisturbed by wayward or lawless feelings:—such is a Quaker-beauty, graceful in reserve.

[...]

The writer seems to have an ear ever on the listen for the accents of charity, patriotism, and religion,—that he may catch their burthen, and prolong their sound: wherever human anguish causes the tear to start, there would he fain be to soothe or alleviate: whatever has really deserved well of fame, he is proud to celebrate: and the choicest and coyest charms of nature have smitten his heart with indelible impressions. [...] That the expression is always on a par with the feeling we cannot say: the writer's style, as it strikes us, is very unequal; and, in the simplicity of conscious sincerity, we sometimes find him common-place in phrase, and careless in construction. It is very easily to be seen that Mr. Barton is not a professional writer [...] Near his most lively images are placed some of the dullest; and common prosing is too frequently hard on the heels of passages of genuine poetry.—We should, on the whole, then, set him down as an amateur of distinguished talent, ready to celebrate any worthy subject that offers itself.

[Francis Jeffrey], Review of *Poems* (1820) in the *Edinburgh Review*

On Barton's style.

The volume before us has all the purity, the piety and gentleness, of the Sect to which its author belongs—with something too much perhaps of their sobriety. The style is rather diffuse and wordy, though generally graceful, flowing, and easy; and though it cannot be said to contain many bright thoughts or original images, it is recommended throughout by a truth of feeling and an unstudied earnestness of manner, that wins both upon the heart and the attention. In these qualities, as well as in the copiousness of the diction and the facility of the versification, it frequently reminds us of the smaller pieces of Cowper,—the author, like that eminent and most amiable writer, never disdaining ordinary words and sentiments when they come in his way, and combining, with his most solemn and contemplative strains, a certain air of homeliness and simplicity, which seems to show that the matter was more in his thoughts than the manner, and that the glory of fine writing was less considered than the clear and complete expression of the sentiments, for the sake of which alone he was induced to become a writer.—Though the volume contains sixty or seventy different pieces, and almost every variety of versification, there is something of uniformity in the strain and tenor of the poetry. There is no story, and of course no incident, nor any characters shown in action. The staple of the whole is description and meditation—description of quiet, home scenery, sweetly and feelingly wrought out—and meditation overshaded with tenderness, and exalted by devotion—but all terminating in soothing and even cheerful views of the condition and prospects of mortality. The book, in short, is evidently the work of a man of a fine and cultivated, rather than of a bold and original mind—of a man who prefers following out the suggestions of his own mild and contemplative spirit, to counterfeiting the raptures of more vehement natures, and thinks it better to work up the genuine though less splendid materials of his actual experience and observation, than to distract himself and his readers with more ambitious and less manageable imaginations. His thoughts and reflections, accordingly, have not only the merit of truth and consistency, but bear the distinct impress of individual character.

Anonymous, 'Sonnet to Bernard Barton'

'On the favourable Notice of his *Poems* in the *Edinburgh Review*'.

> The Critic's praise is just.—His liberal hand
> For thee a lovely wreath has fitly twined;
> While round thy brow its modest flowers expand,
> Be hopes of brighter guerdon all resign'd.
> Ah! where couldst thou more dear encomium find,
> Than thus with COWPER's ever honour'd name
> To hear thine own compared?—May spotless fame,
> Like *his*, be to thy future lays assign'd!—
> See Youth and Innocence confess thy sway,
> With pleased attention round the minstrel bending;
> While the mild glories of th' *Autumnal Day*
> Are to his song their sweet attraction lending:—
> And now—Devotion prompts sublimer lays,
> That blend with Nature's charms their great Creator's praise!

CONTEXTUAL MATERIAL

Bernard Barton, Preface to *Poems*, 2nd edition (1821)
On poetic success and Quaker poetry.

The writer is well aware that the power of absolute talent displayed in this volume, cannot bear comparison with those examples of high poetical genius, which are afforded in the works of several of the popular poets of the present day. He had never imposed upon himself by believing, that he could enter into competition with these in point of ability; but he did think, nevertheless, that it was possible his humble productions might be usefully and not unfitly permitted to take their chance for public favour.

They have found this in a degree beyond his anticipation; and their success, without altering his original estimation of his own talent as a poet, has given him pride as an author beyond what he could have experienced in the assurance of owing that success to genius of the first order.—The indulgence with which these pieces have been received proves to him, that the most poignant temptations, and brilliant seductions, addressed to the public taste and moral sentiment, have not yet extinguished in the public breast, a genuine attachment to the sober and simple exercise of the gentler faculties of the muse.

[…]
The author's religious persuasion having been very commonly alluded to by his critics, he can scarcely avoid referring to this point. That he has not been thought, either to discredit the principles, or dishonour the intellect, of those with whom it is his glory to agree on the most important of all human concerns, cannot but be highly gratifying to him. On the other hand, the liberality with which individuals of different views and habits have connected what is of laudable purpose and salutary tendency in this volume with the tenets and practice of the Society of Friends, ought to be, and no doubt will be, duly appreciated by that body of Christians. That the writer should have been instrumental in procuring this public and affectionate testimony to the honour of a cause which he identifies with truth itself, is a circumstance on which his mind will ever delight to dwell.

Bernard Barton, Preface to *Napoleon, and Other Poems* (1822)
On composition and revision.

It has not been from indolence that the author has not bestowed more elaborate revision on his compositions; nor is it with any affected contempt of refined taste, or in wilful disrespect of critical opinion, that he ventures on publishing what he does; but, in his judgment, his poetry is not of a description which long and laborious revision would essentially improve: what it might gain in elegance appears to him too contingent to be plausibly hoped; what it might lose in simplicity and unstudied earnestness, too probable not to be rationally feared. The *matter* he has been desirous of communicating to his readers, has been, in his hours of composition, of much more moment to him than the *manner*, provided the last were not positively repulsive. Should *his* prove so to those whose taste may have been formed on purer and more classical models, he certainly must regret the circumstance; for he pretends not to undervalue what he is unable to attain: but he has endeavoured to do the best which his education, circumstances, and situation have allowed him.

Charles Lamb, Letter to Bernard Barton, 11 September 1822
On Barton's work and Quakerism.

You have misapprehended me sadly, if you suppose that I meant to impute any inconsistency (in your writing poetry) with your religious profession. I do not remember what I said, but it was spoken sportively [...] I have read Napoleon and the rest with delight. I like them for what they are, and for what they are not. I have sickened on the modern rhodomontade & Byronism, and your plain Quakerish Beauty has captivated me. It is all wholesome cates, aye, and toothsome too, and withal Quakerish. If I were George Fox, and George Fox Licenser of the Press, they should have my absolute IMPRIMATUR. I hope I have removed the impression [of criticism].

I am, like you, a prisoner to the desk. I have been chained to that gally [*sic*] thirty years, a long shot. I have almost grown to the wood. If no imaginative poet, I am sure I am a figurative one. Do "Friends" allow puns? *verbal* equivocations?—they are unjustly accused of it, and I did my little best in the "imperfect Sympathies" [Lamb's essay of 1821] to vindicate them.

Charles Lamb, Letter to Bernard Barton, 9 January 1823
On financial independence and a literary career.

"Throw yourself on the world without any rational plan of support, beyond what the chance employ of Booksellers would afford you"!!! Throw yourself rather, my dear Sir, from the steep Tarpeian rock, slap-dash headlong upon iron spikes. If you had but five consolatory minutes between the desk and the bed, make much of them, and live a century in them, rather than turn slave to the Booksellers.

[...]

Keep to your Bank, and the Bank will keep you. Trust not to the Public, you may hang, starve, drown yourself, for anything that worthy *Personage* cares.

I bless every star that Providence, not seeing good to make me independent, has seen it next good to settle me upon the stable foundation of Leadenhall. Sit down, good B.B., in the Banking Office; what, is there not from six to Eleven P.M. 6 days in a week, and is there not all Sunday? Fie, what a superfluity of man's time,— if you could think so! Enough for relaxation, mirth, converse, poetry, good thoughts, quiet thoughts.

Review of *Poetic Vigils* (1824) in the *Literary Gazette*
On Barton and love.

There is a good feeling, a tone of sensibility, a degree of nature, which at once come from and appeal to the heart. But pray thee, friend Bernard, be not wroth when we say there is a degree of sameness, of quiet almost degenerating into insipidity, in some of thy writings; and this we entirely ascribe to thy not being in love. A poet without a mistress! why, it is a cook without a kitchen, a lord mayor without a coach, a doctor without a fee [...] A brisk flirtation, Mr. Barton, would be of infinite service;—but, *la belle* passion, why, it would do wonders;—it would add at once the tenth string to your lyre. Is there no pretty Friend, whose drab and bright eyes; or, to make your case more poetical, could you not contrive to let your eyes wander beyond the pale of your creed—pit love against duty, the heart against the conscience, gros de Naples *versus* broad-cloth?

Review of *Poetic Vigils* (1824) in the *Monthly Review*
On Barton and his contemporaries.

To those who delight in the happy delineation of the domestic affections, and all the warmer but calmer feelings of the heart, we recommend the verses of Mr. Barton. Were we compelled to define the peculiar characteristic of his poetry, we should term it "the poetry of the affections;" and, to describe it negatively, we should say that it possesses none of the ardent and splendid imagination which burns through the writings of Lord Byron; none of the high lyrical power which gives such grace and dignity to the verse of [Thomas] Campbell; none of the rich narrative of Sir Walter Scott's style; nor any of the mystical obscurity of Wordsworth. It is the simple and pleasing effusion of a warm and poetical heart, poured out in verse eminently suited to the expression of tender feelings;—lucid, correct, and harmonious. At some times, poetry like this possesses greater charms than loftier and nobler compositions; as in music we occasionally prefer a simple and touching air to the most elaborate efforts of the great masters. A relish for this species of poetry seems to argue the existence of natural and unsophisticated feelings [...] Among modern poets,

Burns is certainly most distinguished for the amiable and admirable quality to which we have adverted.

Bernard Barton, Letter to Charles Benjamin Tayler, 1825
On *Poetic Vigils,* Quaker poetry and sectarianism.

One or two of my literary friends do not like my Vigils so well as its precursors—they say it is too Quakerish. Charles Lamb says it is my best, but that I have lugged in religion rather too much. Bowring vituperates it *in toto*—save the Ode to Time; by no means a great favourite with me. I am not put out of conceit with it yet, for all this. Its faults are numerous, but it has more redeeming parts than either of its predecessors. And so it ought; else I had lived two years for nothing. As to its Quakerism, I meant it should be Quakerish. I hope to grow more so in my next—else, why am I a Quaker? My love to the whole visible, ay, and the whole invisible church of Christ, is not lessened by increased affection to the little niche of it in which I may happen to be planted. The bird would not mourn the less the fall of the tree which held its nest, because in that nest was found the first and primary source of its own little hopes and fears. How absurdly some people think and reason about sectarianism! In its purer and better element, it is no bad thing—not a bit worse than patriotism, which need never damp the most generous and enlarged philanthropy. When I no longer love thee, dear Charles, because thou art a Churchman, I will begin to think my Quakerism is degenerating.

[Robert Story], 'Specimen of a Poetical Satire'
A satire on Barton.

> FRIEND.
> Yet every month's review on Bernard's lays
> Exhausts the terms of puffery and praise.
>
> POET.
> Aye, and his rhymes in every Christmas toy
> Rival the cuts in pleasing girl or boy.
> High be his pride, as high his present fame!
> Another age will never see his name;
> Or find it in some old "gazette" bepraised,
> Itself neglected as the name it raised.
> Feeble, inert, his spirit pours along
> No stream magnificent of rolling song—
> But through a level plain, devoid of force,

It bids it wind its slow and sluggish course;
The breaks—the dashings—all so far between,
We turn aside and leave the half unseen—

Bernard Barton, Letter to Thomas Wilkinson, 28 April 1825
On the influence of Wilkinson as a Quaker literary predecessor.

Some years ago, I think long before I had ever written a line of Poetry, certainly before I ever contemplated becoming avowedly an Author, several little Pieces of thine had fallen in [my] way, and the perusal of them had afforded me much gratification. At a later period, but still prior to my venturing aught of my own in print, the perusal of thy affecting & affectionate tribute to the worth & Genius of Elizabeth Smith, had well nigh induced me, though an unknown Stranger, to address a Letter to thee expressive of the pleasure it afforded me to see a Member of our Religious Society coming forward before the Public, *consistently* & *gracefully* in the character of a Poet. And when after much deliberation, I hazarded the experiment of submitting to the public eye a Volume of Poems in which the Author's religious Profession was frankly avowed, I may candidly avow to thee that thy example had some weight in my decision. So thou seest thou hast had more to do in making a Poet of me, if I may use such a colloquial phrase, than thou hast in all probability ever thought of.

Felicia Hemans, 'To the Daughter of Bernard Barton, the Quaker Poet'
To Lucy Barton.

> Happy thou art, the child of one
>   Who in each lowly flower,
> Each leaf that glances to the sun,
>   Or trembles with the shower;
>
> In each soft shadow of the sky,
>   Or sparkle of the stream,
> Will guide thy kindling spirit's eye
>   To trace the Love Supreme.
>
> So shall deep quiet fill thy breast,
>   A joy in wood and wild;—
> And e'en for this I call thee blest,
>   The gentle poet's child!

Bernard Barton, Preface to *Devotional Verses* (1826)
On language in religious poetry.

Nor has he [the poet] even ventured to designate his brief and simple records of thought and feeling by the name of poetry, but has preferred claiming for them the less aspiring appellative of Verses, as more appropriate, not only to what they are, but to what he wishes them to be. At the risque of rendering his pages less attractive to lighter readers, than even *his* modicum of poetic talent might, perhaps, have made them, the Author has endeavoured studiously to avoid all needless ornament, and has been solicitous to "use great plainness of speech;" he has done this, not only in accordance with his own taste in devotional verse, but in compliance with, and reference to, a far more imperative principle,—that of duty.

Review of *Devotional Verses* (1826) in the *Eclectic Review*
On Barton's plainness.

The volume before us is chiefly of a didactic character. It does not rest its claims to the attention of the Christian public on the same grounds as the Author's former volumes,—composed of miscellaneous poetry; nor is it meant as a hymn-book, or as a new set of [Byron's] Hebrew Melodies. Mr. Barton seems rather to have taken for his model, if not in point of style, yet, as regards the character of his work, writers of elder times, such as the admirable Author of the Temple.

[...]

The Author's aim has evidently been, to exhibit Scriptural truth in a striking light, but with little artificial decoration. He has been solicitous, he says, to use "great plainness of speech,"—'not only in accordance with his own taste in devotional verse, but in compliance with an imperative principle of duty.' We are not sure that his theory on this subject will bear investigation, any more than Wordsworth's poetical doctrine, which he has so happily disproved by his own writings. Purity of taste must of necessity produce a love of simplicity, which is the truest elegance; but simplicity, in composition, is nothing but *thought having worked itself clear*. It is not a raw produce. It is a much more recondite thing than finery of diction. When, therefore, Mr. Barton speaks of the 'elaborate and recondite efforts of poetic art,' as opposed to that purity and simplicity of style, that Doric plainness, which befits devotional writing—he appears to us to mistake the matter. If we have any fault to find with his verses, it is that, in some instances, he has departed from the severity of the rule we should lay down, by versification too ingenious.

Bernard Barton, Letter to William Howitt, 15 February 1827

On work and composition.

If the end of existence is what is usually called 'getting on in the world,' poetry is certainly a dead weight in the race, for where one wins the plate fifty are thrown out. In my own case I had nothing to lose. Poetry has gained me little pecuniary profit, but it is a moot point with me if the time spent on it would have turned to much better account. What it might have done is no proof of what it would have done. While I am at the bank I keep verses at arms' length. When I was a younger rhymer, and rode my hobby more furiously, I used to steal a few minutes now and then even to scribble on the sly, and often to con over a couplet or a stanza when my hands were busy smoothing out notes; but at that time I used to have a good deal of such work, so that, without cheating my employers, I could give my thoughts and fancies a roving commission. But of later years my head has had to work as well as my fingers, and I will defy any man to add up or calculate, and compose simultaneously. But when my day's work is done, and I am fairly in my own back-room for the evening, rhyming seems at times my only resource; and so I rhyme, comforting myself, as best I may, that if I might do it better, I might also do it worse.

Review of *A Widow's Tale* (1827) in the *Athenaeum*

On Romantic-era devotional poetry and the evolution of Barton's style.

Though he can hardly be called an imitator of [James] Montgomery, yet he may be strictly said to resemble that poet in the moral and serious tone of his writings […] It is a singular circumstance, that they are the only two authors of religious poetry that possess any degree of popularity in England, or whose names are heard beyond their respective sects; and it is a still more curious circumstance, that of these writers who alone have succeeded in this hitherto unpopular branch of literature, the one is a Moravian and the other a Quaker, members of sects, to which, of all others, we should have last turned our expectation for writers of such successful exertion.

    Bernard Barton, there is little doubt, owed a considerable share of his original notoriety to the circumstance of his being the first openly recognized Quaker poet […] but he is now fairly before the public. His repeated appearances have made us forget his garb, and we are inclined to think his style is every year becoming more ambitious and ornamented. The principal poem in the volume under notice, and several of the minor pieces, are certainly of a generally higher tone, and more imaginative character, than any of our author's former productions.

[Bernard Barton], 'Wolves in Sheep's Clothing': To W.C. Fonnereau, Esq. from a Dissenter

On Tory attacks during the 1835 election campaign.

>   WOLVES IN SHEEP'S CLOTHING! bitter words and big;
>   But who applies them? tell us, if you can:
>   *A suckling Tory!* an apostate Whig!
>   In short, a very silly, weak young man!
>
>   What such an one may either think or say,
>   With sober people will not weigh one pin;
>   In their opinion his own senseless bray
>   PROVES HIM THE ASS WRAPT IN THE LION'S SKIN.

[...]

Sir, you can scarcely be surprised that such an outrageous calumny, as the one above quoted [i.e. that Dissenters are wolves in sheep's clothing], should call forth some slight castigation; but viewing it as I do, as an act of indiscretion and folly, committed under excitement of brimming bumpers and echoing cheers, I have only visited it with a few lines of playful raillery.

Let me, however, add a brief appeal to PHILIP SOBER! Can you suppose that indiscriminate abuse, and vulgar slander, lavished on a body of men whom you think hostile to your Church, are likely to *diminish* that hostility? Are you so confident of your Church's stability, as to think it prudent, by studied insult, to provoke enmity, and offer a premium for aversion and disgust? Rely on it, Sir, that such language, while it only excites in the party vilified, a mingled feeling of contempt and pity, awakens real regret in the minds of sober reflecting Churchmen, who have sense enough to see that the Establishment only requires a few such partisans to ensure its downfall.

One remark more, Sir, and I have done. If, in spite of the mildness and forbearance of this passing rebuke, you persist in publicly slandering us, I give you fair notice, you may not on future occasions be let off so easily.

[...]

Your's, as you hereafter demean yourself, A DISSENTER.

Bernard Barton, Letter to William Martin, 21 January 1837

On science, art and imagination.

As to the Mechanic's Institute my dear fellow I know little more of it than Balaam or even his Ass did [...] I have been to two of the Lectures, though. One on Mental Derangement, and one of a very finely scientific nature, on

Heat. By the first I was much interested; by the latter less so. A mere question or discussion on any matter of pure Science has very little charm for me. The subject of Mental Derangement, on the other hand, is one of deep interest, perhaps not the less so to me from the Poet having said or sung that "The Lover, Lunatic, and Poet are of imagination all compact". Thou wilt tell me, doubtless, that the discoveries of science have such obvious reference to the interests, comforts, & happiness of Man, that they have as strong a claim on one's human interest, as the vagaries of a diseased or excited imagination can, or ought to have, but they have this reference more remotely.

[…]

To hear a man talk by the two hours together about heat & combustion, & reflection & radiation, & all that sort of thing in a technical & professional dialect, and illustrate his positions through diagrams to my eye as unintelligible as the hieroglyphics of Egypt (I can't spell that ere word) puzzles and perplexes me. In truth the vagaries and phantasies of the madman seem to me more comprehensible, for my own fancy, by some hocus pocus process of its own can catch now & then a link of the chain of association which has led the Lunatic astray.

Bernard Barton, Letter to Frances Ann Shawe, 1 September 1837
On maintaining Quaker faith.

My sister [Maria] H.[ack] herself had been previously baptized, three of her children had long before done the same; my brother and his family are all Church-folk, Lucy [his daughter] the same, and I am now almost the sole representative of my father's house, quite the only one of his children, left as an adherent to the creed he adopted from a conscientious conviction of its truth. I am left all alone, like Goldsmith's old widow in the Deserted Village, looking for water-cresses in the brook of Auburn. Lucy tells me I must turn too, but unfortunately, all the results of my reading, reasoning, reflection, observation, and feeling, make me more and more attached to my old faith. It seems only rendered dearer to me by the desertion of those whom I most love. Yet I love them not a whit the less for abandoning it; believing, as I do, that they have done so on principle. Still, principle on their part could be no warrant for a want of it on mine: so I must e'en be a Quaker still.

Bernard Barton, Letter to Frances Ann Shawe, 1839
On ageing and sympathy.

The longer I live the more expedient I find it to endeavour more and more to extend my sympathies and affections. The natural tendency of advancing years is to narrow and contract these feelings. I do not mean that I wish to form a new and sworn friendship every day—to increase my circle of intimates; these are very different affairs. But I find it conduces to my mental health and happiness to find out all I can which is amiable and loveable in all I come in contact with, and to make the most of it. It may fall very short of what I was once wont to dream of; it may not supply the place of what I have known, felt, and tasted; but it is better than nothing—it serves to keep the feelings and affections in exercise—it keeps the heart alive in its humanity; and, till we shall be all spiritual, this is alike our duty and our interest.

Bernard Barton, Letter to Frances Ann Shawe, 8 January 1843
On female preaching and ministry.

Now these two [1 Timothy 2:12 and 1 Corinthians 14:34] are, I think, the only passages interdictory of women's preaching—that their real spirit is not opposed to the lawfulness (under the gospel dispensation) of a female ministry, I am compelled to believe for the following reasons:—First, the entire spirituality of the gospel dispensation, its abolition of all the old Mosaic law of priesthood [...] I believe it to be one of the glorious features of that new priesthood which our Lord himself set up in his church, that it is limited to no sex, or rank, or station. [...] In the second place, the passages referred to in St. Paul's Epistles as interdictory of women's preaching do not appear to me conclusive, because they are in direct contradiction to other passages in his own writings. If he meant, *in toto*, to forbid the ministry of women at all, why give directions what their attire or costume should be when praying or prophesying, and that they should do neither with their heads uncovered? [...] it would be endless to quote all the passages which tend to show, that in the earlier age of the church, and in the primitive purity of its apostolic government, women *did* exercise their gift in the ministry.

With regard to the practical working of this *liberty of prophesying*, in our own Society, I can only say that I believe it has worked well; and that some of the most powerful, effective, and persuasive ministers in the Society have been women,—and still are. I cannot understand why there should be aught of soul in sex which should qualify the one exclusively, and disqualify the other from becoming fit recipients of those influences of the Spirit by the aid of which alone man or woman can speak to edification. In some respects, especially as regards our own Society, I should say that women, among us, taking into account their general training, habits, and the life they lead, have some peculiar advantages, tending to fit and qualify them for the service of the ministry; but on these it is superfluous to dwell.

Bernard Barton, Letter to John Clemesha, 8 July 1843
On London and city experience.

I never fancy to myself that much if aught of *personal* identity can hang about folks in London, that they can see, hear, smell, or think, talk, and feel, as people do in the Country. I can obscurely understand how Cockneys born and bred, or such as are even long resident in Cockaigne, and therefore native to that strange element, may in course of time may [*sic*] acquire a sort of borrow'd Nature, and by virtue of it, a kind of artificial individuality. But I never was in London long enough to get at this, and have always seem'd when there *not to be myself*, but very much as if I were walking in a dream, or like a bit of sea-weed blown off some cliff or beach, and drifting with the current, one knew not why or how. In a coffee room, up one of those queer long dark Inn yards, I have felt far more like myself. There is more of quiet, folks often sit in boxes apart, and talk in a kind of under-tone, or when they do not, the united effect of so many voices becomes a sort of indistinct hum or buzz relieved at intervals by the swinging to & fro of the coffee room door, the clatter of plates, the jingle of glasses, or the rustle of the newspaper often turned over. I have spent an hour or two after my fashion in this way at the Four Swans, Belle Sauvage, Bolt in Tun, Spread Eagle, & other Coach Houses, by no means unpleasantly, seemingly reading the Paper, and sipping my tea or coffee, wine or toddy, but really catching some amusing scraps of the talk going on round, & speculating on the characters of the talkers.

Bernard Barton, Letter to John Clemesha, 13 June 1844
On religious polemic and controversy.

I am not over fond of polemicals, they are almost as bad as galenicals; how our tastes alter with added years & enlarged experience. I was once an eager disputant about matter & spirit, free will & necessity, Unitarianism & Trinitarianism and almost all other isms, and was in a fair [way] of becoming a Sceptic. Happily I found out, I hope in time to avert such a catastrophe, that a Man never stands so fair a chance of making a fool of himself as he does when he begins to fancy himself wiser than all round him.

Bernard Barton, Letter to Matilda Betham, 7 April 1845
On concerts.

L.[ucy?] is gone to a concert, and, truth to tell, I was sorely tempted to go myself: but it was to be performed at the theatre—rather an un-Quakerish locality; and, as J— and A—, though tempted like myself, seemed to think it would not do for them to go, I, who have less music in my ear, though I flatter myself I have some in my soul, could not with decent propriety be the only Quaker there. But I had a vast curiosity to go; for it is not an ordinary concert, but performed on certain pieces of rock, hewn out of Skiddaw, which, struck with some metal instrument, emit sounds of most exquisite sweetness. We have heard of sermons from stones, but I never dreamt of going there for music; but we live in a wondrous age for inventions of all sorts.

Bernard Barton, Letters to Mary Sutton, ?1847

On birthright membership and Quaker discipline.

Touching thy question of membership by birthright; while I admit the objections to it are plausible, still more serious ones present themselves, in my view, to a departure from our present rule. The seceders, if I understand their objections aright, state that birthright conferring membership is one cause why many of our Society grow up in a sort of traditional faith, believing they hardly know what or why. In by-gone days there might be much truth in this [...] but in the present age of discussion and controversy, except in a very few cases, where Friends are very remotely secluded from general intercourse, this can scarcely be the case. Very few of our young Friends can be ignorant of the conflict of opinion which has been called forth, and still fewer I think could be found who must not, in some way or other, have been put upon inquiring and thinking for themselves. The objections to considering none as members who have not attained an age warranting an application from them on the ground of real conviction to be received as such, strike me as serious and formidable. It must, as far as I see aught of its practical working, put all our young people out of the pale of our discipline; for what valid right or plausible plea could we have to extend admonition, or exercise a vigilant and affectionate oversight with respect to parties not in membership[?] [...] As we are now situated, supposing our young people to incline to go to balls, concerts, plays, &c, even where their parents are by no means strict Friends, the thing is not often attempted, because such or such a one would hear of it, and it is hardly worth the fuss which would be made about it. [...] [L]et us look further. As matters now stand, our young folks being all members, none of them could on the mere impulse of a sensibility very common to youth be led to a participation in the ordinances [baptism and Eucharist] now represented as so essential, without the case being brought under notice.

CONTEXTUAL MATERIAL

Bernard Barton, Letters to Mary Sutton, ?1847
On scripture and the inward Light.

I do not like to see one Divine gift pitted against another, as if there were, ought to be, or could be, any rivalry between what must be in their very essence harmonious. I hold with the old faith of our early Friends, who were content thankfully to receive the Scriptures as a blessed and invaluable revelation of God's will; yet so far from understanding them to be the *sole* and *final* one, I conceive that one main end and intent of their being given forth, was to inculcate the knowledge of that Spirit whence they themselves proceeded, to guide us to its teachings, to instruct us to wait for its influences, under a conviction that without its unfoldings even the lively oracles of God's Holy Writ may be to us a dead letter. If I am told there is a danger of these views leading to a fanatical trust in a fanatical inspiration of our own; I can only reply, that I can see no such danger while we seek such aid and guidance in simplicity, godly sincerity, and deep humility. Thus, I believe, were our early predecessors eminently led about and instructed.

Bernard Barton, Letter to William Bodham Donne, 17 February 1849
On his illness.

My desk hours are curtail'd, I now am a Gentleman after four o'clock, and not over wrought up to that hour. The moment Jones [Barton's physician] stated a remission of desk work was essential, it was given in a moment. This is a boon, and when the weather shall be warm so that I can ride out of evenings, it may be a benefit. For the present I cannot dress, or walk across the room, save slowly, without gasping like a fish just hook'd – something in or about the heart, I opine, Angina Pectoris I've a notion, though I know not how to spell it, and I can't make Jones speak out though He and Lu [i.e. Lucy] are both all kindness & vigilant attention. All I can get from my Galen is I must avoid all stimuli do nothing in a hurry, not even catching Head. I am forbidden to button my own buttons, on my boots, I mean, and am in brief a sort of Automaton. However I suffer no very acute pain, beyond the trouble of getting up every breath (now and then) as if "both chain pumps were choked below" but this is not always the case […] [B]ut thank Heaven! my mind is unclouded, my spirits for the most part not below par, and in the main I fudge on very tolerably, specially as I can lay down in bed without suffering from that position only that I cannot lay so long on my side as I used but copy the fashion of the marble Sleepers on the Tombs.

E.V. Lucas, *Bernard Barton and his Friends: A Record of Quiet Lives* (1893)

On Barton's legacy.

By the publicity he gave to his poems he became the pioneer of that Quaker culture which for breadth and grace now holds its own with the best. It needed no reformer to stimulate Quakers to the composition of good prose; for that they have always been able to write. But Bernard Barton was the first Friend to come into prominence as a maker of literary luxuries. It is not too much to assert that had he not done so, the Society would still be more or less ignorant of much that is beautiful and ennobling in Literature and Art.

Probably Bernard Barton would be the last man to claim the title of a revolutionist; nor do we wish to over-estimate his services in the promotion of a reform which unobtrusively was drawing nearer hour by hour. […] What we have to remember is, that the recognized union of Quakerism and Art was hastened by the efforts of the gentle bard of Woodbridge.

NOTES

Barton's *Poems* ran through four editions between 1820 and 1825. Any reference to one applies to later editions unless otherwise stated: so, for instance, a textual variation assigned to the 2nd edition will also occur in the 3rd and 4th editions.

Literary annuals were published for the Christmas market, but were titled 'for' the coming year and are conventionally dated in line with this: as such, a poem in an 1826 annual is, in reality, a poem of late 1825 and so forth.

My Lucy
Published in *Metrical Effusions* (1812).

Lucy Jesup (1781–1808) is a consistent elegiac presence in the early poetry, although this text reflects a rawer sense of loss than a later and more reflective piece like "The Heaven was Cloudless". With its short triplet stanzas and simple refrain, it certainly encapsulates the spontaneous 'effusive' style of Barton's first collection. The epigraph is from Robert Burns' 'The Lament. Occasioned by the Unfortunate Issue of a Friend's Amour' (1786). There are several references to the Scottish poet in *Metrical Effusions*, including an 'Imitation of Burns'.

line 23 – after her mother's death, the infant Lucy was raised by her grandparents and then went to boarding school. E. V. Lucas records in *Bernard Barton and his Friends* (1893) that 'after she became of a companionable and helpful age, father and daughter took up their quarters in what was perhaps the tiniest house ever inhabited by a poet' (p. 34). This is the cottage at 23 Cumberland Street in Woodbridge, marked today by a blue plaque, occupied 1824–35.

line 24 – this refrain is printed without an exclamation mark in *Metrical Effusions*, presumably in error.

Stanzas on the Anniversary of the Abolition of the Slave Trade
Published in *Metrical Effusions* (1812).

Formalising their opposition to slavery as early as 1727, the Quakers played a fundamental role in abolitionist campaigns. Although Barton began writing after the pivotal triumph of 1807 – the abolition of the slave trade – slavery continued in the British Empire until 1833. Barton's lines here act as an optimistic hymn to 1807, hailing the redemption of Africa from its bondage, and Britain from its crimes. Abolitionists are glorified as Christian heroes spearheading a moral enlightenment: as was common at the time, Africans are granted little agency in such discourse. The African Institution, to which the poem is dedicated, was a society founded in 1807 in order to continue the anti-slavery cause and develop the continent after abolition, with a particular focus on supporting (and to an extent administering) Sierra Leone as a colony for freed slaves.

line 2 – the Act for the Abolition of the Slave Trade was formally passed on 25 March 1807.

line 6 – the poetic use of 'Afric', often as a personification, was typical of abolitionist verse.

line 11 – Thomas Clarkson (1760–1846), a leading Anglican Evangelical abolitionist who lived close to Barton in Playford (see Barton's poem of that title in this volume). In 1787, he had been one of the 12 founders of the Society for Effecting the Abolition of the Slave Trade: the majority of the others were Quakers, including Bernard Barton's father, John Barton (1755–89).

line 19 – William Wilberforce (1759–1833), another Evangelical abolitionist and the leader of the parliamentary bloc who campaigned against the slave trade from the 1780s onward.

line 25 – 'Gloster' is Prince William Frederick, Duke of Gloucester and Edinburgh (1776–1834) – he was the African Institution's first president, and provided royal patronage.

lines 30–6 – these lines, of course, refer to the Quakers themselves, and to their joint political causes of abolition and radical pacifism.

line 37 – 'Guinea', at the time, referred to the entire West African slave coast.

line 48 – the line is quoted from the first epistle of Alexander Pope's *An Essay on Man* (1733).

line 53 – the River Jordan is a symbol of miracle and liberation in both Old and New Testaments.

lines 64–5 – missionary and conversionary efforts were key to the broader abolitionist movement. Wilberforce had helped set up the British and

Foreign Bible Society in 1804, in order to distribute scripture, although their work in Africa at this period was negligible compared to Europe and India. Barton included a panegyric to the Bible Society in *Metrical Effusions*.

Ode to an Æolian Harp
Published in *Metrical Effusions* (1812).

One of the very few pieces Barton designated as an ode, this poem draws out a remarkable sound-scape. The aeolian harp – or wind harp – is an unusual instrument where movements of air create random but harmonic music; it has a resonant place in the Romantic era due to famous texts by Coleridge, Percy Bysshe Shelley and others. Rather than making the harp a symbol for his own imaginative faculty or inspired creativity, Barton counterpoints the varying strains of its ethereal sound to the vulgar and vain noise of the world outside. Unlike Coleridge and Shelley, therefore, the poet displaces himself before the instrument, the notes of which become a harbinger of transcendence.

lines 13–16 – William Hayley's *Life of Cowper* (1806, new edition), a text which Barton cited elsewhere in *Metrical Effusions*, spoke of the 'gentle and tranquil dissolution' (IV, p. 188) of the famously tortured poet at his death.
lines 49–52 – the censure of the fashionable world's riotousness is mixed with a timely critique of the glorification of war: Barton would return to the theme in 'Napoleon' (see stanza LVII).
line 58 – 'In a moment, in the twinkling of an eye, at the last trump: for the trumpet shall sound, and the dead shall be raised incorruptible, and we shall be changed' (1 Cor. 15:52).

A Guess at the Contents of Lalla Rookh
Published in the *Suffolk Chronicle* (15 March 1817). Reprinted in *Poems, by an Amateur* (1818).

Barton obviously rated the work of Thomas Moore (1779–1852): see 'Haunts of Childhood' in this volume, which uses his lines for an epigraph. This comic and slightly satiric anticipation of the Irish poet's orientalist romance reminds us of a playful side to the Quaker poet which is easy to overlook. It is titled 'Jeu d'espirit on the forthcoming Poem announced by Thomas Moore, Esq.' in its original newspaper context; I have used the more helpfully descriptive title from *Poems, by an Amateur*. When published, Moore's *Lalla Rookh* (1817) did indeed capture – and sometimes frustrate – reviewers with its hyperbolic and sensuous style, as well as its relentlessly underlined exoticism.

line 3 – 'Cook' is the famous explorer and naval officer, James Cook (1728–79).
lines 7–8 – John Horne Tooke (1736–1812) was a controversial linguist and political radical, known for the philological work *The Diversions of Purley* (1786/1805). The reference to Pluto, Roman god of the underworld, alludes to his recent death.

Stanzas ("The Heaven was Cloudless")

Published in the *Suffolk Chronicle* (20 September 1817). Reprinted in *Poems, by an Amateur* (1818) and *Poems* (1820).

Many of Barton's nature lyrics feature the sea, often as a symbolic resource for reflection and recollection. In this poem, the lucid clarity of the sunlit water shapes a gently elegiac tone, as Barton addresses his dead wife, Lucy Jesup (1781–1808). It adopts two common Romantic tropes of sound: the idea of a word at the edge of language (lines 9–10) and the transcendent murmur of an articulate nature (lines 27–8). Initially published anonymously as 'Stanzas', it was subsequently entitled "The Heaven was Cloudless" (with the double quotation marks) when included in Barton's volumes. The critic Francis Jeffrey (1773–1850), in the *Edinburgh Review* of November 1820, singled the poem out as possessing 'rather more of the ardour and tenderness of love, than we had supposed tolerated in the Society of Friends' (p. 355).

line 20 – 'wast' = 'wert' in the later texts.
line 21 – 'Yet' = 'Yes' in the later texts.

The Convict's Appeal [Stanzas 1–15]

Published as an octavo edition in 1818. See also textual details below.

Originally printed in an untraced issue (prior to spring 1818) of James Montgomery's newspaper *The Sheffield Iris*, this medium-length poem stated its object as the 'Amelioration of our Criminal Code'. As ethical verse – compare Barton's abolitionist and chimney-sweep poetry – it is typical in marrying a position of rational reform to strong sentimental appeals and Christian piety. The convict's dream of his own execution is remarkably vivid, and fulfils Barton's desire to evoke 'a painful, but impressive picture, often realized in its darker shades of hopeless agony' whilst also opening up towards 'brighter hues of humble hope, obtained through sincere repentance' (p. xi). The text's remaining 19 stanzas, not included here, show the convict's prayer for divine mercy answered, and see him directly addressing the reader from a position of faithful repose.

line 11 – executions were popular spectacles: the infamous 1824 hanging of the forger Henry Fauntleroy allegedly drew a crowd of 100,000.

lines 47–8 – the range of minor and non-violent offences that could be punished by death was notorious and a key area for legal reform: in 1823, judges were given discretion to commute sentences for crimes other than treason and murder.

On Silent Worship

Published in the *Suffolk Chronicle* (4 April 1818). Reprinted in *Poems* (1820).

Quaker worship is one of its most distinctive characteristics: anyone may speak, if moved to do so, but meetings may pass entirely in silence. In the quietist tradition, silence is conceived as sublimely prayerful – as waiting for and watching before God. As Quaker theologian Robert Barclay puts it in his 1678 *Apology for True Christian Divinity*, 'it is not only an *outward silence* of the *body*, but an *inward silence* of the *mind*, from all its own imaginations and self-cogitations' (Eleventh Proposition, §10). Barton's poem registers silent worship as the purest form of Christian devotion insofar as it transcends all outward form and expression. The poem originally appeared under the initials B.B; the epigraph from Wordsworth's sonnet 'It is a beauteous Evening' (1807) was discarded in *Poems*, perhaps because Barton no longer needed to diffuse the Quakerism of its theme.

line 7 – clouds fill Solomon's temple during its dedication; see Kings 8:10.
line 18 – 'O GOD!' = 'O Lord!' in *Poems*.
line 22 – the poem's central stanzas are based around the account of Jesus in Samaria in the gospel of John.
line 24 – 'evening' = 'noon-tide' in *Poems*. A significant change: the gospel account mentions 'the sixth hour' (Jn 4:6) which has indeed been interpreted by some as evening (as per Roman time), but is more generally understood as noon (as per Jewish time, which begins at dawn).
line 25 – 'worship' = 'homage' in *Poems*.
line 27 – Solyma is a Greek name for Jerusalem.
lines 29–36 – a paraphrase of Jesus's words to the Samaritan woman from John 4:21-24.

Playford. A Descriptive Fragment.—1817
Published in *Poems, by an Amateur* (1818). Reprinted in *Poems* (1820).

'Playford' describes a Suffolk village close to Barton's home which held an important place in his life, not least because of his friendship with the abolitionist Thomas Clarkson (1760–1846), who lived in Playford Hall. The poem's shifting and irregular rhyme scheme mirrors the heterogeneity of its perspectives on landscape: from the dramatic evening tempest to notes of the picturesque in the rustic cottages, and from gentle woodland beauties to the twisted dead tree which becomes the landscape's final symbolic centrepiece. The spiritual repose Barton evokes at the fragment's end is tellingly irenic: the Anglican bells have ceased (permitting an appropriately Quaker silence to emerge) but the church still has its place in the scene.

line 22 – the moated Playford Hall, which dates from *c.* 1590.
line 32 – St. Mary's Church in Playford, still situated by a sharply rising path.
line 37 – 'the bell's loud summons' = 'the bell's last summons' in *Poems* (1820).
line 45 – the 'leafless tree' would fall some time before 1828, as evidenced by the poem 'A Veteran's Memorial; or Verses on the Fall of an Old Tree in Playford Church-yard' in *A New Year's Eve*.
lines 49–54 – these lines are indented differently in the 2nd edition of *Poems* (1821).
line 75 – 'outstretch'd meadows' = 'peaceful meadows' in the 3rd edition of *Poems* (1822).

Written in a Lady's Album
Published in *Poems, by an Amateur* (1818). Reprinted in *Poems* (1820).

The practice of recording a few lines of verse in an album or autograph book was one of the most informal types of poetry in the early nineteenth century and, as in this example, the theme of such lines was often reflexive – simply the physical event of writing in the album itself. Nevertheless, album verses did not always remain in a purely private context: Barton printed several, of varying registers and lengths, across his major volumes. As a spontaneous act of inscription which was also a form of social and cultural memory, they raised in a light manner issues of posterity, poetic ownership and literary fame.

When reprinted in *Poems* (1820), the poem was re-titled 'Written in an Album' and the date rendered in the Quaker form: '1st Mo. 5, 1818'.

Stanzas, Addressed to Some Friends Going to the Sea-Side
Published in *Poems, by an Amateur* (1818). Reprinted in *Poems* (1820).

Perhaps indebted to Samuel Taylor Coleridge's famous 'This Lime-Tree Bower My Prison' (1797) in envisaging companionable, roving walks from which the poet is excluded, this piece expresses Barton's strong love for the coast. If, as is likely, 'To Some Friends Returning From the Sea-Side' is a pendant piece, then the friends may be Anne Knight (1792–1860, née Waspe) and her sisters Phoebe and Hannah, since that text refers to 'sisterly converse'. They were recurrent companions at the time: see the notes to 'The Valley of Fern'.

line 5 – 'I can easily picture' = 'My fancy can picture' in the 3rd edition of *Poems* (1822).
line 14 – the striking vehicle of Barton's simile, lit coal beacons were used as navigational marks in Britain as late as 1822 (they were replaced by catoptric oil lights). Reportedly one was placed in the tower of Orford Castle, some 10 miles east of Woodbridge.
line 20 – Cornelian, or carnelian, is a reddish-brown mineral.
line 41 – 'pensive enjoyment' = 'soothing enjoyment' in the 3rd edition of *Poems* (1822).

Sonnet to the Deben ['Thou hast thrown aside thy summer loveliness']

Published in *Poems, by an Amateur* (1818).

Barton wrote repeatedly about the rivers of Suffolk, especially the Deben, which is a 30-mile long watercourse that flows through his native Woodbridge. This sonnet addressed to the Deben – not the only one of its title in the 1818 volume – uses its opening line and volta to inscribe a characteristically Bartonian preference for the charms of a less obviously appealing landscape.

line 4 – the topographer Samuel Lewis's *Book of English Rivers* (1855) refers to the countryside around Woodbridge as embracing 'pleasant walks, and fine views of the broad river Deben' (p. 98).

Stanzas, to Helen M— M—

Published in *Poems, by an Amateur* (1818). Reprinted in *Poems* (1820).

This is a poem of leave-taking for Helen Maria Mathew, one of the subscribers to Barton's 1818 volume. Born in Calcutta in 1803, the daughter of Henry Mathew, a merchant with Suffolk connections, she appears to have spent her childhood in England. A Miss H. M. Mathew is mentioned in the *Asiatic Journal and Monthly Register* of July 1820 as a passenger destined for Bengal. Not least because of Helen's age in 1818, the second and third stanzas' insistence that he is not in love with her is striking, and curiously self-conscious of his inclination to idealise and effuse over young female friends. Mathew was to die in Calcutta on 10 February 1822 of typhus fever, aged 19: Barton included two elegiac poems in 1824's *Poetic Vigils*.

The epigram, only present in 1818, is from Lord Byron's 'To Ianthe', which was a prefatory lyric added to the 1814 edition of *Childe Harold's Pilgrimage*. Lady Charlotte Harley, the prototype for Ianthe, was 11 years old when Byron first met her, in 1812.

Haunts of Childhood

Published in *Poems, by an Amateur* (1818).

Here Barton reminiscences about the Tottenham mansion of his grandfather Thomas Horne (*c*. 1727–1802, technically the father of his step-mother). See the extract from FitzGerald's memoir in this volume for a version of the same material, including evocations of the citrus trees, aloe and pond-side walk. Although reflecting on the mechanics of imaginative reverie, it wears its Romantic themes of childhood and memory lightly. Stylistically, it is loosely conversational, even prosaic, and along with the use of starred breaks it can be positioned as similar to the fragment poem 'Playford'.

The epigraph is a slightly misquoted extract from 'Farewell!—but, whenever you welcome the hour', included in the fifth number of Thomas Moore's *A Selection of Irish Melodies* (1814).

Sonnets to Charlotte M— [1818 and 1828]

First sonnet published in *Poems, by an Amateur* (1818). Reprinted in *Poems* (1820). Second sonnet published in *A New Year's Eve, and Other Poems* (1828).

These paired poems, a decade apart in date, are almost certainly addressed to Charlotte Moor (1804–1878), the daughter of the orientalist scholar and retired soldier, Major Edward Moor (1771–1848). Charlotte – who later married a barrister and Liberal MP who became Lord Chancellor – would have thus been around 14 and 24 years old at the times of writing. Although self-consciously 'idle rhyme', they are excellent examples of the verse which flowed profusely from the poet's Suffolk friendships and social connections. The first sonnet is described as one of Barton's 'very best—extremely good' (p. 774) in *Blackwood's Magazine* of December 1822.

1828 sonnet, line 8 – the poem 'To Charlotte', in *Poetic Vigils*, is strong evidence that one of the 'loved, lamented dead' is Helen Maria Mathew, hailed there as a mutual friend (see the notes to 'Stanzas, to Helen M— M—').

Drab Bonnets

Published in the *Liverpool Mercury* (4 September 1818). This text based on the version included in the *London Magazine* 2.9 (September 1820). Reprinted in the 2nd (1821) and 3rd (1822) editions of *Poems* only. See also textual details below.

A paradoxically lively poem mounting an affectionate defence of the plain dress characteristic of the Society of Friends. Dull colours, lack of decoration or ornament and a disregard for fashion aligned Quaker clothing with their overall ethic of simplicity and humility: Barton himself was uncertain about sporting a modestly fashionable waistcoat made for him by his daughter. The anapaestic rhythms and proliferation of feminine rhymes give it a light feel, and one might speculate that treating Quakerism with such playfulness was one reason for the unexplained withdrawal of the poem from the 4th edition of *Poems*. The source for and subject of the epigraph has not been located.

The earliest version I have traced is unattributed, entitled 'Original Lines Sent to a Young Lady, Member of the Society of Friends', and appears with the initials D.B.P.E. in a Liverpool newspaper (and was rapidly re-circulated in several other newspapers at the time). Barton had lived in Liverpool briefly after Lucy's death. I have not used it as the reading text because its provenance and circumstances are unclear. The *Mercury* version does share similarities with a signed holograph in Barton's handwriting (with an 1819 watermark) held in the Carl H. Pforzheimer Collection at NYPL (Misc 3587). The latter appears to be an intermediate revision, and is cited with the permission of the New York Public Library, Astor, Lenox and Tilden Foundations.

line 1 – 'cant of costumes, and of brilliant head-dresses' = 'rant of their costume, and brilliant head-dresses' in *Liverpool Mercury* (*LM*).
line 2 – 'in the Greek style, in the French style'. Typical epithets to describe the most fashionable attire: in the period, head-dresses were made of luxurious materials such as silk, lavishly ornamented with feathers, flowers or jewels.
line 5 – 'Yet to my partial glance, I confess the drab bonnet' = 'Yet, when all's said and done, to my eye the *drab bonnet*' in *LM*; 'Yet, to my partial eye, I confess the drab bonnet' in Pforzheimer MS.
line 6 – 'most when it bears' = 'chief when it wears' in *LM*.
line 8 – 'Benevolence wears' = 'Benevolence bears' in *LM*.
line 11 – the periodical press did indeed record and illustrate the changing fashions, month by month. Curiously, this very poem was reprinted in the October 1824 issue of one such journal, the *Lady's Monthly Museum*, which must be one of the most unlikely settings for Barton's work.
line 12 – 'sweetest to me' = 'neatest to me' in *LM*.
line 16 – 'its ribbons so glossy' = 'its ribbons so brilliant' in *LM*.

line 17 – 'Yet still I must own, although none may seem duller' = 'Yet somehow, or other, though none can seem duller' in *LM*.

line 20 – 'Around which my fancy delightedly plays:—' = 'Round which, with fresh fondness, my fancy still plays,' in *LM* and (with slightly different punctuation) in Pforzheimer MS.

line 24 – the turban was another *á la mode* item. *The Lady's Monthly Museum* of February 1820 records of Parisian fashion that 'the most fashionable style of head-dress in grand costume, is a scarf composed of crape, gauze, cachemire, or silver tissue; which is put on something in the turban style; but yet so contrived as to display a great deal of the hair' (p. 112).

lines 25–8 – lines alluding to Thomas Gray's 'Elegy in a Country Churchyard' (1751):

> Full many a gem of purest ray serene,
> The dark unfathomed caves of ocean bear:
> Full many a flower is born to blush unseen,
> And waste its sweetness on the desert air.

line 27 – 'And many a floweret, its beauties unvaunted' = 'And "full many a flower," its beauties uncounted' in *LM*. See above for the quotation from Gray.

line 30 – 'Array'd in the liv'ry' = 'Arrayed in that liberty' in *LM*.

line 31 – 'as e'er rose' = 'as e'er flash'd' in *LM*.

line 35 – 'If my heart-felt attachment ignobly concealing' = 'If my heart felt attachment, and fondness concealing' in *LM*.

line 36 – 'past unhonour'd' = 'were unhonoured' in *LM*.

line 37 – 'in the blaze of both beauty and fashion' = 'in the full blaze of beauty and fashion' in *LM*.

line 38 – 'with gifts' = 'in gifts' in *LM*.

line 40 – 'what sorrow must bear' = 'what sorrow must share' in *LM*.

line 42 – 'Far the highest enjoyment' = 'Still the highest enjoyment' in *LM*.

line 43 – 'most fondly, most dearly' = 'most fondly and dearly' in *LM*.

line 45 – as so often in Barton's verse, the elegiac presence of Lucy Jesup (1781–1808) hangs over the poem. Textually, 'my pleasure,—my pride!' = 'my pleasure and pride' in *LM*.

line 46 – 'o'er the dark-heaving sea' = 'in the deep heaving sea' in *LM*.

line 48 – 'is still beauteous to me' = 'is the sweetest to me' in *LM*; 'still is beauteous to me' in Pforzheimer MS.

The Ivy, Addressed to a Young Friend

Published in the *London Magazine* 1.1 (January 1820). Reprinted in *Poems* (1820).

A well-reviewed and frequently reprinted piece, this was the earliest of Barton's stream of contributions to the *London Magazine* in the early 1820s.

Framed through an affectionate but didactic address to a younger friend, it offers an iconographic treatment of the indomitable ivy wrapped around a dying tree. Several motifs – the nostalgic recall of Barton's spring-like youth, the attention drawn to an unbeautiful object, the insistence on a moral lesson in nature – are absolutely characteristic.

The *London Magazine* subtitle is 'Addressed to —— ——', but I have adopted the less obscure title used in *Poems*. There is an undated manuscript version in the University of Leeds Brotherton collection (BC MS 19th C Barton, envelope 2), which is cited with the permission of Special Collections, Leeds University Library.

line 24 – 'Perhaps I see beauty' = 'I can still see beauty' in Brotherton MS.

line 35 – 'I can draw, from that mould'ring tree' = 'I can find in that mouldering Tree' in Brotherton MS.

line 42 – the *London* actually reads '[sheds…] leaves on the dead'. As the Brotherton MS and *Poems* agree on 'leaves not the dead' (i.e. abandons not) and the poem revolves precisely around the evergreen character of the ivy, I have assumed the former is a printer's error and adopted the latter reading.

line 44 – 'let him ask of God, that giveth to all men liberally, and upbraideth not' (Jas 1:5).

line 48 – 'Greenness, and beauty, and strength' = 'Beauty, and Grace, and Strength' in Brotherton MS.

The Valley of Fern

Published in *Poems* (1820). See also textual details below.

'The Valley of Fern' could well be the quintessential nature poem in Barton's oeuvre, and it is not coincidentally positioned second (after his 'Verses' on a Quaker burial ground) in all editions of *Poems*. It is a particularly striking example of Barton's litotic stance: that is, privileging a lowly landscape consciously contrasted to more spectacular scenes. It evolves into a melancholic account of such a landscape's destruction, which connects it to a current in Romantic writing most famously expressed by John Clare (1793–1864).

The first part, written in 1817 and originally published as a standalone piece in *Poems, by an Amateur* (1818), is combined with a second part (written 1819) that describes the despoiling of the valley. This gives us the two part 1820 text. The religious poetics of the original tend towards joyous natural theology; the sequel moves towards reflections on the transience of created things. Both strains echo one of Barton's favourite poets, William Cowper (1731–1800). The 1818 poem which became 'Part I' differs in some punctuation and minor verbal variants (e.g. hath/has; may/shall) alongside the revisions recorded below.

line 1 – the location of the 'lone valley' is identified in John Glyde's *New Suffolk Garland* (1866), which cites a letter from Barton's friend and fellow Quaker Anne Knight (1792–1860) recounting the genesis of the poem: '"The Valley of Fern" is a beautiful little wild, sequestered spot, lying on the left of the high-road leading to Melton, and behind what is called Leeks hill, never noticed, I dare say, until the Poet immortalized it. I well remember going through it, for the first time, one summer day, with him and my two sisters [Hannah and Phoebe Waspe], and enjoying its romantic stillness. The next day he brought in the first part of the poem and read it to us, when we suggested a few verbal alterations' (p. 365). Textually, 'can it' = 'it can' in 1818.

line 2 – the River Tweed; Barton is comparing the gentle Suffolk landscape to the Romantic sublimity of Northumberland and the Scottish borders.

line 8 – 'wind's sigh' = 'winds' sigh' in 1818.

lines 17–19 – fern, furze and broom are hardy plants typical of Suffolk heathland.

lines 31–2 – perhaps an echo of Wordsworth's 'Tintern Abbey' (1798), where 'the heavy and the weary weight / Of all this unintelligible world, / Is lightened'.

line 38 – the notion of 'one beautiful whole', reflecting benevolent and harmonious design, is an assertion typical of eighteenth-century natural theology and the poetry inspired by it.

line 68 – 'its charms' = 'thy charms' in 1818.

line 73 – Barton does not offer details of the vale's destruction, but Arthur Young's *General View of the Agriculture of the County of Suffolk* (1797) gives a sense of radical changes to landscape urged at the time: 'there are in Suffolk many thousands of acres of poor, wet, cold, hungry pastures and neglected meadows [...] abounding with too few good plants to render their improvement easy without breaking up: all such should be pared and burnt [...] the dry rough sheep-walks covered with ling, furze, broom, &c. should also be broken up in the same manner' (pp. 163–4).

line 77 – the spoiler is a repeated figure of destruction in the Book of Jeremiah – e.g. 'And the spoiler shall come upon every city, and no city shall escape: the valley also shall perish, and the plain shall be destroyed' (Jer. 48:8).

line 83 – ling is a name given to heather.

line 84 – this line was not correctly indented until the 4th edition of *Poems* (1825).

line 86 – 'Nature or Art' suggests that it is indeed a process of agricultural improvement that has altered the valley.

lines 111–12 – the 'inward and holy revealings' gesture to the Quaker doctrine of the inward Light.

line 117 – an allusion to Jacob's ladder (Gen. 28:12).

line 118 – 'beheld with the patriarch's eye' = 'which rose on the patriarch's eye' in the 4th edition of *Poems* (1825).

line 136 – probably the Waspe sisters (see the note to line 1).

line 140 – figuring 'all space' as 'the temple of God' is an established idea – Pope had done it in his 'Universal Prayer' (published 1738), and it has Romantic and pantheistic overtones – but in the Quaker context likely alludes to an insistence on purely spiritual (not material) worship.

Verses, Supposed to be Written in a Burial-Ground Belonging to the Society of Friends

Published in *Poems* (1820).

These Spenserian verses allude directly to Thomas Gray's famous 'Elegy Written in a Country Churchyard' (1751), perhaps the most cited, parodied and imitated poem of the age. However, where Gray's poem had interrogated the value of ornate monuments and elaborate epitaphs, Barton's is shaped by the more radical Quaker custom of leaving graves entirely unmarked. Indeed, the poet wrote in 1846 that he only had an uncertain idea of where his wife, Lucy, was buried in Woodbridge (see *SPL*, p. 40). The poem defends Quaker practices of mourning and memorial, and more broadly hails the burial ground as a place which inscribes the identity and imagined community of the Society of Friends.

lines 1–2 – a 1717 epistle from the London Yearly Meeting had formalised the Quaker opposition to physical memorial: 'This meeting being informed, that friends in some places have gone into the vain custom of erecting monuments over the dead bodies of friends, by stones, inscriptions, &c. it is therefore the advice of this meeting, that all such monuments should be removed […] and that none be any where made or set up, near, or over, the dead bodies of friends or others, in friends' burying-places for time to come'. See *Extracts from the Minutes and Advices of the Yearly Meeting of Friends* (1802), p. 55.

lines 15–16 – a paraphrase of Luke 20:37-8, emphasising a resurrectionary God.

line 31 – 'the first fruits of the dead' is a motif from 1 Corinthians 15:20.

line 35 – 'shadowy vale'. Probably a citation from Beilby Porteus' Seatonian prize-winning poem *Death* (1759): 'I seek the shadowy vale / of DEATH'.

line 39 – from Gray's 'Elegy': 'many a holy text around she strews, / That teaches the rustic moralist to die'.

lines 43–7 – Barton refers to the parable of the rich man and Lazarus the beggar: although not named, the rich man is traditionally dubbed Dives. After dying and finding himself in hell, Dives pleads that Lazarus (a soul now in heaven) be sent back to urge his family to repent. The lesson is that the witness of scripture should be enough: 'if they hear not Moses and the prophets, neither will they be persuaded, though one rose from the dead' (Lk 16:31).

line 68 – 'had no business there'. An allusion to Laurence Sterne's *A Sentimental Journey through France and Italy* (1768). Sterne's hero, Yorick, weeps on the grave of Father Lorenzo when he pulls up nettles 'which had no business to grow there'.

line 69 – Thomas Clarkson notes the 'solemn silent pause' (II, p. 31) at the heart of the Quaker funeral in his *Portraiture of Quakerism* (1806).

line 95 – 'pomp of circumstance'. See Shakespeare, *Othello*, III.iii.359.

line 119 – 'it is sown a natural body; it is raised a spiritual body' (1 Cor. 15:44).

line 127 – the identity of the Friend is not recorded: Suffolk Quaker registers record a Mary Head, who died aged 34 on the 14 November 1819, which is the date appended to the poem (although she was not buried until the 19th).

line 135 – an allusion to the parable of the talents (see Matt. 25:14-30).

Leiston Abbey
Published in *Poems* (1820).

Originally founded in 1182, Leiston Abbey belonged to the Premonstratensian Order: the largely fourteenth-century ruins described by Barton lie around 15 miles north-east of Woodbridge. The opening of the poem oscillates between sublime and picturesque effects, contemplating the crumbling stonework as it lies open to the surrounding landscape. This is a typically Bartonian strain of 'fitful breezes' and 'clinging moss', but shifts into historical and theological reflection during a digressive middle section. Although Roman Catholic formalism is inimical to Quakerism, the Friends were known for their tolerant bent; as Barton avers in another poem on Leiston, 'The Abbot Turned Anchorite' (1824), 'I love to trace the latent good / Which dwells in widely diff'rent creeds'. The ruin, although a remnant of superstition, is also a monument to awe-inspiring piety and hence possesses lasting value both aesthetically and spiritually. The poem closes in a more intimate style, with memories of a coastal walk with a friend.

line 27 – 'Couldst never have given birth to music more sublime' = 'No music couldst have known more awfully sublime' in the 3rd edition of *Poems* (1822).

lines 73–5 – a reference to the dissolution of the monasteries: Leiston was suppressed in 1536.

line 86 – Marian prayer, crucifixes and prayer-beads were all evocative shorthand for Roman Catholic ceremonialism during the Romantic era.

line 102 – despite later persecution of Quakers, Barton is respectful of the broader history of English Protestantism: see, for instance, his reference to the Oxford martyrs in 'A Memorial of Mary Dyer'.

line 105 – originating in George Fox's critique of 'professors', Quakerism was extremely sceptical of clergy; 'priestcraft' also has a wider resonance in the period, implying the deliberate manipulation of believers by clerics.

line 123 – the quotation – one of Barton's favourites – is from Proverbs 4:18.

lines 134–5 – lines altered to 'Their influence would instruct him how to draw / His life upon the line of God's unerring Law' in the 2nd edition of *Poems* (1821).

line 154 – the identity of the 'young friend' who dwells near the Ouse (probably the River Great Ouse in eastern England) is unclear.

line 158 – 'ween', i.e. think.

line 184 – the ruins are situated two miles from the Suffolk coastline; the original site of the abbey was closer to the sea.

Stanzas, Addressed to Percy Bysshe Shelley
Published in *Poems* (1820).

Although one could hardly think of two more different contemporaries, Barton admired Shelley's work and this poem is a nuanced response to his atheism and his genius alike. Its first stanza deliberately inhabits the sparkling liquidity and ethereality of Shelley's own style, but only in order to cast such sublime flights as doomed transgressions. Soaring idealism is broken on the bleak earth evoked by this poem's key intertext – Shelley's 'Mont Blanc' (published 1817) – and Barton offers instead the divine ray: leading, arguably, to a subtly Quaker attestation of the inward Light. Ultimately, Barton bids Shelley's muse to descend from its heights to a more humble valley, and 'fancy's restless spell' is rejected.

Barton's own note reads: 'no one can more admire the genius of this highly-gifted man, than I do; but, in exact proportion to my admiration, is the regret I feel, for what I consider as the perversion of powers so rare, the misapplication of talents so splendid'.

line 1 – compare 'The fields, the lakes, the forests, and the streams' ('Mont Blanc').

lines 12–23 – these allusions to Genesis 3 (with particular emphasis on proper and improper knowledge) position Romantic sublimity as a repetition of the Fall.

line 22 – cf. 'the very spirit fails, / Driven like a homeless cloud from steep to steep' ('Mont Blanc').

lines 32–3 – compare the 'rude, bare, and high' summits in 'Mont Blanc'. More generally Barton's fourth stanza seems to track the themes and imagery of Shelley's third strophe.

line 36 – 'Thou hast a voice, great Mountain, to repeal / Large codes of fraud and woe' ('Mont Blanc').

line 37 – the quotation is adapted from the fourth epistle of Pope's 'Essay on Man' (1734), a definitive eighteenth-century statement of epistemological moderation.

line 44 – 'the path of the just is as the shining light, that shineth more and more unto the perfect day' (Prov. 4:18).

To Lydia

Published in *Poems* (1820).

As with much verse referring to Barton's closest circles, 'To Lydia' presents a frustratingly mysterious addressee. More certain than the identity of Lydia is the echoing of Book IV of Cowper's *The Task* (1785) and Coleridge's 'Frost at Midnight' (1798). These both set the fire-lit imagination of the poet against a silent nocturnal world and possess a meditative, conversational style. Coleridge's lyric also philosophises over his sleeping infant son Hartley; Barton cleaves instead to the sentimental conventions of contemporary lyrics to sleeping children (Lydia is probably a child) by depicting an innocent surrounded by gently protective presences.

lines 2–4 – intently observing the low-burning fire plays a central role in both the Cowper and Coleridge poems mentioned above. Although Barton does not go into detail, the 'faint and fitful noise' may be caused by the film on the grate mentioned conspicuously by both writers. Such a film was said to portend the arrival of a stranger.

Winter

Published in *Poems* (1820).

An extended sonnet in form, the frequently reprinted 'Winter' illustrates Barton's characteristic desire to register the beauty of all seasons. The echo of Keats' anti-pastoral line from his 1819 ode 'To Autumn' – 'thou hast thy music too' – in Barton's 'thou hast thy decorations too' is telling but coincidental given the dates involved.

line 12 – Golconda, near Hyderabad in India, was famous for the mining of diamonds, and became synonymous with them in the era.

A Dream
Published in *Poems* (1820).

One of the most positively received of Barton's poems, cited in reviews by both *Blackwood's Magazine* (December 1822) and the *British Review* (June 1820), this is another elegiac text for Lucy Jesup (1781–1808). Elevated into a metaphysical vision with broad Dantean echoes, it involves a particularly uncanny place for the poet-visionary who is the only figure to understand Lucy as a heavenly creature. It also expresses fascination with the boundary between dream and wakefulness: as in Keats's 'Ode to a Nightingale', and several other Romantic-era texts, the most vivid of dreams cannot simply be dismissed as unreal, but involve their own affective and epistemological value.

line 1 – 'not one of the living' = 'not of the living' in the 3rd edition of *Poems* (1822).
line 24 – a commonplace of dream theory at the time was that the will was suspended in dreaming, hence the chaotic and fanciful forms produced by the unregulated imagination: Barton denies his dream is like this.
line 41 – an idiosyncratic use of 'passionless' to mean unearthly and pure rather than bereft of feeling.
line 78 – a note in *SPL* (p. 288) suggests that the dream which inspired this poem was, in fact, the only time Barton ever wept in adulthood.

A Day in Autumn
Published as a quarto edition in 1820. This text is based on the revised version included in *Poetic Vigils* (1824).

'A Day in Autumn' is a 540 line piece cast in Barton's favoured Spenserian stanzas. Indebted to the eighteenth-century tradition of the long meditative poem, its conversational tone and 'occasional' quality recall William Cowper's *The Task* (1785). The poem ranges loosely, narrating a breakfast picnic, representing the Suffolk countryside, reflecting on the literary culture of the day, praising friendship and sociability, and concluding with an apostrophe to night. When first published alone as a quarto in late 1820, it received favourable reviews suggesting that Barton had added more power and imaginative force to his poetry. The *Monthly Review* was more negative, disappointed by the poem's placid theme, supposedly awkward versification and imitation of the Lake School (Southey, Wordsworth and others).

Due to the unusually extensive revisions made by Barton to this poem, I have adopted the later 1824 version as the reading text. The River Orwell extract begins on p. 72, roughly two thirds of the way through the poem.

[Invocation to Autumn]

lines 1–2 – the opening lines are cited from Robert Southey's *Madoc* (1805). The 1820 quarto is prefaced with a letter to Southey, whilst *Poetic Vigils* replaces this with a short poem addressed to him.
line 2 – 'and may Memory' = 'May its memory' in quarto.
line 6 – 'Most lovely season' = 'Delightfullest season' in quarto.
line 8 – 'sere', i.e. dry or withered.
line 17 – 'That its delight may be' = 'That its fix'd frame may be' in quarto.
line 23 – Flora is the Roman goddess of Spring (and flowers).

[The River Orwell]

line 5 – 'essay', i.e. attempt.
line 6 – 'To trace its tranquil pleasures' = 'To register its pleasures' in quarto.
line 9 – 'Those lovely scenes attir'd' = 'The lovely scenes spread round' in quarto.
line 12 – 'colours far above' = 'beauty far above' in quarto.
line 13 – 'Spring's gayest flowers, or turf of freshest green' = 'Spring's gayest hues, or brightest freshest green' in quarto.
line 17 – 'Assum'd more gorgeous beauty; others, gray' = 'Assum'd more gorgeous colours: others—grey,' in quarto.
line 22 – the river Orwell lies entirely within Suffolk, broadening into an estuary at Ipswich, and was a favoured poetic subject for Barton. Frederic Shoberl's *Suffolk; or, Original Delineations Topographical, Historical, and Descriptive* (1818) describes it as 'one of the finest salt-rivers in the kingdom [...] bordered on either side almost the whole way with gently rising hills, enriched with gentleman's seats, villages with their churches, woods, noble avenues, parks stocked with deer, extending to the water's edge; and, in a word, almost every object that can give variety to a land-scape' (p. 261).
lines 25–7 – these lines suggest that the location described by Barton is a few miles below Ipswich, at Downham Reach: the same observation of a land-locked appearance is made by others.
line 28 – 'And on its bosom' = 'Yet on its bosom' in quarto.
line 30 – 'A single vessel' = 'A puny vessel' in quarto.
line 35 – 'those soft shadowy lines' = 'even those shadowy lines' in quarto.
lines 37–8 – lines had read 'Orwell! lov'd stream; may I not fitly pause, / And pay the tribute thou from me must claim?' in quarto.
line 41 – 'thy cherish'd name' = 'thy humble name' in quarto.

line 51 – 'half hide' = 'half hid' in quarto.
line 52 – 'storm has seldom lower'd' = 'seldom has storm lower'd' in quarto.
line 54 – an echo of Wordsworth's 'harvest of a quiet eye' from 'A Poet's Epitaph' (1800).
lines 55–63 – this stanza self-consciously rejects the aesthetic effects of sublimity, such as obscurity, power and astonishment.
lines 55–8 – the quarto had read:

> The bolder charms of savage scenery may,
> Auspiciously beheld, *demand* delight,
> Enforcing admiration, and delay,
> Which thy weak charms more winningly *invite*:

line 60 – 'ere long' = 'yet soon' in quarto.
lines 68–90 – this digression on the consolations of memory, although a recurrent Bartonian theme, may be broadly influenced by Samuel Rogers' *The Pleasures of Memory* (1792), also composed in Spenserian stanzas.
line 68 – 'while thereon we trace' = 'while on it we trace' in quarto.
line 76 – 'By loveliness' = 'By witchery' in quarto.
line 77 – 'that life' = 'the life' in quarto.
line 84 – 'And on the soul far more than' = 'And on the mind such more than' in quarto.
line 88 – 'Alas! too rare' = 'But, all too rare' in quarto.
lines 90–1 – between these two stanzas, the quarto had inserted this stanza:

> But Orwell! I have wander'd far from thee;
> And now I turn, 'tis but to say "Adieu!"
> Much might I add, would I set fancy free,
> And give full scope to faithful memory too,
> Of many a beautiful and peaceful view
> Upon thy quiet banks; of feelings born,
> And nourish'd there; of early thoughts that grew
> Beside thy waters, in life's happy morn;
> And idle schemes of bliss, which reason now would scorn.

line 91 – 'Orwell, farewell! thy cherish'd image must' = 'Farewell! then, and for ever! though thou must' in quarto.
line 96 – 'perchance' = 'perhaps' in quarto.
lines 101–2 – lines had read 'The house of dinner;—round us gathers eve:— / And he who frames this legend must, at last,' in quarto.
line 107 – 'sweet thoughts' = 'fond thoughts' in quarto.

The Quaker Poet. Verses on Seeing Myself So Designated
Published in the 2nd edition of *Poems* (1821).

This is among Barton's most sustained reflections on the possibility of Quaker poetry. A little like for John Clare (1793–1864), for whom the russet nightingale evokes a peasant-songster, the poem highlights the drab plumage of the most literary of birds, and connects it to Quaker plainness. Further characteristic *litotes* underwrite an assertion of deep over superficial feeling, interlinked with an ethical rejection of fashion and the world. The poem closes with the universality of various divine gifts: in effect, reversing the anticipated objection by stating it is stranger that Quakers have *not* written in the past than that they have started to write now. In an echo of Barton's own developing aesthetic, a simple style 'abhorring affectation' is claimed as the particular province of the Friends.

line 1 – as early as November 1820, *The British Stage and Literary Cabinet* was referring to 'Bernard Barton, the Quaker Poet, whose talents have lately attracted much notice' (p. 314).

line 35 – the Quaker interdiction against 'pride and immodesty in apparel, and all vain and superfluous fashions of the world' is first formalised in an epistle of 1691. See *Extracts from the Minutes and Advices of the Yearly Meeting of Friends* (1802), p. 130.

lines 57–60 – from the 3rd edition (1822), these lines read

> And thus the muse her gifts assigns,
> With no sectarian spirit;
> For ALL the wreath of fame she twines
> Who fame and favour merit.

line 65 – 'from Lapland's snows, from Persia's bowers' is a rhetorical but resonant geography. Interest in Persian poetry had been sparked by the translations of Sir William Jones (1746–1794). Several Laplander songs circulated in the eighteenth century, deriving from the translations of Swedish writer Johannes Schefferus (1621–1679).

line 71 – 'peculiar' was a resonant word: the oft-cited New Testament verse that 'ye are a chosen generation, a royal priesthood, an holy nation, a peculiar people' (1 Pet. 2:9) was central to Quaker identity.

To L.E.L.
Published in the *Literary Gazette* 264 (9 February 1822).

Letitia Elizabeth Landon (1802–1838), better known as L.E.L., was one of the most scintillating writers of the Romantic age. Like Barton, her success and celebrity were in no small part driven by the culture of periodicals and literary annuals. These lines attest to the hypnotic effect of Landon's style – which in the rhetoric of 'gushing', 'falling' and 'witching' Barton captures relatively well – as well as her mysterious literary persona. Soon after this poem was published, Landon would become one of Barton's more unlikely letter-writing correspondents.

In the *Literary Gazette* – which published early Landon poems and this response – the following note was added: 'We have pleasure in saying that the sweet poems under this signature are by a lady, yet in her teens! The admiration with which they have been so generally read, could not delight their fair author more than it has those who in the *Literary Gazette* cherished her infant genius.—*Ed*.'

line 12 – Nourmahal is an Eastern concubine who enchants a sultan with singing and lute-playing in one of the tales of Thomas Moore's *Lalla Rookh* (1817). See Barton's 'A Guess at the Contents of Lalla Rookh' in this volume.

Napoleon [Stanzas 28–90]

Published in *Napoleon, and Other Poems* (1822). Reprinted in *Minor Poems, including Napoleon* (1824).

At 118 Spenserian stanzas, *Napoleon* is by far Barton's longest work, albeit a rather uneven one. Predictably shaped by Quakerism's radically anti-war stance, the poem is both an intervention in Britain's post-war discourse, as well as a more abstract moral reflection on the vanity of great men – the *Literary Speculum*'s (rather sceptical) review of June 1822 suggested it could have been as well entitled 'Julius Caesar', 'Alexander' or 'Tamerlane'. Across its rather rambling full length, *Napoleon* covers much ground. A meditative opening becomes a reflection on Napoleon's reputation, and then shifts – via a prayer-like blessing – to a long disquisition on the principles of Christian pacifism. Like many anti-war poems of the era, Barton takes aim at militaristic sentiment at home, before turning to the poem's centrepiece: a sentimentally drawn pastoral idyll which is only imagined in order to be violated by the horrors of war. The poem then circles back to Napoleon's legacy, and the image of his death on a 'surf-surrounded rock', concluding with a kind of pacifist sublime that draws moral and historical lessons from the ruined grandeur of Napoleonic ambition. Urging pacifism as imperative, the text closes with a pious affirmation of divine sovereignty.

By 1822, Barton was relatively well-known: letters from the time show he was disappointed at the limited critical notice given to *Napoleon* (see *LCBB*, pp. 53–4 and pp. 57–8). Nevertheless, its ambitiously ranging scope and descriptive passages received praise from periodicals such as the *British Review*, *Eclectic Review*, *Literary Chronicle* and *Kaleidoscope*, although Barton's radical anti-war stance and even-handed sympathy for Napoleon were considered problematic by some readers.

line 32 – see Lord Byron's 'Ode to Napoleon Buonaparte' (1814), written after his abdication: 'Nor till thy fall could mortals guess / Ambition's less than littleness'.

lines 46–63 – these two stanzas, along with XXXIX and XLI, were critiqued by the *Eclectic Review* of August 1822 as possessing 'a rhythm too closely bordering on prose' (p. 157).

lines 71–2 – the annunciation to the shepherds (Lk 2:14).

line 73 – the 'prince of peace' is a messianic title derived from Isaiah 9:6.

lines 86–7 – in Isaiah 28:6, the prophet promises 'strength to them that turn the battle to the gate'.

lines 105–6 – see John 18:36. John 18 recounts the arrest of Jesus.

lines 109–10 – see John 18:11.

line 115 – the quotation is from Romans 12:19, which itself refers to Deuteronomy 32:35.

lines 127–8 – 'for the wrath of man worketh not the righteousness of God' (Jas 1:20).

line 136 – 'This is an hard saying; who can hear it?' (Jn 6:60).

lines 172–3 – a citation of the Lord's prayer.

line 176 – Jan Hus (*c.* 1370–1415), a Czech theologian and reformer who inspired the pre-Protestant Bohemian Reformation.

line 177 – Jan Žižka (*c.* 1360–1424), a famous Hussite general.

line 178 – sciolists are those with superficial knowledge.

line 208 – a sizeable Napoleonic barracks was sited at Woodbridge, and through it Barton knew several military officers.

line 225 – 'By this shall all men know that ye are my disciples, if ye have love one to another' (Jn 13:35).

line 233 – 'in sorrow, not in anger' is an idiom derived from Shakespeare's *Hamlet* (I.ii.229).

lines 235–6 – a slight misquotation of the seventh part (1744) of Edward Young's *Night-Thoughts*: 'Die for thy Country?—thou romantic Fool! / Seize, seize the Plank thyself, and let her sink'.

line 256 – the vine and fig-tree image is from Micah 4:4.

line 260 – Moloch is a Canaanite deity recurrently associated with sacrifice.

line 263 – a quotation from Samuel Johnson's 'The Vanity of Human Wishes' (1749).

line 264 – a reference to temporary structures erected in celebration of victory as part of decorative 'illuminations'. Permanent triumphal arches were quickly planned, however: the most famous was Marble Arch, originally sited at Buckingham Palace and completed in 1833.

line 270 – a reference to Luke 23:34.

lines 280–97 – these two stanzas were detached from their context and included under the title 'River Scene' in *SPL*.

line 285 – 'second childhood', i.e. the frailty of old age.

lines 307–15 – this stanza was detached from its context and included under the title 'A Village Church' in *SPL*.

lines 339–42 – the *Literary Speculum*'s negative review of June 1822, relatively kind to the pastoral middle of the poem, accurately describes these lines as 'a couple of portraits, borrowed from the collection of Mr. Wordsworth' (p. 46).

line 378 – a paraphrase of Job 1:21.

line 412 – the Edenic nature of the scene is reinforced by this reference to the tree of knowledge (cf. Gen. 2:17).

line 461 – pioneers were specialist military units who made fortifications and entrenchments, and cleared the way for other units, often wearing a distinctive apron and armed with axes and other tools.

lines 511–13 – an allusion to Napoleon's marriage (initially by proxy) to Marie-Louise, Duchess of Parma (1791–1847). Occurring in 1810, it marked the decisive containment of a much reduced Habsburg Empire (the 'elder throne') by France.

line 514 – Barton's counter-factual 'ten years ago' accurately locates 1811–12 as the apogee of Napoleon's power, prior to his disastrous invasion of Russia. French domination of Europe at this time stretched from Spain's border with Portugal in the west to the Duchy of Warsaw and a cowed Austrian Empire in the east.

line 523 – Napoleon died on St. Helena, the remote South Atlantic island, on 5 May 1821.

lines 527–8 – imperial eagles were the standards of Napoleonic regiments; the star of honour was the insignia of the Legion of Honour, established in 1802. Barton had written satiric verses on both symbols in 1818's *Poems, by an Amateur*.

line 543 – see the third epistle of Alexander Pope's 'Essay on Man' (1733): 'all mankind's concern is charity: / All must be false that thwart this one great end; / And all of God, that bless mankind or mend'.

line 555 – British national debt was indeed staggeringly high at the end of the Napoleonic Wars.

line 556 – 'statists' are politicians in general but probably more specifically, as a separate sense recorded by the OED suggests, those politicians who sacrifice principle to expediency.

The Contrast

Published in *Napoleon, and Other Poems* (1822). Reprinted in *Minor Poems, including Napoleon* (1824).

The Quaker doctrine of the inward Light granted potential spiritual inspiration to every individual Friend, and a strong prophetic tradition runs through Quaker writing. 'The Contrast' is a strikingly hallucinatory vision-poem, juxtaposing two Biblical episodes – Babel and Pentecost – in order to imagine both the splintering and re-gathering of humanity under the divine will. The form, loosely modelled on the Spenserian stanza but with shorter line lengths, is unusual: Byron used it in 'And thou art dead, as young and fair' (1812).

line 1 – Shinar is the Biblical name for Babylonia.
line 14 – an unusually explicit Bartonian meditation on the imaginative process: the vision is positioned as neither untruth nor mere dream, but an act of historical empathy.
line 17 – 'compeers', i.e. companions.
line 22 – 'let us make us a name, lest we be scattered abroad' (Gen. 11:4).
line 27 – the Pyramids. Although several collapsed medieval spires had been taller, they were the tallest structures in the world during Barton's lifetime.
line 46 – 'And the Lord came down to see the city and the tower, which the children of men builded' (Gen. 11:5).
line 75 – Pentecost is a Jewish festival, but marked in the New Testament as the time when the Holy Spirit descended upon the Apostles and filled them with the gift of tongues. As a linguistic event, it is traditionally seen as the mirror image of Babel.
line 76 – 'they were all with one accord in one place' (Acts 2:1).
lines 82–3 – 'And suddenly there came a sound from heaven as of a rushing mighty wind' (Acts 2:2).
lines 87–90 – 'And there appeared unto them cloven tongues like as of fire, and it sat upon each of them. And they were all filled with the Holy Ghost, and began to speak with other tongues, as the Spirit gave them utterance' (Acts 2:3-4).
lines 93–4 – these are some of the many races mentioned in the New Testament narrative: Parthia, Elam and Media were territories in modern

Iran; Barton adds Moor where the Bible separately mentions dwellers of Egypt and Libya.

To a Robin
Published in *Napoleon, and Other Poems* (1822). Reprinted in *Minor Poems, including Napoleon* (1824).

A conversational and meditative poem that characteristically selects a modest subject, rejecting feted Romantic birds such as nightingale and skylark in favour of the humble robin. Concrete description gives way to stanzas of meandering moral reflection, freshened by the recollections of boyhood. As in the Wordsworthian ethics to which the poem directly alludes, childhood joys emerge with lasting consolatory power. Barton concludes by hailing the robin as a model for his own authorship: artless, overlooked but sweetly tender.

lines 61–2 – folk wisdom suggested that robins lay moss on dead bodies, and references to robins participating in funeral ceremonies are found in, for example, Shakespeare's *Cymbeline*.

line 71 – 'The child be father of the man'. A paraphrase of the famous line from William Wordsworth's 'My Heart Leaps Up', written in 1802 and published in 1807.

Verses on the Death of Bloomfield, the Suffolk Poet
Published in the *Suffolk Chronicle* (6 September 1823). Reprinted in *Poetic Vigils* (1824). See also textual details below.

As a writer steeped in his locality, Barton shares an intense relation to place with the era's so-called peasant poets. Like the Quaker, Robert Bloomfield (1766–1823) was from Eastern England, and this elegy claims him with particular focus as a Suffolk poet. It also involves a vindication of aesthetic values close to Barton's own: the poem defines his rusticity neither as an unsophisticated departure from classical norms nor merely as the quaint effect of rural dialect, but as a mode of authentic pastoral. Bloomfield died on 19 August 1823; the poem was thus evidently composed at speed. Charles Lamb discusses some 'Stanzas on Bloomfield' with Barton in a letter of 17 September 1823 (see *Lamb*, pp. 668–70), and his critique clearly influenced later revisions.

The poem was reprinted from the *Suffolk Chronicle* several times: see the *London Magazine* 8 (October 1823), the *Gentleman's Magazine* 93 (December 1823), and the locally printed anthology *Tributary Verses to the Memory of Robert Bloomfield* (1823). The first is identical to the original; however, revisions leading towards the final version found in *Poetic Vigils* can be tracked in the latter pair – I have not recorded every instance of this below to avoid overburdening the notes with minor detail. In *Poetic Vigils*, the title reads 'to the Memory of' rather than 'on the Death of'.

line 2 – echoing Sir Walter Scott's line 'Unwept, unhonoured, unsung' from the sixth canto of *The Lay of the Last Minstrel* (1805).

line 8 – *The Farmer's Boy* (1800) was Bloomfield's first and best-known poem.

line 14 – 'common wild', i.e. common land.

line 9 – 'Could' = 'Did' in *Poetic Vigils*. No other text includes this revision.

line 17 – 'The merry HORKEY's passing cup' = 'The HARVEST HOME's rejoicing cup' in *Poetic Vigils*. Lamb disliked the sound of the original reading, presumably prompting the revision. Both versions of the line refer to harvest festivals, with Horkey naming a traditional celebration in East Anglia which features in Bloomfield's work. *Tributary Verses* also includes this alteration.

line 19 – an allusion to Bloomfield's 'The Widow to her Hour-Glass' (1802).

lines 25–9 – lines referring to several poems from Bloomfield's *Wild Flowers, or, Pastoral and Local Poetry* (1806): 'To my Old Oak Table', 'Abner and the Widow Jones, a Familiar Ballad' and 'The Broken Crutch. A Tale' (Gilbert Meldrum is a protagonist in the latter).

lines 39–40 – these lines allude to places mentioned in the ambulatory poem 'Barnham Water', another piece from *Wild Flowers*.

line 42 – 'The memory of thy song, and thee' = 'Thy memory and its tablets be' in *Poetic Vigils*.

lines 47–8 – these are characters in two eponymous narrative poems from Bloomfield's *Rural Tales, Ballads, and Songs* (1802).

line 50 – the Doric, a Greek term, implied rusticity in dialect and simplicity in art. Lamb's letter describes this poem as itself 'sweet with Doric delicacy' (p. 668).

line 68 – 'Castaly' was a fountain of Mount Parnassus, sacred to the muses.

line 69 – 'Aganippe' was a well at the foot of Mount Helicon, also sacred to the muses.

line 85 – 'But 'tis not these' = 'It is not *these*' in *Poetic Vigils*.

lines 97–104 – this stanza is omitted in *Poetic Vigils*, and indeed all texts other than the identical *Suffolk* and *London* versions. Lamb critiques it in his letter, noting 'I shall omit in my own copy the one stanza which alludes to Lord B.[yron] I suppose. It spoils the sweetness and oneness of the feeling. Cannot we think of Burns, or Thomson, without sullying the thought with a reflection out of place upon Lord Rochester? These verses might have been inscribed upon a tomb […] satire does not look pretty upon a tomb-stone' (p. 669).

line 103 – a quotation from the fourth epistle of Pope's *Essay on Man* (1734): 'See Cromwell, damn'd to everlasting Fame!'
line 105 – 'Better, and nobler' = 'How wise, how noble' in *Poetic Vigils*.
line 112 – Theocritus, the third-century BCE Greek writer, was a seminal pastoral poet.
lines 116–18 – Bloomfield's final years were blighted by ill health and financial difficulties.
line 126 – 'lowliest' = 'humblest' in *Poetic Vigils*.
line 130 – 'thy Verse' = 'thy song' in *Poetic Vigils* (relocating the original line 42). No other text includes this revision.

Bishop Hubert

Published in the literary annual *Forget-Me-Not; a Christmas and New Year's Present for 1824* (1824). Reprinted in *Poetic Vigils* (1824).

A Wordsworthian piece in its dramatization of a chastening dialogue between adult presumption and the holy wisdom of children. The encounter described is a legend usually associated with the life of Saint Augustine of Hippo, notably in Jacobus de Voragine's hagiographical anthology, *Legenda Aurea*. Bishop Hubert is likely Hubert Walter (*c.* 1160–1205), who has a connection with the founding of Leiston Abbey: I have found no written evidence linking the tale with him instead of Augustine, although it may have circulated orally. In its first printed context – Frederic Shoberl's *Forget-Me-Not* literary annual – the poem was accompanied by an engraving by J. S. Agar after a drawing by the German artist Ludwig Rullman (1765–1822).

line 5 – 'lonely thought' = 'earnest thought' in *Poetic Vigils*.
line 15 – Hubert Walter accompanied Richard I, as Archbishop of Canterbury, on the Third Crusade, which would explain this evocation of a desert landscape.
line 56 – 'On his pilgrimage' = 'While a Pilgrim here' in *Poetic Vigils*.

Pity for Poor Little Sweeps

Published in *Poetic Vigils* (1824).

Echoing the title of William Cowper's 'Pity for Poor Africans' (1788), this text is a sharp but characteristically emotive interrogation of the working conditions of chimney sweeps. Like abolition, the campaign to reform this particularly brutal form of child labour was driven by the religious sentiment of Evangelical and Quaker Christianity. Barton also contributed poems to the 1824 anthology *The Chimney-Sweeper's Friend, and Climbing Boy's Album*, but this text is identified as earlier: the preface to *Poetic Vigils* states that 'at the time of writing [Pity for Poor Little Sweeps], the Author had not seen a line of Poetry on the subject' (p. vii). The *Chimney Sweepers Act* of 1834 legislated against the worst elements of the trade, although further parliamentary acts were introduced throughout the Victorian period in order to extend and enforce regulation.

line 30 – see Shakespeare's *Macbeth*: 'Methought I heard a voice cry, "Sleep no more, / Macbeth does murder Sleep"' (II.ii.33–4).

lines 61–72 – these two stanzas describing the terrible working conditions, broken bodies and cruel masters of sweeps conform readily to contemporary accounts, such as Samuel Roberts' 'On the Employment of Climbing Boys', excerpted in *The Chimney-Sweeper's Friend*:

> The initiating of these tender infants in their horrid, difficult, and laborious calling, is *invariably* accompanied with more or less of laceration; their backs, their knees, their elbows, their shoulders, and their toes, are always rendered sore; and very often they are, when in this state of suffering, compelled, in the severest weather, to wander at the most unseasonable hours through frost and snow, and climb the rough and rugged flues till their wounds frequently ulcerate and become incurable. Their eyes are generally rendered inflamed, and their heads swoln. They are scantily clothed, poorly fed, ill lodged and exposed to the most unrestrained capricious cruelty of one of the most ignorant, violent, and depraved classes of human beings in this or perhaps any other civilised kingdom. (pp. 12–13)

A Memorial of John Woolman; a Minister of the Gospel, Among the Quakers

Published in *Poetic Vigils* (1824).

John Woolman (1720–1772) was a New Jersey Quaker minister and preacher whose tireless campaigning in favour of abolition was important in defining an anti-slavery position amongst the Society of Friends in America. Despite his political engagement, his spirituality was quietist, and his beautifully reflective journal became an iconic work of Quaker literature – and one of Barton's most cherished books. The poem hails Woolman as a contemporary apostle: not through any outward miraculous works but through the force of inner faith. Charles Lamb objected to the lilting, anapaestic rhythms of this piece, preferring the stately iambic 'A Memorial of James Nayler' (see *Lamb*, p. 692).

line 8 – the 'chaplet of bay' was a Roman symbol of military victory.

line 14 – myrtle was sacred to Venus, and frequently used as a symbol for poetry.

line 36 – the Lion of Judah unseals the apocalyptic book in Revelation 5:5. Woolman's *Journal* begins with a childhood memory of reading the Book of Revelation, and it is an important and recurrent intertext for Barton's poem.

line 39 – 'lavation', i.e. washing. A common metaphor for Christ's salvationary grace.

lines 45–8 – broadly, this passage echoes the song sung to the Lamb in Revelation 5:9–14.

line 45 – the triple repetition of holy is marked in Revelation 4:8, as well as Isaiah 6:3.

line 62 – 'primitive age' refers to the earliest, apostolic days of Christianity. Whether miracles had now ceased was a common theological debate of the time.

A Memorial of James Nayler, the Reproach and Glory of Quakerism

Printed in *Poetic Vigils* (1824).

James Nayler (1618–1660), as the title of this poem indicates, was a deeply controversial figure. A charismatic and radical preacher with a messianic streak, he clashed with both George Fox and the leading Quakers in London. This tension came to a head in 1656, when he rode into Bristol in imitation of Christ entering Jerusalem. Disowned by the Friends, he was then tried and brutally punished by the religious authorities, flogged, branded and his tongue bored. He was later released from prison and reconciled with Fox. Barton's poem aligns with the attitude of many later Quakers, who condemned Nayler's spiritual fall but were drawn by his repentance.

Barton's own explanatory note to the poem reads: 'in the fifth, sixth, seventh, and eighth stanzas of this Poem, I have attempted to embody in verse some of Nayler's expressions on his death-bed, as given in Sewell's History. That I have done very inadequate justice to the original, I cheerfully concede; but the difficulty of success can be only appreciated by those who feel the beauty of that original; and they, I am sure, would forgive even a failure more complete, for the sake of the feelings which led to the attempt.—There is a simple sublimity, a spiritual unction, if I may so term it, in the style of Nayler's age, which a modern poetical paraphrase can scarcely hope to convey'.

lines 13–14 – the legacy of Nayler had indeed been much contested, and his works much censored. See Erin Bell, 'Eighteenth-Century Quakerism and the Rehabilitation of James Nayler, Seventeenth-Century Radical', *Journal of Ecclesiastical History* 59.3 (2008), pp. 426–46.

lines 41–80 – as Barton's note indicates, these lines are adapted from the death-bed testimony recorded in William Sewel's *History of the Rise, Increase, and Progress of the Christian People Called Quakers* (English translation, 1722). The passage is as follows:

> There is a Spirit which I feel, that delights to do no Evil, nor to revenge any Wrong, but delights to endure all Things, in hope to enjoy its own in the End: Its Hope is to out-live all Wrath and Contention, and to weary out all Exaltation and Cruelty, or whatever is of a Nature contrary to itself. It sees to the End of all Temptations: As it bears no Evil in itself, so it conceives none in Thoughts to any other: If it be betray'd it bears it, for its Ground and Spring is the Mercies and Forgiveness of God: Its Crown is Meekness, its Life is everlasting Love unfeigned, and takes its Kingdom with Entreaty, and not with Contention, and keeps it by Lowliness of Mind: In God alone it can rejoice, though none else regard it, or can own its Life: It's conceived in Sorrow, and brought forth without any to pity it; nor doth it murmur at Grief and Oppression: It never rejoiceth but thro' Sufferings; for with the World's Joy it is murder'd: I found it alone, and being forsaken; I have Fellowship therein with them who lived in Dens, and desolate Places in the Earth, who through Death obtain'd this Resurrection and eternal holy Life. *J.N.* (p. 159)

line 97 – 'watch unto prayer' (1 Pet. 4:7).

line 112 – enthusiasm denotes emotionally intense and visionary religious experience, usually used pejoratively and most frequently applied to Methodism in Barton's own time.

A Memorial of Mary Dyer, One of the Early Worthies and Martyrs in the Society of Quakers

Published in *Poetic Vigils* (1824).

Mary Dyer (d. 1660) emigrated to Massachusetts and, sensationally, was reported to have given birth to a monstrous stillborn child. Travelling back to England in the early 1650s, she became a Quaker. She was eventually executed in Boston. Barton's poem alludes to the persecution of Anglicans in its praise of Dyer, attesting to the general power of martyrdom narratives over both childhood and adult imagination.

line 6 – 'Latimer, and his compeers' are Hugh Latimer, Nicholas Ridley and Thomas Cranmer, the so-called Oxford martyrs, burnt in 1555–56 for their Protestant beliefs.

Verses on the Approach of Spring, Addressed to my Little Play-Fellow
Published in *Poetic Vigils* (1824).

A sentimental but oft-reprinted vernal lyric. Its characteristically extensive use of feminine rhymes, and the striking repetitions between fourth and fifth lines in each stanza, give it an appositely sprightly and childish air. Nevertheless, the poem's tenderness lies as much in Barton's rejection of melancholy in order to play with the child, as it does in the idealised charm of the 'little play-fellow'. The child could well be Emma Knight (b. 1819), nicknamed 'Puck', the daughter of Barton's friend Anne Knight, with whom Barton lodged in the early 1820s. The *New Suffolk Garland* (1866) identifies Emma as the addressee of a similar poem from the time, 'A Winter Evening Ditty', and notes 'this dear child he petted almost as much as his own' (p. 362).

line 6 – the primrose was typically marked as one of the first flowers of spring.

Bealings House
Published in *Poetic Vigils* (1824).

Barton's connection with the tiny village of Great Bealings, a few miles west of Woodbridge, was largely through the Moor family (see the sonnets to Charlotte M— in this volume). Bealings House was a fine house occupied by Major Edward Moor in his retirement. He authored *Bealings Bells* (1841) after supposedly witnessing ghostly ringing in the mansion; Barton contributed introductory verses. This sonnet is rooted in more conventional themes: an elegant celebration of English gardens, domesticity and 'social converse'.

line 1 – Bealings house, which still stands and is now listed, is a Georgian mansion with a rear courtyard and considerable grounds.
lines 3–4 – the seamless refinement of nature by art was a commonplace of Romantic-era gardening practices; the octet repeatedly evoke values of the picturesque, such as sweeping and undulating lines, and visual variation.

To a Butterfly. Translated from the French
Published in *Minor Poems, including Napoleon* (1824).

The source text is Alphonse de Lamartine's 'Le Papillon', from his *Nouvelles Méditations Poétiques* (1823), a collection which perhaps not coincidentally included a meditation on the death of Napoleon. The original's 10 alexandrines are expanded into 6 quatrains, with feminine rhymes marking the second and fourth lines of each. Lamartine (1790–1869) was known as a bold versifier who drew from English models: his devotional bent and reflective intensity suited Barton well. For the British reception of Lamartine, see 'Living French Poets.—No. II.', *New Monthly Magazine* 6, no. 85 (1823), pp. 467–73, and 'French Poetry', *Edinburgh Review* 37, no. 74 (November 1822), pp. 407–32.

On a Portrait of Beatrice Cenci

Published in *Minor Poems, including Napoleon* (1824).

As indicated by Barton, this painting was in the collection of John FitzGerald (1775–1852), father of the writer Edward. It would have been a copy (untraced) of Guido Reni's famous and much reproduced *Portrait of Beatrice Cenci* (1599) which hangs in the Palazzo Barberini in Rome. As with many writers who saw the original in Italy, from Percy Bysshe Shelley to Charles Dickens, the poet is mesmerised by the ethereal glance of the young girl clad in white, cast over her shoulder at the viewer. Cenci was a real sixteenth-century personage who murdered her father, reputedly after incestuous rape. Shelley's play *The Cenci* (1819) is the most famous Romantic-era treatment.

On the Death of Samuel Alexander, of Needham-Market

Published in the 4th edition of *Poems* (1825).

The empty seat in the meeting house, described in the seventh stanza, is the pathos-laden centrepiece of this fulsome elegy. *Poetic Vigils* had included several memorials to past Quaker worthies; here Barton memorialises a contemporary with whom the poet had personal connections. The Alexanders were Ipswich bankers who intermarried with several major Quaker families (e.g. the Tukes, the Gurneys), and Barton worked in Alexander's Bank in Woodbridge for most of his life. Samuel Alexander (1749–1824) had stepped back from business early, however, and became a respected Quaker minister.

The epigraph is taken from Congregationalist poet Josiah Conder's 'To the Memory of Edward Powell', collected in *The Star in the East; with Other Poems* (1824).

line 41 – Alexander's death notice in the *Gentleman's Magazine* for December 1824 reports that 'his charity for those who differed from him in sentiment was well worthy of imitation; and by the poor, to whom he was a liberal benefactor, his loss will be felt most sensibly' (p. 566). His will bequeathed an annuity to support widows in the almshouses at Needham Market.

line 56 – 'silent eloquence' alludes to the ideals of Quaker devotion (see 'On Silent Worship'). An account of Alexander notes that 'he was cautious not to move in the exercise of his gift as a minister, without a clear apprehension of required duty […] in our meetings for discipline, it was instructively obvious to his brethren, by his reverent deportment, that he was often concerned to wait before the Lord for the arising of his power'. See Josiah Forster, *Piety Promoted; in Brief Biographical Memorials, of some of the Religious Society of Friends. The Eleventh Part* (1829), p. 333.

lines 71–2 – the balance of 'inward guide' and 'God's written law' suggests that Alexander, like Barton himself, reconciled the traditional Quaker notion of the inward Light with the authority of scripture.

Bow Hill

Published in the 4th edition of *Poems* (1825).

A nature lyric shadowed by ancient monuments, written in so-called fourteener couplets. The long seven-stress heptameters have internal rhymes and an implicit caesura on the eighth syllable, effectively meaning every pair of lines can be read as a quatrain in common metre (8.6.8.6). 'Bow Hill' is also a nocturne: Barton repeatedly set poems as night-scenes, and described the silent and ethereal beauty of moonlit landscapes.

Barton's own explanatory note to the poem reads: 'Bow Hill is an eminence near Chichester. For an interesting account of it, as well as for a very pleasing description of the beautiful and extensive prospect from its summit, the author refers his readers to the opening chapter of [Barton's sister] Maria Hack's "English Stories."'

lines 10–12 – the interaction between the poet's subjectivity and the objectivity of landscape was a Romantic commonplace, most famously expressed in Wordsworth's theory that the imagination half-created the perceptual world.

line 16 – in *Poems*, Barton juxtaposed 'Bow Hill' with a sonnet to the vale at Kingley Bottom.

line 18 – the tombs are Bronze-Age barrows. However, local folklore suggested that they were the graves of Viking raiders. James Dallaway's *History of the Western Division of the County of Sussex* (1815) records that 'it is conjectured, that this is the site of that dreadful slaughter of the marauding Danes by the men of Chichester, of which the chroniclers speak, as having happened about the year 900. Their sea-kings, or piratical chiefs, were then probably slain, and interred in the barrows on the summit' (I, p. 111).

line 26 – the vale was renowned for its ancient yew-tree woodland, which still stands today.

A Grandsire's Tale

Published in the literary annual *The Literary Souvenir; or, Cabinet of Poetry and Romance* (1826). Reprinted in *A Widow's Tale, and Other Poems* (1827).

Along with the pastoral mid-section of *Napoleon*, this is one of Barton's most obvious attempts to mimic the narrative aspect of Wordsworth, although its unapologetically direct piousness also recalls fellow *Literary Souvenir* contributor, Felicia Hemans (1793–1835). 'A Grandsire's Tale' was first published in Alaric Watts' annual, before becoming the longest piece (aside from the title poem) in *A Widow's Tale*. Notable are its tale-telling frame, the sentimentalised deathbed as a site of transcendence (again Hemansesque) and the otherworldly figuring of the young girl.

lines 51–2 – in an undated letter of 1827, Charles Lamb described this as an 'exquisite simile'; he also praised the eleventh stanza as 'equally good' (*Lamb*, p. 775).
line 62 – 'impervious to the noontide ray' = 'imperious to the moontide ray' in *A Widow's Tale*. The latter reading is odd and may be a printer's error.
line 77 – 'Though 'rightly fancy had its close portrayed' = 'Though fancy had too well its close pourtray'd' in *A Widow's Tale*.
line 87 – 'glories bright'ning' = 'radiance brightening' in *A Widow's Tale*.
line 102 – 'morning meal' = 'matin meal' in *A Widow's Tale*.

Stanzas, Composed During a Tempest

Published in the literary annual *Friendship's Offering* (1826). Reprinted in *A Widow's Tale, and Other Poems* (1827).

A dynamic and richly imagined storm lyric, with a concluding theological sentiment based around the sublime. Barton contributed several poems to the long-running annual *Friendship's Offering* in the 1820s. The version of 'Stanzas' in *A Widow's Tale* is typographically different and less fragmentary, using dashes far more sparingly.

line 2 – 'shewing' = 'showing' in *A Widow's Tale*.
line 6 – 'Soft moonlight on the ocean;—' = 'Fair—moonlight on the ocean,' in *A Widow's Tale*.

A Prophet's Old Age

Published in *Devotional Verses* (1826).

This is the first of seven poems I have selected from *Devotional Verses*, Barton's most unified poetic volume, which sought to illustrate spiritual and scriptural truth with a plain and spare verse style (see the extract from Barton's preface in the contextual material).

As a poet who came to verse relatively late and when widowed, Barton frequently wrote from a position of self-conscious and often elegiac ageing: in 'A Prophet's Old Age', he meditates on the ageing of the patriarchs. Mirroring a pattern found across *Devotional Verses*, the Biblical narrative is supplemented with a moral reflection: while Moses bears the mark of a directly bestowed divine gift, his long life is also an allegorical sign for the promise of resurrection.

line 5 – a 'green old age' was proverbial, and used in poetry by Alexander Pope, Oliver Goldsmith and others.
line 12 – this image was used, in a similar context, in Barton's poem to the Quaker Elizabeth Fry, 'To E.F.'

Ruth's Love
Published in *Devotional Verses* (1826).

The female characters of scripture would receive their most sophisticated Romantic-era treatment in Felicia Hemans' 1834 sonnet sequence of that name; while *Devotional Verses* touched only lightly on Biblical women, this poem about Ruth illustrates that Barton's domestic strain suited the subject well. In scripture, Ruth travels with Naomi from Moab to Bethlehem, whilst Orpah stays in her own homeland.

line 8 – Ruth and Orpah are actually Naomi's daughters-in-law.
lines 27–8 – David is the great grandson of Ruth; Ruth is one of the few women noted in Jesus' genealogy (see Matt. 1:5).

The Vanity of Human Knowledge
Published in *Devotional Verses* (1826).

Although this poem possesses no direct echoes of Samuel Johnson's 'The Vanity of Human Wishes' (1749), Barton's Quaker piety accords relatively well with an eighteenth-century ethic of setting boundaries to humanity's reach and ambition, also seen in Pope's 'Essay on Man' (1733–34). His use of short trimeter couplets mingled with slightly longer tail rhymes give the verse a vivid, compressed clarity which is indeed more akin to these literary forbears than the Book of Job, which provides the epigraph.

line 14 – Cistus flowers, or rock roses, were a symbol of fragility and transience.

A Soliloquy
Published in *Devotional Verses* (1826).

The germ of *Devotional Verses* was a recommendation in 1822 by his publishers – Baldwin, Cradock and Joy – to attempt some 'Essays in Devotional Poetry' (see the letter to Robert Southey in *LCBB*, p. 59). Not only was the genesis of the project lengthy, it was relatively painstaking: the memoir penned by Edward FitzGerald notes that the volume represented an exception to Barton's usually rapid processes of authorship (see *SPL*, p. xvi). This drawn out labour explains 'A Soliloquy', which is preceded by the following note: 'after the composition of the preceding Verses, the further progress of this little volume had been, for some time, suspended; indeed its author had for a little while felt little ability or inclination to proceed in it, its completion appearing to him almost a hopeless contingency. A candid statement of this circumstance may perhaps explain, if not justify the insertion of the following'. In this light, we can see the poem as a reflection on different sides – secular and religious – to Barton's poetic vocation in the mid-1820s, a theme also recurrent in 1824's *Poetic Vigils*.

line 38 – 'for we walk by faith, not by sight' (2 Cor. 5:7).
lines 43–48 – an allusion to Ezekiel 37:1–10, and a relatively rare assertion of a prophetic aspect to Barton's usually modest authorship.

A Reflection
Published in *Devotional Verses* (1826).

As in 'The Contrast', literature is positioned in 'A Reflection' as an act of historical imagination and translation. The poem is also a self-conscious pivot within the structure of *Devotional Verses*, as Barton moves from Hebraic figures and episodes to the world of the New Testament, and engages the theological transformation this implies. Despite the scriptural grandeur of the places Barton surveys from his 'ideal eminence', the tone is conversational and the landscape characteristically illumined with gentle beauty.

line 6 – a strong assertion of a theology of grace. In the nineteenth century, British Quakerism was being altered and indeed split by Evangelical currents, which introduced new understandings of grace, sin and atonement. Barton eschewed doctrinal disputes, but averred a traditional Quaker belief in the universality of grace.
line 17 – Barton's evocation of Bethlehem in this stanza includes the site of Jesus' crucifixion (Calvary) and ascent to heaven (the Mount of Olives).

lines 21–22 – in Exodus 24:16, Mount Sinai is obscured by cloud as Moses receives the Ten Commandments.

line 32 – the music of the spheres is a classical philosophical concept expressing celestial harmony; Barton's image allows divine music to enact an apocalypse of the physical heavens.

Tears
Published in *Devotional Verses* (1826).

Barton's poem combines a Romantic fascination with tears as a kind of language (inherited and modified from the eighteenth-century discourse of sensibility) with a Christian lachrymatory tradition that runs from the Psalms to Renaissance religious lyric. As often in *Devotional Verses*, secular feelings are evoked only to be redoubled in strength through a religious context.

line 26 – Lazarus of Bethany; in the Gospel of John, Jesus is moved to weeping by the mourning of the people before he proceeds to the tomb to raise Lazarus from the dead.

Walking in the Light
Published in *Devotional Verses* (1826).

Written in common metre (8.6.8.6), this poem of Barton's became a very popular hymn, usually sung to 'Manoah'. Spiritually optimistic, its Quaker origins can be traced in the rhetorical celebration of Christ as a principle of light.

line 12 – 'God is light, and in him is no darkness at all' (1 Jn 1:5).
line 16 – 'the path of the just is as the shining light, that shineth more and more unto the perfect day' (Prov. 4:18).

Which Things Are a Shadow
Published in the literary annual *Friendship's Offering* (1827). Reprinted in *A Widow's Tale, and Other Poems* (1827).

By the end of the 1820s, Barton was one of the leading devotional poets of the era. In no small part, this was down to lucid and meditative verse like this poem, described by the *Literary Magnet* in 1827 as 'a gem of the first water' (III, p. 248). Read alongside a contemporary example of his nature verse – such as 'Summer Musings' – the harmonious overlap between Barton's religious and landscape modes is evident. The title is adapted from Colossians 2:17.

line 8 – 'the glorious West' = 'the glowing west' in *A Widow's Tale*.
lines 17–22 – the imagery here is taken from John the Baptist's preaching: see Matthew 3:10 and Luke 3:9.
line 24 – perhaps an echo of Milton's *Paradise Lost*: 'disciplined / From shadowy types to truth' (XII.302–3).
line 28 – 'above the sky' = 'beyond the sky!' in *A Widow's Tale*.

Prefatory Sonnet [to *A Widow's Tale, and Other Poems*]
Published in *A Widow's Tale, and Other Poems* (1827).

The guttering of a lamp as darkness falls may be a highly stylised (and highly Romantic) image of poetic creativity, but Barton's writing practices – at least when maintained at the level of intensity apparent in the 1810s and 1820s – were of necessity nocturnal. He describes working after midnight to various correspondents, including fellow poets Robert Southey and Thomas Wilkinson, and it is clear that combining literary and professional life did exhaust him at times. This sonnet, however, transfigures such exhaustion into a gesture towards posterity.

Caractacus
Published in *A Widow's Tale, and Other Poems* (1827).

Caractacus was a British chieftain notorious for resisting Roman rule and, in the account given by Tacitus, for speaking with noble eloquence when taken to Rome as a captive. As an icon of British liberty, he models a strain of patriotic vigour and broadly Whig politics in Barton's work: indeed, the most famous literary depiction of Caractacus was a tragedy of 1759 by the Whig writer, William Mason. The poem uses common metre (alternating tetrameters and trimeters) modified with stanza-ending couplets: an appropriately economical and dynamic form for the oratorical scene.

line 32 – Claudius, Roman emperor from 41–54 CE.
lines 49–52 – 'If to the nobility of birth [...] I had united the virtues of moderation, Rome had beheld me, not in captivity, but a royal visitor, and a friend'. See *The Works of Cornelius Tacitus*, trans. Arthur Murphy (1793), II, p. 75.
lines 67–72 – 'Had I acted otherwise, where, on your part, had been the glory of conquest, and where, on mine, the honour of a brave resistance?' (Murphy, p. 75).
lines 73–8 – 'I am now in your power: if you are bent on vengeance, execute your purpose; the bloody scene will soon be over, and the name of

Caractacus will sink into oblivion. Preserve my life, and I shall be, to late posterity, a monument of Roman clemency' (Murphy, p. 75).

lines 83–4 – *The Juvenile Speaker*, an elocutionary anthology published in 1829, renders the final couplet as 'The conqueror was *their* captive then; / —He bade the slave be free again'. This alteration stands in later nineteenth-century reprints. Given a review of *A Widow's Tale* in the *Literary Chronicle* of 10 March 1827 had singled out the final stanza as a blot, and the editor of *The Juvenile Speaker* states in its preface that he obtained permissions from living authors, it is probable that this is Barton's own revision.

Sonnet; To a Grandmother
Published in *A Widow's Tale, and Other Poems* (1827).

Described by Charles Lamb as a 'downright good sonnet' (*Lamb*, p. 775) in an undated letter of 1827, this lyric sets off in playful refutation of its slightly misquoted epigraph, taken from James Macpherson's Ossianic poem 'Carthon', dated 1761/2. (The works of Ossian were purportedly ancient Scottish poetry, incredibly popular but always suspected as being forgeries). The octet rises to gentle and conventional piety; the sestet is more vivid in its sharply observed celebration of domesticity.

Stanzas, Written for a Blank Leaf in Sewell's History of the Quakers
Published in *A Widow's Tale, and Other Poems* (1827).

The posthumous auction catalogue of Barton's possessions lists a 1774 edition of William Sewel's *History of the Quakers*, a text also cited in 'A Memorial of James Nayler'. One of several 'blank leaf' poems in Barton's oeuvre, the 'Stanzas' reflect on the progress of Quakerism: from a persecuted sect born in the violent crucible of seventeenth-century religious politics to the calm prosperity of its existence in the 1800s. Like other Romantic-era Dissenters looking back on denominational histories – the Unitarian Anna Letitia Barbauld (1743–1825) would be a good example – Barton mixes appreciation for present stability with a touch of nostalgia for the purity of spiritual origins. Couched in typically Bartonian pastoral strains, the image of the rising sun frames this historical understanding allegorically.

line 4 – an understanding of persecution is central to all of Barton's poems on Quaker history.

line 8 – 'Presbytery' and 'Church' refer to the religious landscape of the republican Commonwealth (1649–60) and restored monarchy (1660 onward) respectively. Traditionally, the Church of England has been organised through episcopacy – a hierarchical system of bishops. Presbyterian church government, by contrast, is through councils of elders, and while Presbyterians were not the only faction influencing events at the time, the episcopacy had been abolished by the Long Parliament in 1646. Barton's point, of course, is that the shifting balance of power changed little for the Quakers, who were oppressed regardless.

line 9 – Charles II (reigned 1660–85) and James II (reigned 1685–88) were both Stuart monarchs; the latter effectively brought in an era of formal toleration for the Quakers.

line 10 – Oliver Cromwell, Lord Protector between 1653 and 1658.

line 12 – 'off-scow'ring', i.e. that which is scoured off, the rejected or outcast. The word is used scripturally in Lamentations 3:45 and 1 Corinthians 4:13.

lines 41–3 – 'unto you that fear my name shall the Sun of righteousness arise with healing in his wings' (Mal. 4:2).

line 50 – Ecclesiastes 12:5 prophesises that 'the grasshopper shall be a burden'.

line 65 – 'my peace I give unto you: not as the world giveth' (Jn 14:27).

The Vale of Tears
Concluding Verses, to a Child Seven Years Old

Published in *A Widow's Tale, and Other Poems* (1827).

Self-consciously juxtaposed, these two poems follow each other as an ordered pair to close Barton's 1827 volume, *A Widow's Tale*. The allegorical darkening of a vernal landscape traced in 'The Vale of Tears' is reversed in 'Concluding Verses', which recuperate the contrast between spring and later seasons by mapping it on to Barton's consoling friendship with a young child. Several Wordsworthian tropes, such as the radiance of infancy and the child as philosopher, echo through the latter piece. The identity of the child is unknown: it could be Emma Knight (see 'Verses on the Approach of Spring') who turned seven in July 1826.

'Vale', line 30 – perhaps an echo of Milton's famous closing lines from *Paradise Lost*: 'They hand in hand with wandering steps and slow, / Through Eden took their solitary way' (XII.648–9).

'Vale', line 32 – 'the grasshopper shall be a burden' (Eccles. 12:5).

'Vale', lines 33–4 – 'Or ever the silver cord be loosed, or the golden bowl be broken, or the pitcher be broken at the fountain, or the wheel broken at the cistern' (Eccles. 12:6).

'Concluding', lines 1–2 – i.e. Barton's 'Prefatory Sonnet' to the collection (also included in this volume), and 'The Vale of Tears' respectively.

'**Concluding', line 5** – 'we were troubled on every side; without were fightings, within were fears' (2 Cor. 7:5).
'**Concluding', line 21** – a quotation from John Scott's 'Elegy. Written at Amwell' (1768); Scott (1731–1783) was the best-known Quaker poet prior to Barton.
'**Concluding', line 45** – 'ruth', i.e. pity.
'**Concluding', lines 55–7** – 'Then were there brought unto him little children, that he should put his hands on them, and pray: and the disciples rebuked them. But Jesus said, Suffer little children, and forbid them not, to come unto me: for of such is the kingdom of heaven' (Matt. 19:13–14).

Sonnet to William and Mary Howitt
Sonnet to the Same

Published in *A New Year's Eve, and Other Poems* (1828).

William and Mary Howitt (1792–1879 and 1799–1888) were probably the most prominent literary Quakers of the nineteenth century after Barton, and Barton recommended them himself to the literary editor William Jerdan (see *LCBB*, pp. 68–70). His first sonnet to William and Mary luxuriates in the pastoral tropes of the couple's collection *The Forest Minstrel* (1823); the second, winter-tinged, urges other styles: sentimental, domestic, conversational, historical and legendary. Coincidentally, the Howitts' next publication – *The Desolation of Eyam* (1827), which was dedicated to Barton – does indeed adopt a broader range of tones, including its title poem's account of a seventeenth-century plague. Barton responded to the dedication with some grateful and friendly lines penned for the *Literary Magnet* of July 1827.

Sonnet to W&MH, line 10 – the Howitts were Nottingham poets and the folklore around Robin Hood does feature in their work.
Sonnet to W&MH, line 14 – 'your minstrel lay', a direct allusion to *The Forest Minstrel*.
Sonnet to the Same, line 6 – 'your forest fountain', another allusion to *The Forest Minstrel*.

The Daughter of Herodias

Published in *A New Year's Eve, and Other Poems* (1828). See also textual details below.

A Biblical lyric closely modelled on the longer of two gospel accounts of the princess Salome, that given in Mark. As the critic Adriana Cracuin points out in *Fatal Women of Romanticism* (2002), it eschews the moral complexity and circumspection of Mary Lamb's 'Salome' (1818), a line of which is cited. Barton's lyric, briefly enchanted by the sinuous grace of the dance, registers only unambiguous horror, although reserves even worse censure for the mother. In that way, it is a poem recoiling from the perceived perversion of an array of conservative feminine ideals.

It was reprinted in an anthology of contributions to *Fulcher's Ladies Memorandum Book* (2nd edition, 1841). This Suffolk literary annual began in 1825, although I have not been able to trace the exact volume that included this poem so it is uncertain whether *Fulcher* represents an earlier or later text.

line 2 – Herod, Tetrarch of Galilee, is described as celebrating his birthday in the Biblical account, when Salome enters dancing.
line 6 – 'Hatred, cruelty, or guile' in *Fulcher*.
line 20 – Barton compares Salome to a siren, the fatally alluring female creatures famous from Greek myth and legend.
lines 21–32 – in dialogue and action, this broadly follows Mark 6:22–27, concluding with the death of John the Baptist.
lines 31–2 – 'Doomed the saint that death to die / Hatred had invented' in *Fulcher*.
line 42 – see Mary Lamb's 'Salome':

> When painters would by art express
> Beauty in unloveliness,
> Thee, Herodias' daughter, thee,
> They fittest subject take to be.

line 47 – in Mark's account, Salome's mother Herodias is the one who advises her to ask for John the Baptist's head. Barton elides this earlier in the poem, but refers to it here.

Godiva

Published in *A New Year's Eve, and Other Poems* (1828).

This poem, an extended sonnet in form, hails a figure at the intersection of legend and history who embodies virtuous British liberty. This was a frequent mode for Barton in the late 1820s: 'Caractacus', included in this volume, is another example. In folklore, Lady Godiva rode naked through the streets of Coventry in order to release the people from the burden of oppressive taxation: interestingly, Barton elides the 'peeping Tom' traditionally included in the tale. Here, her nakedness is an 'unblenched' sign of moral purity. Charles Lamb described 'Godiva', in a letter to the poet in December 1828, as 'delicately touch'd [...] a beautiful story characteristic of old English times' (*Lamb*, p. 842).

line 11 – an allusion to Genesis 2:25: 'And they were both naked, the man and his wife, and were not ashamed'.

On a Portrait by Spagnoletto
Published in *A New Year's Eve, and Other Poems* (1828).

Passionate about the visual arts, Barton wrote much ekphrastic verse describing paintings and drawings and this is one of the finest examples. Its subject – Lo Spagnoletto, or Jesupe de Ribera (1591–1652) – was a Spanish-Italian painter whose profile was heightened along with other Spanish artists by an influx of imports after the Peninsular War. Although it is not clear how or when Barton saw it, the image described can be reliably identified with a painting that hangs today in the Gösta Serlachius Fine Arts Foundation in Finland, which acquired it in London in 1938. In the poem, the painting's dark and brooding manner is highlighted: there are notes of gothic or Byronism in the speculations about the identity of the sitter, and Ribera's stylistic difference from Barton's usual tastes is consciously marked. Across the text, the poet plays with a tension between the directness of the human and imaginative connection evoked by its subject, and various forms of obscurity and antiquity that surround the painting as an object.

The painting's likely provenance can be tracked during the Romantic era as follows, although this is inexact and could indeed conflate multiple items or copies: naturally the Ipswich sale stands out, although the tambourine is not mentioned and neither buyer nor seller specified. Further information is detailed in the Getty Provenance Index.

a) A sale in London on 25 May 1798. Ribera, 'His portrait, with a flask and hoop – size of life – vigorously painted'. Ligt number 5769.
b) A sale in London on 23 May 1817. Ribera, 'An Italian Musician, with a flask in one hand, and a tamboureen in the other'. Ligt number 9144.
c) A sale in Ipswich on 1 August 1825. Ribera, 'Man with Flask'. Ligt number 10960.
d) A sale in London on 19 May 1837. Ribera, 'A man, with a flask and a tambourine; powerfully painted'. Ligt number 14723.

> **line 23** – Rembrandt van Rijn (1606–1669), the Dutch master. Barton identifies the use of dramatic *chiaroscuro*, although Ribera's direct influence here would be the Italian artist Caravaggio (1571–1610) rather than Rembrandt.
> **line 37** – *Man, Wine Bottle and Tambourine* is dated 1631.

line 60 – only the 1798 sale (if it is indeed the same painting) assumes the painting to be a self-portrait.
line 88 – 'ween', i.e. think.

Fireside Quatrains, to Charles Lamb
Published in *A New Year's Eve, and Other Poems* (1828).

The 'Fireside Quatrains' stem from the gift of a coloured print (in a rather comically ill-fitting frame) from Lamb to Barton: see *Lamb*, p. 778–81 for details. The poem's intimate notes span familiar themes of friendship, piety and home, but also evidence his love for decorating domestic space with pictures. This was unusual; Clarkson's *Portraiture of Quakerism* (1806) suggests images, if owned by Quakers, would be usually bound away in portfolios (I, p. 295). By contrast, Barton avidly collected and mounted pictures, continually adding to and altering his collection. It is worth noting that two of the other pictures identifiable in the poem (see below) were also gifts and spurred verse-writing: a clear indication of how remembrance and friendship can consecrate objects with feeling in Barton's poetics.

line 11 – 'Stanzas on Receiving from a Friend an Early Sketch of Gainsborough's' is also included in *A New Year's Eve*. Thomas Gainsborough (1727–1788) was a Suffolk-born painter whose landscape work was ultimately overshadowed by his fame as a portrait artist.
line 13 – probably the 'Holy Family in a Landscape' by Flemish artist Hendrik Van Balen (*c.* 1575–1632) recorded in the posthumous catalogue of Barton's possessions. *A Widow's Tale* (1827) includes a poem entitled 'To Mrs. [Mary Frances] Fitzgerald; On her Presenting the Author with a Beautiful painting by Van Balen', which describes it as a Virgin and Child with angels.

England's Oak
Published in *A New Year's Eve, and Other Poems* (1828).

Litotic gestures – privileging the lesser thing despite and indeed via a comparison to something 'better' – are absolutely recurrent in Barton's verse, and 'England's Oak' turns that rhetorical strategy to national identity and patriotic affections. Like William Cowper's rather more complex 'Yardley Oak' (written 1791–92), 'England's Oak' alludes to the construction of ships from oak, as well as the trees' iconic place in English landscape. However, where Cowper's poem contemplates long timescales and an arboreal 'memory' of historical duration, Barton's text links the tree to the ageing of an individual human life.

line 10 – 'Araby', i.e. Arabia.
line 11 – 'Libanus', i.e. Lebanon.

line 12 – Gilead is a Biblical name for the region east of the River Jordan; a curative balm (or balsam) was derived from shrubby trees growing there.
line 27 – 'dight', i.e. clothed or adorned.
line 68 – Barton figures the proselytising ventures of Christian missionaries as parallel to the voyage of Noah's ark, as recounted in Genesis 7–8. Suffolk was historically a centre of shipbuilding.

Summer Musings

Published in *A New Year's Eve, and Other Poems* (1828).

The poem's bright marshalling of Romantic-era pastoral tropes (balmy air, warbling birds, sprays, bees) gives way to reflections on mortality and time, animated with Christian values of hope. Despite the neat sestets, the titling of the poem evokes a spontaneous and desultory authorship, which was a recurrent rhetorical claim in Barton's work.

lines 41–2 – the extended symbolism by which mental gleaming points towards the spiritual light of a redeemed existence, framed through a reflection on earthly sunlight or daylight, is recurrent in Barton and resonates with the Quaker doctrine of the inward Light. See, for instance, the 'unending day' (line 116) of 'The Valley of Fern', or the 'far more than sunshine' (line 84) of the River Orwell section of 'A Day in Autumn'.

Epistle to the Editor of Friendship's Offering

Published in the literary annual *Friendship's Offering* (1829).

Barton contributed several poems to *Friendship's Offering* across the late 1820s – see 'Stanzas, Composed During a Tempest' and 'Which Things Are a Shadow' in this volume – although this poetic epistle to its new editor Thomas Pringle (1789–1834) appears to be his last. When so much of the Quaker's authorial self-fashioning was solemn or sentimental, it is a lively reminder not just that Barton could write in different modes, including the comic, but of his inevitable entanglement in the commercial realities of literature, exemplified by London.

line 7 – A pun, of course, on 'muse', referring back to 'the Nine' muses referenced in line 2.
line 9 – 'cui bono?' is Latin for 'who benefits?'
line 10 – Mechanics' Institutes were founded in many towns to provide technical education: see the extract from Barton's 1837 letter to William Martin in the contextual material for an account of attending two such lectures.

line 12 – stock market vocabulary: an omnium is an aggregate of stock, scrip is a share certificate, and bull and bear markets are characterised by rising and fallings prices respectively.

line 15 – the Thames Tunnel, linking Wapping and Rotherhithe, had been begun in 1825, although recurrent difficulties, including floods, meant that it was not completed until 1843.

line 16 – the previously exiled Miguel I (1802–1866) had seized the Portuguese throne in 1828, sparking several years of war between liberals and absolutists: Britain took a keen diplomatic and military interest in these developments.

lines 17–20 – the champagne of Charles Wright and the shoe blacking of Robert Warren were two products of the period notably, and heavily, advertised using poetry: see John Strachan, *Advertising and Satirical Culture in the Romantic Period* (2007), especially pp. 38–42.

line 32 – Sir William Curtis (1752–1829) was a famous businessman who also served as a Tory M.P. Sir Walter Scott (1771–1832) is, of course, the famous Scottish writer.

The Coronation of Ines de Castro

Published in the literary annual *The Amulet: A Christian and Literary Remembrancer* (1830). Reprinted in *The Reliquary* (1836).

This tale of medieval Portugal underwent something of an artistic vogue in the late Romantic period and was famously treated by Barton's contemporary Felicia Hemans in 1828. Barton's version is sparer, not least because of the compressed trimeter lines. Inês de Castro (1325–1355) was the paramour of Dom Pedro: she was killed by Pedro's father, Afonso IV, after failed attempts to keep the lovers apart. According to legend, when Pedro became king himself he exhumed her body and had her coronated. The scene painted by Barton is gothic in tone and yet retains a certain grandeur.

In *The Reliquary*, the following headnote is provided: 'in the year 1350, six years after her interment, the remains of Donna Inez de Castro were taken out of her tomb, and she was proclaimed Queen of Portugal, in the Church of Sancta Clara, by order of her husband, Don Pedro'.

line 1 – 'dight', i.e. clothed or adorned.

line 2 – 'mellow sunbeams' = 'mellow'd sunbeams' in *The Reliquary*.

line 4 – The monastery of Santa Clara-a-Velha in Coimbra is where Inês de Castro was initially buried.

line 6 – 'Robed priests' = 'With priests' in *The Reliquary*.

line 9 – 'young and fair' = 'young and gay' in *The Reliquary*.

line 16 – 'Surveys' = 'Beholds' in *The Reliquary*.
line 22 – 'tongue' = 'speech' in *The Reliquary*.
line 27 – 'His thoughts and feelings' = 'What thoughts and feelings' in *The Reliquary*.
line 32 – 'splendid state' = 'solemn state' in *The Reliquary*.
lines 33 and **35** – 'Its' = 'The' in *The Reliquary*.
line 43 – 'But not one' = 'And not one' in *The Reliquary*.

To the White Jasmine
Published in *The Gem, A Literary Annual* (1830). Reprinted in *The Reliquary* (1836).

Although Barton's nature lyrics had always expressed religious and moral themes, his work of the 1830s often concentrated this strain into condensed allegorical forms. This example of a flower poem, initially printed in *The Gem*, bears some of the sensory richness of late-1820s verse authored by women such as Letitia Landon (1802–1838) and Felicia Hemans (1793–1835), for whom night-blowing flowers were potent symbols.

line 2 – 'sunny hour' = garish hour' in *The Reliquary*.
line 3 – a frequently referenced property. For example, the botanical volume of William Bingley's natural history work *Useful Knowledge* (1816) states that jasmines 'exhale a sweet, and penetrating odour, particularly after rain, and in the night' (II, p. 13). Textually, 'rich perfume' = 'beauteous bloom' in *The Reliquary*.
line 5 – 'sunny ray' = 'dazzling ray' in *The Reliquary*.
line 6 – 'the glare of day' = 'the glow of day' in *The Reliquary*.

To Wm. Kirby, Rector of Barham, Suffolk
Published in *The Aurora Borealis, a Literary Annual* (1833). Reprinted in *The Reliquary* (1836).

Barton was friends with several Suffolk clergyman, of whom William Kirby (1759–1850) had perhaps the most unconventional career. Despite being a country pastor, Kirby was also a renowned entomologist, Royal Society Fellow and the author of major scientific studies and papers – beginning with work on bees collected from his own parish. Barton's poem follows the contours of pre-Darwinian natural theology in seeing Kirby's pastoral researches leading to knowledge of design and, ultimately, typologies of spiritual experience. The *Introduction to Entomology* mentioned under the poem's title was published in four volumes between 1815 and 1826, co-authored with William Spence.

One of Barton's letters, dated 19 January 1832 and included in John Freeman's *Life of the Rev. William Kirby* (1852), requests the only copy of what can be assumed to be this poem back from Kirby, in order to revise and publish (see pp. 459–60). It was first printed in the short-lived Quaker annual *Aurora Borealis*. A version marked 'Woodbridge, July 1829' appears in the *Annals and Magazine of Natural History* for July 1843: it was passed on by Kirby's friend and fellow scientist Henry Denny (1803–1871), and may better represent the original MS (as well as identifying the likely date of composition).

line 10 – 'while both have surely' = 'the second must have' in Denny.
line 13 – 'ween', i.e. think.
line 25 – 'lore' = 'love' in Denny.
line 29 – 'For precept must be upon precept, precept upon precept; line upon line, line upon line; here a little, and there a little' (Isa. 28:10).
line 35 – 'Despite the beauty' = 'Whate'er of beauty' in Denny.
line 41 – this line is omitted in Denny.

The Sea-Shell

Published in *The Amethyst, or Christian's Annual* (1834). Reprinted in *The Reliquary* (1836).

A well-reviewed and frequently disseminated lyric. As in 'To the White Jasmine', the natural object is primarily a vehicle for allegory, with the oceanic echoes within the shell being parallel to the traces of heaven retained by the soul on earth. In this sense, the poem gives a religious turn to ideas of exile and yearning most famously explored by Wordsworth in his 1807 Immortality Ode.

line 7 – although proverbial, the belief that a shell carried the sound of the sea was novel enough to require a footnote in Lord Byron's *The Island* (1823). Byron's note alluded to an eight line passage in Walter Savage Landor's *Gebir* (1798), often considered to be the earliest poetic treatment; Wordsworth figures the universe itself as a shell for the 'ear of faith' in Book IV of *The Excursion* (1814).

A Negro Mother's Cradle-Song

Published in *The Bow in the Cloud; or, The Negro's Memorial* (1834).

The Bow in the Cloud was an anti-slavery anthology edited by Mary Anne Rawson (1801–1887), conceived long before its eventual publication in 1834: this poem actually belongs amidst Barton's verse of the mid-1820s. The ventriloquization of an African speaker and the dramatization of a piteous scene of sensibility, although problematic from a modern perspective, are characteristic of the Romantic era (e.g. William Cowper's 1788 poem 'The Negro's Complaint'). The expression of suicidal despair was strikingly dark for Barton, and indeed found a deliberate counter-balance in another poem he contributed to *The Bow* on a slave's conversion and salvation, 'A Christian Negro's Thanks and Prayer'. In a letter to Rawson accompanying the manuscripts, held by the John Rylands library in Manchester, the poet explains that he had aimed 'to express some of those bitter feelings which I cannot but think the common dictates of <u>Nature</u> must incite in the unfortunate Slave Mother, in reference to her equally miserable child' (Eng MSS 414/2). There is no significant textual variation in the 1826 holograph.

line 24 – an allusion to Sir Walter Scott's *The Lady of the Lake* (1810): 'Sleep the sleep that knows not breaking, / Morn of toil, nor night of waking'.

The Bible ['Lamp of our feet!']
Published in the *Ipswich Journal* (30 August 1834). This text based on the revised version included in *The Reliquary* (1836).

This composition in common metre became, like 'Walking in the Light', a popular inclusion in hymnals. With its scriptural focus and an almost Evangelical intensity, it might initially seem an odd poem for an avowedly traditional Quaker. Yet, as his scriptural poems in *Devotional Verses* also illustrate, Barton saw no clash between the authority of the Bible and Quaker ideas of inward intuition. 'Lamp of our feet' is a phrase drawn from Psalm 119, and the stanzas are well-stocked with Psalmic images of faith, such as rock, tower or shield and buckler.

As the poem's afterlife as a hymn was based on the version in *The Reliquary*, I have used this as my source, rather than the slightly different *Ipswich Journal* text. A version omitting the eighth stanza, but otherwise identical to the newspaper version, is printed in the January 1835 issue of the short-lived *Educational Magazine, and Journal of Christian Philanthropy*, edited by Barton's friend William Martin (1801–1867).

line 1 – 'thy word is a lamp unto my feet, and a light unto my path' (Ps. 119:105).
line 2 – 'when wont to stray' = 'as here we stray' in the *Ipswich Journal* (*IJ*).
line 6 – 'True Manna' = 'Our Manna' in *IJ*.
line 9 – see Exodus 13:21.
lines 11–16 – maritime metaphors for spiritual strife were recurrent in the imaginary of eighteenth- and nineteenth-century 'heart religion'.

line 16 – 'deep-sea lead' = 'plummet-line' in *IJ*.
line 19 – 'the LORD is thy shade upon thy right hand' (Ps. 121:5).
line 22 – 'Victory's triumphant palm!' = 'Of Victory's hour the Palm!' in *IJ*.
line 24 – the balm of Gilead (also referenced in 'England's Oak') is a famous medicinal perfume mentioned in the Bible.
line 25 – 'Childhood's preceptor!' = 'Childhood's Instructor!' in *IJ*.
line 31 – a reference to Delphi, the famous Greek Oracle.
line 41 – 'if we aright would learn' = 'if we would rightly learn' in *IJ*.

A Clerico-Politico Portrait
Published in the *Suffolk Chronicle* (13 December 1834).

The 1830s was a turbulent decade posing reform-minded Whigs and liberals against a reactionary Tory establishment, with one particularly divisive issue being the compulsory payment of Anglican church rates. Suffolk was far from untouched by the tumult, as this venomous satire from the 1835 electoral campaign indicates: it illustrates a very different side, albeit anonymous, to Barton's literary talents (see also 'Wolves in Sheep's Clothing' in the contextual material). As the text itself indicates, Etough (1783–1853) was a local clergyman: he addressed a raucous public dinner of some 200 guests, detailed in an *Ipswich Journal* report of 6 December 1834, and his anti-Dissenting speech was the direct spur for the poem. It can be confirmed as the poet's work through a redacted and shortened version in a footnote of *SPL*, accompanied with the observation that 'the quiet Quaker *could* strike' (p. xxx). In the election itself (won nationally by the Whigs), Barton's friend and liberal M. P. Robert Newton Shawe (1784–1855) lost his seat in the two-member East Suffolk constituency. Church rates were not abolished until 1868.

The epigraph comes from a minor novel of 1830; corbie is a Scottish dialect word for a raven or crow.

line 4 – the quotation comes from Shakespeare's *Hamlet*, I.ii.133.
line 8 – as the *Ipswich Journal* records, Etough's speech followed a toast of 'Church and King' and did indeed repeatedly return to variations of the phrase.
line 11 – the Whigs and the Radicals formed a loose alliance in the nineteenth century: the Quaker M.P. John Bright (1811–1889) would become one of the most famous Radicals when elected in 1843.
line 17 – High Toryism is traditionalist, often aristocratic, and deeply protective of the Church of England.

line 24 – the 'voluntary system' or voluntary principle was the proposal that the Anglican church should rely on freely given contributions from its own parishioners, rather than a system mandated by law.
line 27 – 'Episcopacy' is the organisation of the church through a hierarchical system of bishops.
line 28 – Etough held a D.D., a 'Doctor of Divinity' degree from Cambridge.
lines 29–30 – adapted from Alexander Pope's satiric 'Epistle to Dr. Arbuthnot' (1735): 'Who but must laugh, if such a man there be? / Who would not weep, if *Atticus* were he?'

First Scripture Lessons
Published in the literary annual *Fisher's Juvenile Scrap-Book* (1839).

A spin-off for younger readers from Fisher and Son's successful *Drawing-Room Scrap-Book* annual, *Fisher's Juvenile Scrap-Book* was co-edited by Barton in the 1830s. This poem from its pages, evoking a pedagogical scene of mother and child, is striking in its simplicity but possesses an undertow of nostalgia. As explained by Barton's note (see below), the child is Dissenting theologian Philip Doddridge (1702–1751). In an 1845 letter, Barton wrote that he had forgotten the poem until someone sent him a child's handkerchief inscribed with some of its lines, declaring 'this handkerchief celebrity tickles me somewhat' (*SPL*, p. 91). He also wrote a poem for adults on the same theme and image – 'Look on our pictur'd page!' – for the 1838 *Fisher's Drawing-Room Scrap-Book*.

Barton's own note reads: 'It is recorded of the justly celebrated Dr. Doddridge, that his "First Scripture Lessons" were taught him by his mother from the Dutch tiles round their home-fire. The annexed plate is an illustration of that maternal instruction: and the accompanying verses are furnished by one who is not ashamed to own himself a lover of those rude yet ready accessaries [*sic*] to early instruction.' The manuscript version is found in a letter of 30 July 1838, sent 'in haste' to Robert Fisher. This is held by the Library of the Society of Friends, London (MS Box 12[4]5).

line 2 – 'for its blaze' = 'from its blaze' in MS.
line 25 – 'Dutch tiles' were renowned in the seventeenth and eighteenth centuries, spurred by the influence of Chinese porcelain carried along early Dutch imperial trade routes. Those illustrating Biblical scenes (*bijbeltegels*) were highly popular.
line 39 – 'the sling' = 'his sling' in MS.
lines 39–40 – see 1 Samuel 17.
lines 41–4 – see Genesis 37:18–36.

lines 45–6 – see Ruth 2:1–3; and Barton's own poem 'Ruth's Love' in this volume.

line 45 – crossings out in the MS show the cancelled reading 'And so was that of Ruth, who went'.

lines 47–8 – see 2 Kings 5:9–15. Naaman was a Syrian general healed of leprosy when bade to wash in the River Jordan seven times by the prophet Elisha.

lines 49–50 – see Luke 2:46.

lines 51–2 – a reference to the gospel episode of Jesus walking across the Sea of Galilee.

On a Drawing of the Cottage at Aldborough, Where Crabbe Lived in Boyhood

Published in the literary annual *Fulcher's Ladies' Memorandum Book*, also known as *The Sudbury Pocket-Book* (1839). This text based on the revised version included in *Household Verses* (1845).

One of Barton's favourite poets was George Crabbe (1754–1832), a fellow Suffolker whose narrative verse describing rural life was robustly realistic, but critiqued as unpoetic in its unflinching and minutely-drawn detail. This poem defends such a counter-pastoral strain in a way not dissimilar to 'Verses on the Death of Bloomfield'. Crabbe is positioned as a poet of absolute mimetic fidelity, and from such fidelity can come sympathy for the full range of human sorrows. 'On a Drawing' is also a text of personal county connections: its first appearance was in a locally printed literary annual published by George Fulcher (1795–1855), and at the time Barton already had a friendship and correspondence with Crabbe's son, also named George (1785–1857), the rector of nearby Bredfield. In its first printed context, the poem's ekphrastic character is clearer, as the *Memorandum Book* includes an impressive foldout frontispiece depicting a humble domestic scene in the cottage's interior, engraved by J.[ohn?] Hawksworth after a painting by the Suffolk artist Perry Nursey (1771–1840).

Due to the unusually extensive revisions made by Barton to this poem, I have adopted the later 1845 version as the reading text. The epigraph is only included in the 1845 version, and is taken from another poem of Barton's on the same subject.

line 2 – 'better' = 'earlier' in *Fulcher*.

line 8 – a line closely adapted from Robert Blair's gothic poem *The Grave* (1743), marked as a quotation in *Fulcher*.

line 13 – 'charm' = 'spell' in *Fulcher*.

line 17 – the quotation is Lord Byron's judgement on Crabbe in *English Bards and Scotch Reviewers* (1809).

line 18 – 'his verses' truest test' = 'and this its deepest zest' in *Fulcher*.
line 22 – the 'classic models' are the traditions of Greek pastoral and their later re-articulation in English literature.
line 24 – an allusion to Crabbe's own anti-pastoral gesture in Book I of *The Village* (1783): 'Here joyless roam a wild amphibious race, / With sullen woe display'd in every face'.
line 27 – 'few and far between' is marked as a quotation in *Fulcher*, deriving from Thomas Campbell's line 'like angel visits, few and far between', from *The Pleasures of Hope* (1799).
line 30 – see Shakespeare's *Othello*: 'the very head and front of my offending' (I.iii.80); it was a widely used and adapted idiom in the period.
line 32 – 'no artist's play' = 'no push-pin play' in *Fulcher*. The latter was a child's game.
lines 45–6 – between these two stanzas, the version in *Fulcher* had inserted this stanza on John Bradford (1510–1555), which follows the traditional attribution of the idiom 'there but for the grace of God' to the Protestant martyr:

> Bradford, the Martyr, when he once beheld
>   A criminal to execution led,
> Exclaim'd "had not the grace of God with-held
>   My feet from wandering in a path as dread,
>   Such portion had been mine!" 'Twas nobly said;
> And he who, on the Gospel's humbling plan,
>   Forbears to judge another, but instead,
> Turns inward his own evil there to scan,
> Feels sympathy for *all*, bearing the name of Man!

lines 52–4 – in *Fulcher*, these lines had read: 'To bear in mind the warfare they may wage, / The rougher tide which they may have to stem, / A lesson, taught aright, which leads to pity them.'
line 64 – 'know and feel our Poet's worth' = 'truly know, and feel his worth' in *Fulcher*.
lines 71–2 – in *Fulcher*, the poem closed with this alternative couplet: 'That in our human hearts must aye combine, / May fitly frame a wreath his honour'd brow to twine!'

An Epistle to a Phonographic Friend; Or a Few Words on Phonography

Published in the *Suffolk Chronicle* (17 May 1845).

This satirical piece was published in the same provincial newspaper with which Barton had begun his career three decades earlier. Its target – the phonography of Isaac Pitman (1813–97) – was not just a system of shorthand, but a visionary proposal to revolutionise orthography by replacing the English alphabet with phonetically consistent symbols. Barton wrote this mocking critique of Pitman's schemes after so-called Phonographic Soirees were held in Woodbridge and Ipswich: a long account of the latter meeting, entitled 'The Writing and Printing Reformation', appears in the same issue of the newspaper as Barton's piece. The poet's intervention appears to have ruffled feathers: it provoked several poems against Barton, and a defensive letter from Pitman himself, all printed in the following week's *Chronicle*.

The epigraph is an ironic reworking of *Macbeth* V.v.25-7.

line 11 – 'crotchets' probably encompasses two senses: a fanciful and perverse conceit or device, and the musical note which would evoke phonographic symbols.

line 27 – Barton refers to the straight and curved strokes, dots, hooks, loops and other marks which constitute Pitman's system of phonographic writing.

line 32 – phonography had been explicitly compared to railway technology at the Ipswich meeting, and steam was a recurrent Victorian metaphor for speed, mechanisation and modernity. In 1846, Barton expressed his 'perfect hatred' of railways, but nonetheless opposed a plan by the Eastern Union Railway to leave Woodbridge unconnected – see his letter of 6 June 1846 to J. W. Candler, held by the Library of the Society of Friends, London (MS. Box 5/8).

line 40 – the leading phonographers Isaac Pitman, his brother Joseph, and Thomas Allen Reid were present at the Soirees. These meetings were held across the country in order to promote phonography.

line 49 – one supposed advantage of Pitman's system was that it could be universalised to capture the phonetics of any language, modern or (as in Barton's five examples) ancient.

line 53 – 'gull', i.e. a gullible person.

line 54 – 'sconce' is a jocular term for the head; phrenology was a Victorian pseudo-science attempting to read character through skull shape.

line 55 – mesmerism, or animal magnetism, was a Victorian pseudo-science claiming to manipulate an invisible field around the body.

line 57 – the explosive growth of the railways in the 1840s provoked a famous speculative financial bubble.

To the B.B Schooner, on Seeing Her Sail Down the Deben for Liverpool

Published in *Household Verses* (1845).

One of Barton's more curious literary legacies was the launch, on 20 April 1840 in Woodbridge, of a small mercantile schooner bearing his name – in many ways an apposite image for the poet's fame and legacy, given the life-long entwining of commerce and literature in his career. These verses on the vessel construct his authorship in a fashion well-established since the 1810s: self-effacing and with a privileging of the local. There is an undated holograph in the autograph album of Hannah Maria Philip, held by the Cadbury Research Library at the University of Birmingham (HMP/139), which is cited with their permission.

line 5 – in a letter to Frances Ann Shawe of 2 May 1840, Barton cites the old blessing 'God speed the good ship, and send her safe to her desired port' in a discussion of his personal attachment to the schooner: he confesses that 'the B.B. is a bit of a pet with me' (*SPL*, p. 20).
line 12 – 'verse' = 'guerdon' in Philip.
line 20 – 'unasked' = 'unsought' in Philip.

Sonnet, to a Friend Never Yet Seen, But Corresponded with for Above Twenty Years
Published in *Household Verses* (1845).

As is confirmed in the poem's later printing in *SPL*, the friend 'unknown to sight' is the Cumberland Quaker, Mary Sutton (dates unknown). Barton's correspondence with her includes some of his most explicit theological statements (see the letters extracted in the contextual material). The sonnet – which holds that epistolary, affective and spiritual patterns of interchange and union can transcend physical distance – is appositely framed through ABBA units of rhyming, always circling back in a motion of enclosure and completion.

lines 11–12 – 'Bear ye one another's burdens, and so fulfil the law of Christ' (Gal. 6:2).

A Postscript to 'To the Dead in Christ'
Published in *Household Verses* (1845).

Perhaps because his wife's death preceded his emergence as a poet, an elegiac note runs across Barton's work and the presence of the dead among us is a theme he returns to frequently, with a mixture of wonder and consolation. These short stanzas, appended to 'To the Dead in Christ', are a late iteration of the theme.

line 6 – the amaranth is a symbol of constancy (indeed, its etymology means 'not fading') and employed poetically as a flower of immortality.

line 8 – 'After this I looked, and, behold a door was opened in heaven: and the first voice which I heard was as it were of a trumpet talking with me; which said, Come up hither, and I will shew thee things which must be hereafter' (Rev. 4:1).

The Yellow-Hammer; A Song, by a Suffolk Villager
Published in *Household Verses* (1845).

Unusually for Barton, a dramatic monologue in the voice of a rustic: repetitions and refrains give it the song-like quality promised by the title. Nevertheless most of the themes – blissful yet irrecoverable summer scenes, gently pastoral landscapes, notes of loss and *pathos* – are stereotypically Bartonian. The yellowhammer is a small songbird of the bunting family; the most famous Romantic poem on it is John Clare's 'The Yellowhammer's Nest' (1835).

line 3 – the yellowhammer song is a repeated monotone with an emphasised final note. A nineteenth-century ornithologist notes that 'the cow-boys, from their own feelings, no doubt, have composed words to his short and plaintive song, viz. A lit–tle bit of bread, but no cheese' – see J. Main, 'Some Account of the British Song Birds', *Magazine of Natural History* 4, no. 21 (September 1831), p. 416.

line 9 – the unpoetic 'dun cow' aligns Barton with a radical simplicity associated with the Lake School: it was the kind of motif used to satirise Wordsworth.

line 26 – collecting nuts, or nutting, was a common rural pastime for children; again, it finds literary expression in Wordsworth.

line 35 – 'cheerly', i.e. cheerfully.

To E.F., On Her Reappearance Among Her Friends at the Yearly Meeting, 1845
Published in *Household Verses* (1845).

Elizabeth Fry (1780–1845) was a major social reformer of the nineteenth century. Born as a Gurney, and hence into the network of East Anglian Quaker families that Barton knew well, she contributed to the causes of abolition, education, nursing and above all prison reform. In May 1845, critically ill and only five months from her death, she did indeed attend the Women's Yearly Meeting of Friends in London and spoke passionately on two instances: see the account in Susanna Corder's *Life of Elizabeth Fry* (1853), pp. 624–5.

line 1 – Fry's melodious and affecting voice was commented upon, described by a witness in 1818 as 'saintly […] like the voice of a mother to her suffering child' (recounted in Corder's *Life*, p. 280).

line 13 – 'faith, hope and love', the famous triptych of virtues enunciated in 1 Corinthians 13.

line 16 – as in his elegy to Samuel Alexander twenty years earlier, Barton concludes with an image of irradiating light, which has a resonant place within Quaker theology.

Sonnet, to Job's Three Friends
Published in *Household Verses* (1845).

Job's three friends are Eliphaz the Temanite, Bildad the Shuhite and Zophar the Naamathite. In the Biblical account, their attempts to explain Job's suffering – in sum, that it is a punishment – are discounted and they are ultimately rebuked by God himself. Barton's sonnet – acknowledging that they 'err in after speech' – concentrates instead on their compassionate silence as they first approach the desolate Job. The eloquence of voiceless mourning is an apposite theme in the broader context of Quaker practice and belief.

line 4 – 'him of Uz', i.e. Job.

line 9 – 'So they sat down with him upon the ground seven days and seven nights, and none spake a word unto him: for they saw that his grief was very great' (Job 2:13).

Sonnets, Written at Burstal
Published in *Household Verses* (1845).

Barton wrote sonnets of many types, sometimes in pairs, but this appears to be his only sonnet sequence. It is set in the landscape around Burstal (sometimes Burstall), a tiny village just west of Ipswich. The first three poems build outwards from a prospect view towards an assertion of God's hand in natural beauty and the devotional power of the 'visible creation'. Barton's reiteration of what is basically eighteenth-century natural theology shows exactly how tenacious these ideas were, despite well-known challenges to Victorian faith. The sequences goes on to trace a series of vignettes – characteristic *litotes* framing a lakelet, a pair of oaks, and an impressionistic evening sketch – before concluding with the cycling of the seasons.

A note in *SPL* records that 'these eight sonnets were composed during a day's visit to the village of Burstal [...] in some grounds belonging to John [Biddle] Alexander' (p. 353). The Alexanders were a wealthy Quaker banking family: see 'On the Death of Samuel Alexander' in this volume. Barton worked in Alexander's bank, and one of John B. Alexander's children was named Bernard Barton Alexander on his birth in 1849. The poet also had a strong connection to the locale via the clergyman John Charlesworth (1782–1864) and his family, who lived nearby.

Sonnet I, line 5 – the almost childlike 'lovely spot' is a phrasing also used in 'Playford' and 'The Valley of Fern'.

Sonnet IV, lines 5–11 – the insistence that nature is potentially a 'master-key' to spiritual truth, but also transient and secondary in the last analysis, recalls the theology of the influential poet William Cowper (1731–1800)

Sonnet IV, line 12 – 'threescore', i.e. 60. Barton turned 60 on 31 January 1844.

Sonnet V, lines 1–2 – references to the Lake District: Ullswater is the second largest of its lakes; the town of Keswick lies close to the shores of Derwentwater.

Sonnet VI, line 9 – given the dates, the 'wedded pair' split by death could conceivably be John's parents, Samuel (1773–1838) and Rebecca (1777–1849, née Biddle). The latter, unusually, became a female partner in the bank on her husband's death.

Sonnet VII, line 1 – the first line of Wordsworth's sonnet 'Composed Upon Westminster Bridge' (1802).

Sonnet VIII, line 9 – 'ween', i.e. think.

Poetical Illustrations from *Natural History of the Holy Land*
Published in Lucy Barton's *Natural History of the Holy Land* (1856).

Natural History of the Holy Land was published by Barton's daughter Lucy in 1856. Richly illustrated, the work mingled discussion of scripture, zoological descriptions and the observations of travellers. It also covered a huge range of flora and fauna, from lions to beetles. Barton contributed simple but sometimes intriguing verses to accompany the engravings, of which these are five examples.

This text bears an unclear relation to Lucy Barton's earlier *Scripture Natural History for the Young*, published in 1848 by Peter Jackson, and advertised as having 82 engravings accompanied by Barton's poetry (the 1856 *Natural History* has 81). Unfortunately, I have been unable to trace a surviving copy of the earlier work, although of course it seems certain that the *Natural History* is a reworked version in some fashion, using the same verse and plates. This would suggest, logically enough, that Barton's lines were likely composed some time around 1847–48.

'Heron', line 4 – in 'Syr Heron', a poem from 1828's *A New-Year's Eve*, Barton had described a heron in similar terms as 'moveless in dream-like silence lone, / Some spectre bird, or sculptured stone'.

'**Serpent', lines 3–4** – Mary Trimmer's *Natural History* (1825) records that 'in 1799, a Malay seaman was almost instantaneously crushed to death, in the island of Celebes, by one of these serpents thirty feet in length, which seized him by the right wrist, and twined round his head, neck, breast and thigh' (p. 212). Lucy Barton repeats this tale in her explanatory text. Celebes is the Indonesian island of Sulawesi.

'**Barbary Ape', line 2** – Barton conceives the resemblance between primates and humans in traditional terms: Darwin's *Descent of Man* would be published in 1871 and create a more fundamental trembling in anthropocentric pride.

A Prefatory Appeal for Poetry and Poets
Published in *The Reliquary* (1836).

This text is Barton's only significant essay on poetic principles, printed as the preface to *The Reliquary*. This volume was jointly authored with his daughter Lucy, and gathered together much of the verse of his middle period. Although framed as a post-Romantic aesthetic statement – and indeed critical of a 'mannerist' excess associated with the 1810s and 1820s – the preface reiterates a defence of poetry indebted to the manifestoes of canonical Romanticism. Linking poetic expression to childhood emotions, the ideal of the meditative poet in retirement, and the sympathetic re-creation of feeling in the reader's mind are all positions familiar from Wordsworth, Shelley and others. Poetry is defined not technically but spiritually – as the expression of human nature in its highest aspects. This lies beyond narrowly conceived utility or scientific materialism and ultimately binds the poetic vocation, for Barton at least, to Christianity. Again in tune with certain tendencies of his time (e.g. the Oxford Movement), Barton asserts that the poetic aspect of religion is the natural mirror of the religious essence of poetry.

"**increase of appetite could grow…**" – an allusion to *Hamlet* I.ii.148–9.

throwing off the artificial trammels and technical phraseology – a standard self-understanding of how Romantic-era poets altered eighteenth-century poetic tradition.

milk and water – Barton, along with minor poets Barry Cornwall [Bryan Waller Proctor] and George Croly, had been attacked as the Milk and Water School: see Barton's letter of 20 February 1822 to William Jerdan, in *LCBB*, pp. 51–3.

"**the world's dread laugh**" – a quotation from the 'Autumn' section of James Thomson's *The Seasons* (1730): 'still the world prevail'd, and its dread laugh / Which scarce the firm philosopher can scorn'.

Utilitarians – the philosophical school associated with Jeremy Bentham (1747–1832).

"making the past and the future predominate..." – adapted from Samuel Johnson's *A Journey to the Western Islands of Scotland* (1775).

the giver of every good and perfect gift – see James 1:17; this is the most conspicuous allusion in a passage rich in scriptural imagery.

their sway is that of the affections – Barton's conservative understanding of separate masculine and feminine spheres is characteristic of the time; it is interesting to see him acknowledge the importance of female readers but not female writers (such as Landon, Hemans and indeed his own daughter).

penates – Roman deities of the household.

the one talent intrusted to him – an allusion to the parable of the talents, see Matthew 25:14–30. Barton was drawn to the 'one talent' motif: in an 1827 letter to Thomas Wilkinson, he reflected that he would sacrifice his health for the sake of his one talent, and that his motto was 'better wear out than rust out'. The letter is archived in the British Library, Add MS 60580, ff. 115–16.

All the following contextual material, except the Hemans poem, is in extract form.

Edward Fitzgerald, 'Memoir of Bernard Barton'

SPL, pp. ix–xxxvi. Alcinous, King of the Phaeacians, appears in Homer's *Odyssey* and his garden is proverbially idyllic; battledore and shuttlecock is a historical game similar to badminton. See 'Haunts of Childhood' in this volume for a poetic treatment of these memories.

Lord Byron, Letter to Bernard Barton, 1 June 1812

SPL, pp. xviii–xix [footnote]. Mr Rogers is the poet Samuel Rogers (1763–1855); the printed volume would be *Metrical Effusions* (1812).

B.B. [Bernard Barton?], 'The Friends: To the Editor of the Examiner'

The Examiner 404 (24 September 1815), p. 621. This letter, dated 13 September, responds to and cites from William Hazlitt's 'Round Table' essay on sects in the 10 September 1816 issue of Leigh Hunt's periodical *The Examiner*. Handel is the eighteenth-century composer G. F. Handel (1685–1759); Apelles is a painter of ancient Greece; *Rasselas* is a 1759 philosophical novel by Samuel Johnson.

Robert Southey, Letter to Bernard Barton, 21 January 1820

SPL, pp. 110–11. John Scott of Amwell (1730–1783) was a friend of Samuel Johnson and the best known Quaker poet prior to Barton; Charles Lloyd the Elder (1748–1828) had translated Homer and the epistles of Horace between 1807 and 1812, mostly printing them privately in Birmingham.

Review of *Poems* (1820) in the *London Magazine*

London Magazine 2, no. 8 (August 1820), pp. 194–7. This periodical was a major outlet for Barton in the early 1820s. A letter of 1 July 1822 to the publishers Taylor and Hessey reveals he had seen the *London* as crucial to building a literary reputation, but felt increasingly sidelined, not least by the periodical's enthusiasm for 'Johnny [i.e. John] Clare'. See *LCBB*, pp. 57–8.

[Francis Jeffrey], Review of *Poems* (1820) in the *Edinburgh Review*

Edinburgh Review 34, no. 68 (November 1820), pp. 348–57. Edited by Francis Jeffrey (1773–1850), the Whig-leaning *Edinburgh Review* was hugely influential and this review was therefore a landmark critical assessment of Barton's work; see *LCBB*, pp. 48–9 for Barton's own response to it.

Anonymous, 'Sonnet to Bernard Barton'

London Magazine 3, no. 15 (March 1821), p. 303. See the above review for context. '*Autumnal Day*' alludes to Barton's *A Day in Autumn*, published in quarto in 1820.

Bernard Barton, Preface to *Poems*, 2nd edition (1821)

Poems, 2nd ed., pp. ix–xii. This is usefully read alongside 'The Quaker Poet'.

Bernard Barton, Preface to *Napoleon, and Other Poems* (1822)

Napoleon, and Other Poems, pp. ix–xv.

Charles Lamb, Letter to Bernard Barton, 11 September 1822

Lamb, pp. 617–18. Rhodomontade is bluster; cates are food; George Fox (1624–1691) was the founder of the Quakers.

Charles Lamb, Letter to Bernard Barton, 9 January 1823

Lamb, pp. 640–2. Barton was a clerk at Alexander's bank in Woodbridge; the Tarpeian Rock was a Roman execution site; Leadenhall is Leadenhall Street in London, where Lamb worked as a clerk in East India House. This is perhaps the most famous of all letters written to Barton.

Review of *Poetic Vigils* (1824) in the *Literary Gazette*

Literary Gazette 385 (5 June 1824), pp. 354–5. Gros de Naples was a type of highly fashionable silk, which the reviewer opposes to plain and simple broadcloth.

Review of *Poetic Vigils* (1824) in the *Monthly Review*

Monthly Review 104 (August 1824), pp. 435–9. Thomas Campbell (1777–1844) was most famous as the author of *The Pleasures of Hope* (1799) and *Gertrude of Wyoming* (1809).

Bernard Barton, Letter to Charles Benjamin Tayler, 1825

SPL, pp. 3–4. Tayler (1797–1875) was the curate of Hadleigh in Suffolk and an author. Bowring is the polyglot intellectual and writer John Bowring (1792–1872), with whom Barton corresponded.

[Robert Story], 'Specimen of a Poetical Satire'

Newcastle Magazine 4, no. 2 (February 1825), pp. 57–8. The authorship of minor Tory poet Robert Story (1795–1860) can be adduced from a version of these lines inserted into his work *The Critics and Scribblers of the Day* (1827). 'Christmas toy' refers to the literary annuals, which were published at the year's end and proved central to Barton's career in the 1820s; the 'cuts' were the engraved illustrations within them.

Bernard Barton, Letter to Thomas Wilkinson, 28 April 1825

Original in the British Library, Add MS 60580, ff. 105–6. Punctuation regularised. Previously printed in Mary Carr, *Thomas Wilkinson: A Friend of Wordsworth* (1905), re-transcription permitted courtesy of the British Library Board. Wilkinson (1751–1836) was a Quaker writer from the Lake District: he knew Wordsworth and was also an abolitionist poet. The 'tribute' to scholar and translator Elizabeth Smith (1776–1806) is Wilkinson's poem 'How dark this river murmuring on its way', included in Smith's posthumous *Fragments in Prose and Verse* (1808).

Felicia Hemans, 'To the Daughter of Bernard Barton, the Quaker Poet'

Works of Mrs Hemans: With a Memoir of Her Life, 7 vols (1839), VI, p. 141. The holograph of this poem (held at the National Library of Wales) dates it to June 1825.

Bernard Barton, Preface to *Devotional Verses* (1826)

Devotional Verses, pp. v–xiii. The quotation is from 2 Corinthians 3:12.

Review of *Devotional Verses* (1826) in the *Eclectic Review*

Eclectic Review 25 (March 1826), pp. 236–44. Byron's *Hebrew Melodies* (1815) was a collection of lyrics; *The Temple* was a devotional collection by the seventeenth-century poet George Herbert (1593–1633). 'Wordsworth's poetical doctrine' is the famous injunction to write poetry in the real language of men, from the 1800 Preface to *Lyrical Ballads*.

Bernard Barton, Letter to William Howitt, 15 February 1827

Margaret Howitt, 'Some Letters from Bernard Barton', *Good Words* (December 1895), pp. 236–44. William Howitt (1792–1879) was a Nottingham Quaker writer with a long and fascinating Victorian career interlinked with that of his wife, Mary (1799–1888). See 'Sonnet to William and Mary Howitt' and 'Sonnet to the Same' in this volume.

Review of *A Widow's Tale* (1827) in the *Athenaeum*

Athenaeum 3 (16 January 1828), p. 36. James Montgomery (1771–1854) was a Scottish poet from a Moravian background: his hymns were very popular.

[Bernard Barton], 'Wolves in Sheep's Clothing': To W.C. Fonnereau, Esq. from a Dissenter

Suffolk Chronicle (31 January 1835), p. 3. This epigram and public rebuke emerge from the same contentious election campaign as 'A Clerico-Politico Portrait'.

William Charles Fonnereau (1804–1855) was a Suffolk landowner, turned Tory from a Whig background. Fonnereau's slander – that Dissenters like Barton are wolves in sheep's clothing – comes from Aesop; to appeal to Philip Sober is idiomatic, deriving from an historical anecdote about Philip II of Macedon. Barton's authorship is presumed through the epigram's appearance in *SPL*, p. xxxi.

Bernard Barton, Letter to William Martin, 21 January 1837

Original in the Friends Historical Library, Swarthmore College. SFHL-RG5-311, letter 82. Punctuation regularised. Previously printed in *LCBB*, re-transcription permitted courtesy of Swarthmore College. Martin (1801–1867) was a Woodbridge-based children's writer and educationalist. The Woodbridge Literary and Mechanics' Institution was established in the autumn of 1836: the lectures on mental derangement were given by John Kirkman of the Suffolk lunatic asylum on 16 and 28 November; and those on heat by local surgeon William Welton on 11 and 25 January 1837. Other subjects in the opening season were the Institution itself; the inhabitation of other worlds; British manufactures; the customs of early Britons; and coal formations. Balaam and the Ass is a Biblical story from Numbers 22; Barton's quotation is from Shakespeare's *A Midsummer Night's Dream*, V.i.7–8.

Bernard Barton, Letter to Frances Ann Shawe, 1 September 1837

SPL, pp. 11–12. Shawe (1783–1856) was the wife of Suffolk landowner and sometime liberal M.P., Robert Newton Shawe; they lived in Kesgrave Hall, 5 miles south west of Woodbridge. The brother mentioned is the political economist, John Barton (1789–1852); *The Deserted Village* (1770) was a poem written by Oliver Goldsmith.

Bernard Barton, Letter to Frances Ann Shawe, 1839

SPL, p. 19.

Bernard Barton, Letter to Frances Ann Shawe, 8 January 1843

SPL, pp. 21–5. Elsewhere in this letter Barton cites Philippians 4:3 and Acts 2:17–18 as scriptural passages which imply the legitimacy of women preaching. Female ministry had always been a notable Quaker practice.

Bernard Barton, Letter to John Clemesha, 8 July 1843

Original in the Library of the Society of Friends, London. Temp MSS 60/1, letter 36 in Clemesha correspondence. Punctuation regularised. Previously printed in *SPL*, re-transcription permitted courtesy of the Library of the Society of Friends. Clemesha (possible dates 1796–1874) was a Quaker merchant and a regular correspondent. The Land of Cockaigne in Barton's punning reference is a legendary land of plenty.

Bernard Barton, Letter to John Clemesha, 13 June 1844

Original in the Library of the Society of Friends, London. Temp MSS 60/1, letter 64 in Clemesha correspondence. Punctuation regularised. Previously printed in *SPL*, re-transcription permitted courtesy of the Library of the Society of Friends. Galenicals are medicines.

Bernard Barton, Letter to Matilda Betham, 7 April 1845

SPL, p. 86. Betham (1776–1852) was a Suffolk-born poet and writer who lived much of her life in London. The performance to which the letter refers is by Richardson's 'rock band', which played classical pieces on a 'petrachord' constructed from different sized stones hung from a wooden frame. Several concerts were given locally at the time. Skiddaw is in the Lake District; 'sermons from stones' is an allusion to Shakespeare's *As You Like It*, II.i.17.

Bernard Barton, Letters to Mary Sutton, ?1847

SPL, pp. 43–59. In *SPL*, a multitude of letter fragments are included within this page range but only the first is dated (as written on 23 October 1847). Sutton (dates unknown) was a Cumberland Quaker and the subject of the 'Sonnet, to a Friend Never Yet Seen'. Both extracts need to be read in the context of the transformation of nineteenth-century British Quakerism by Evangelical impulses, and Barton's own fidelity to more traditional forms. Birthright membership had been formalised in the 1730s but was attacked for preventing spiritual vibrancy and growth. In the first extract, Barton defends it on the grounds that without it Quaker discipline cannot legitimately protect young Friends, from both secular pleasures and conversion to other forms of Christianity. The 'seceders' are those who left over such issues, especially after the 1835–36 Beaconite Controversy. The second extract is typical of Barton's open theological attitude: whilst it was another issue provoking tension and schisms within the Society, he argues that individual spiritual discerning (the inward Light) and the authority of scripture are complementary.

Bernard Barton, Letter to William Bodham Donne, 17 February 1849

Original in the Library of the Society of Friends, London. MS. Box 12(5)3. Punctuation regularized. Previously printed in *LCBB*, re-transcription permitted courtesy of the Library of the Society of Friends. Donne (1807–82) was a writer with family connections to William Cowper, and an important friend to Barton in his final years. The quotation comes from a ballad variously entitled 'The Storm' or 'The Tempest', attributed to George Alexander Stevens (1710–1780).

E.V. Lucas, *Bernard Barton and his Friends: A Record of Quiet Lives* (1893)

Lucas, pp. 187–8.

BIBLIOGRAPHY

a) Barton's Major Works

Metrical Effusions, or Verses on Various Occasions (Woodbridge: S. Loder, 1812) [published anonymously].
The Triumph of the Orwell, with a Dedicatory Sonnet and Prefatory Stanzas (Woodbridge: Smith and Jarrold, 1817) [published anonymously].
The Convict's Appeal (London: Darton, Harvey and Darton, 1818) [published anonymously].
Poems, by an Amateur (London: J. McCreery, 1818) [published anonymously].
Poems (London: Harvey and Darton, 1820).
A Day in Autumn; A Poem (London: Baldwin, Cradock, and Joy, 1820).
Poems, 2nd edn, with additions (London: Baldwin, Cradock, and Joy, 1821).
Napoleon, and Other Poems (London: Thomas Boys, 1822).
Poems, 3rd edn, with additions (London: Baldwin, Cradock, and Joy, 1822).
Verses on the Death of Percy Bysshe Shelley (London: Baldwin, Cradock, and Joy, 1822).
Minor Poems, including Napoleon (London: Thomas Boys, 1824).
Poetic Vigils (London: Baldwin, Cradock, and Joy, 1824).
Poems, 4th edn, with additions (London: Baldwin, Cradock, and Joy, 1825).
Devotional Verses; Founded on, and Illustrative of Selected Texts of Scripture (London: B.J. Holdsworth, 1826).
A Missionary's Memorial; or, Verses on the Death of John Lawson, Late Missionary at Calcutta (London: Frederick Westley, 1826).
A Widow's Tale, and Other Poems (London: B.J. Holdsworth, 1827).
A New Year's Eve, and Other Poems (London: John Hatchard, 1828).
The Reliquary (London: John W. Parker, 1836) [jointly authored with Lucy Barton].
Household Verses (London: George Virtue, 1845).
Sea-Weeds; Gathered at Aldborough; Suffolk (printed for private circulation, 1846).
A Memorial of Joseph John Gurney (London: Charles Gilpin, 1847).
On the Sign of the Times (Woodbridge: Edward Pite, 1848).
Ichabod! (Woodbridge: Edward Pite, 1848).
Natural History of the Holy Land, and Other Places Mentioned in the Bible, with Poetical Illustrations, Original and Selected (London: Thomas Allman, 1856) [jointly authored with Lucy Barton].

b) Further Reading and Resources

Angell, Stephen W., and Pink Dandelion (eds), *The Oxford Handbook of Quaker Studies* (Oxford: Oxford University Press, 2013) [an authoritative reference to Quaker thought, practice and culture].

SELECTED POEMS OF BERNARD BARTON

Barcus, James E. (ed.), *The Literary Correspondence of Bernard Barton* (Philadelphia: University of Pennsylvania Press, 1966) [the best collection of Barton's letters available, edited to modern scholarly standards].

Barton, Lucy (ed.), *Selections from the Poems and Letters of Bernard Barton* (London: Hall, Virtue and Co., 1849) [includes Edward FitzGerald's 'Memoir' and many interesting letters].

Bevan, Joseph Gurney (ed.), *Piety Promoted, in Brief Memorials and Dying Expressions of Some of the Society of Friends. The Tenth Part* (London: William Phillips, 1810) [includes a short biography and some brief writings of Lucy Jesup, Barton's wife].

A Catalogue of the Property of Bernard Barton, Esq. Deceased; to be Sold at Auction by B. Moulton (Woodbridge, 1849) [includes a list of books and artworks owned by Barton].

Clarkson, Thomas, *A Portraiture of Quakerism*, 3 vols (London: Longman, Hurst, Rees and Orme, 1806) [a copious account of Quaker culture in the Romantic era by a friend of Barton's].

Harris, Katherine, 'Index of Bernard Barton's Contributions to British Literary Annuals', *Forget Me Not: A Hypertextual Archive* (2005) http://www.orgs.miamioh.edu/anthologies/fmn/Authors_Barton.htm [a useful bibliography covering a major part of Barton's output].

Lucas, Edward Verrall, *Bernard Barton and his Friends: A Record of Quiet Lives* (London: Edward Hicks, 1893) [still the most comprehensive biographical account of Barton's life].

Punshon, John, *Portrait in Grey: A Short History of the Quakers*, 2nd edn (London: Quaker Books, 2006) [a contemporary and accessible introduction to the Society of Friends].

Stokes, Christopher, 'Poetics at the Religious Margin: Bernard Barton and Quaker Romanticism', *Review of English Studies* 70, no. 295 (2019), pp. 509–26 [figures Barton in terms of his reworking of Romantic-era modes and styles; the first modern critical analysis of Barton's work].

Vigus, James, 'Informal Religion: Lakers on Quakers'. In *Informal Romanticism*, ed. James Vigus (Trier: Wissenschaftlicher Verlag Trier, 2012), pp. 97–114 [a recent scholarly analysis of early Romantic responses to Quakerism].

INDEX OF TITLES AND FIRST LINES

A bullying, brawling Champion of the Church 208
A cloudless sky once more is ours 192
A modest Mansion, with its garden ground 134
Again the rapid flight of time brings round 21

Barbary Ape & Ouran Outang 231
Barbary Ape! Ouran Outang! 231
Bealings House 134
Beautiful fabric! even in decay 65
Before proud Rome's imperial throne 166
Believe not that absence can banish 41
Belov'd, rever'd, and mourn'd,—Farewell! 139
Bible, The ['Lamp of our feet!'] 206
Bird of the lonely lake 230
Bishop Hubert 118
Born with the balmy breath of Spring 135
Bow Hill 142
Butterflies 230

Caractacus 166
Clerico-Politico Portrait, A 208
Cloudless and lovely is the night, the stars are bright on high 142
Concluding Verses, to a Child Seven Years Old 175
Contrast, The 106
Convict's Appeal, The 29
Coronation of Ines de Castro, The 199

Daughter of Herodias, The 180
Day in Autumn, A 78
Dazzling may seem the noontide sky 151
Dost thou not love, in the season of spring 53

Drab Bonnets 48
Dream, A 75

"Earth has not any thing to show more fair!" 228
Elk, The 230
England's Oak 189
Epistle to a Phonographic Friend; Or a Few Words on Phonography, An 217
Epistle to the Editor of Friendship's Offering 194

Fair Earth! thou surely wert not meant to be 227
Fireside Quatrains, to Charles Lamb 187
First Scripture Lessons 211
Forests, and lakes, the majesty of mountains 71

Glide gently down thy native stream 219
Godiva 182
Grandsire's Tale, A 147
Guess at the Contents of Lalla Rookh, A 26

Hast thou a heart to prove the power 34
Hast thou heard of a shell on the margin of ocean 204
Haunts of Childhood 43
Heron, The 230
His birth of yesterday 156
Honoured and gifted Friend 194
How lightly o'er thy guarded head 152
How sweet it were, methinks, to sojourn here 229
However ye might err in after speech 225

I know not which to envy most 202
I know thy fall to some appears 127

I saw a stream whose waves were bright 164
I stood, in thought, on SHINAR's plain 106
In visions which are not of night, a shadowy vale I see 173
It haunts me still! that lovely face 137
It is a mild and lovely winter night 187
It stood beside the broad and billowy deep 214
"It was a day that sent into the heart["] 78
It was a happy thought—upon the brow 226
It were, methinks, no very daring flight 227
Ivy, Addressed to a Young Friend, The 53

Jasmine! thy fair and star-like flower with honours should be crown'd 201

Lamp of our feet! whereby we trace 206
Leiston Abbey 65
Let India boast its spicy trees 189
Like one who, fruitlessly perchance 37
Look back unto the morning of our day 170

Memorial of James Nayler, the Reproach and Glory of Quakerism, A 127
Memorial of John Woolman; a Minister of the Gospel, Among the Quakers, A 124
Memorial of Mary Dyer, One of the Early Worthies and Martyrs in the Society of Quakers, A 131
Midnight has stol'n upon me! sound is none 73
Mild melodist! whose artless note 110
My Lucy 19
My opening numbers told of strength's decline 175

Napoleon 88
Negro Mother's Cradle-Song, A 205
Not worthless are the tears 161

O sad yellow-hammer! that singest to me 222
O say not so! A bright old age is thine 169
Ode to an Æolian Harp 24

Oh, Thou! from earth for ever fled! 19
Oh! were I borne in spirit to the time 159
On a Drawing of the Cottage at Aldborough, Where Crabbe Lived in Boyhood 214
On a Portrait by Spagnoletto 184
On a Portrait of Beatrice Cenci 137
On his royal throne of state 180
On Silent Worship 32
On the Death of Samuel Alexander, of Needham-Market 139
Once more, lov'd solace of my lonely hours 157
Once more thy well-known voice lift up 224

Pity for Poor Little Sweeps 121
Playford. A Descriptive Fragment.—1817 34
Postscript to 'To the Dead in Christ', A 221
Prefatory Sonnet [to A Widow's Tale, and Other Poems*]* 165
Prophet's Old Age, A 152

Quaker Poet. Verses On Seeing Myself So Designated, The 84

Reflection, A 159
Rejoice, my little merry mate! 132
Ruth's Love 154

Sea-Shell, The 204
Serpent of the Isle of Celebes 230
Since Summer invites you to visit once more 38
Sinuous monster! long and lithe 230
Sleep, my child! and might the prayer 205
Soliloquy, A 157
Sonnet, to a Friend Never Yet Seen, But Corresponded With For Above Twenty Years 220
Sonnet; to a Grandmother 169
Sonnets to Charlotte M— 46
Sonnet, to Job's Three Friends 225
Sonnet to the Deben ['Thou hast thrown aside thy summer loveliness'] 40
Sonnet to the Same [William and Mary Howitt] 179
Sonnet to William and Mary Howitt 178

330

INDEX OF TITLES AND FIRST LINES

Sonnets, Written at Burstal 226
Stanzas ("The Heaven was Cloudless") 27
Stanzas, Addressed to Percy Bysshe Shelley 71
Stanzas, Addressed to Some Friends Going to the Sea-Side 38
Stanzas, Composed During a Tempest 151
Stanzas on the Anniversary of the Abolition of the Slave Trade 21
Stanzas, to Helen M— M— 41
Stanzas, Written for a Blank Leaf in Sewell's History of the Quakers 170
Summer Musings 192
Sunshine and Moonshine by hook or by crook 26
Sweet instrument! whose tones beguile the ear 24
Sweet is it thus at times to feel 221

Tears 161
The breath of Spring is stirring in the wood 178
The dweller on *Ullswater's* grander shore 227
The Heaven was cloudless—the Ocean was calm 27
The hours fly fast, and soon the beam 29
The lamp will shed a feeble glimmering light 165
The morn was dark, the wind was high 121
"The Quaker Poet!"—is such name 84
The spacious streets were silent as the grave! 182
The tale I tell was told me long ago 147
There are, among the leafy monarchs round 228
There is a lone valley, few charms can it number 55
There is glory to me in thy Name 124
They may cant of costumes, and of brilliant head-dresses 48
Thou art but in life's morning, and as yet 46
"Thou art but in life's morning!"—Years have sped 46
Thou art not one of the living now 75

Thou bear'st thy branchy Antlers well 230
Thou hast thrown aside thy summer loveliness 40
Thou hast thy beauties: sterner ones, I own 74
Thou shouldst not to the grave descend 114
Though glorious, O GOD! must thy temple have been 32
Though prouder names than thine may live 154
Through windows richly dight 199
'Tis not the subject!—More than this 184
'Tis the hour of even now 118
'Tis winter, and the fire burns bright 211
To a Butterfly. Translated from the French 135
To a Robin 110
To E.F., On Her Reappearance Among Her Friends at the Yearly Meeting, 1845 224
To L.E.L. 87
To Lydia 73
To me there's more of Minstrel stealth 87
To the B.B Schooner, on Seeing Her Sail Down the Deben for Liverpool 219
To the White Jasmine 201
To Wm. Kirby, Rector of Barham, Suffolk 202

Unknown to sight! for more than twenty years 220

Vale of Tears, The 173
Valley of Fern, The 55
Vanity of Human Knowledge, The 156
Verses on the Approach of Spring, Addressed to my Little Play-Fellow 132
Verses on the Death of Bloomfield, the Suffolk Poet 114
Verses, Supposed to be Written in a Burial-Ground Belonging to the Society of Friends 60

Walk in the light! So shalt thou know 163
Walking in the Light 163
We too have had our Martyrs. Such wert Thou 131
What though no sculptur'd monuments around 60
When I am weary of my Mother-tongue 217

Which Things Are a Shadow 164
Who gave this spot the name of Berry's Hill 226
Who has not known and felt the soothing charm 43
Winter 74

Winter hath bound the brooks in icy chains 179
Written in a Lady's Album 37

Yellow-Hammer; A Song, by a Suffolk Villager, The 222

www.ingramcontent.com/pod-product-compliance
Lightning Source LLC
Chambersburg PA
CBHW021135230426
43667CB00005B/124